Concern for Church Mission and Spiritual Gifts

Concern for Church Mission and Spiritual Gifts

Essays on Faith and Culture,
1958–1968

CONCERN: A Pamphlet Series for
Questions of Christian Renewal

EDITED BY
Laura Schmidt Roberts

WIPF & STOCK · Eugene, Oregon

CONCERN FOR CHURCH MISSION AND SPIRITUAL GIFTS
Essays on Faith and Culture, 1958–1968

CONCERN: A Pamphlet Series for Questions of Christian Renewal

Copyright © 2022 Wipf and Stock Publishers. All rights reserved. Except for brief quotations in critical publications or reviews, no part of this book may be reproduced in any manner without prior written permission from the publisher. Write: Permissions, Wipf and Stock Publishers, 199 W. 8th Ave., Suite 3, Eugene, OR 97401.

Wipf & Stock
An Imprint of Wipf and Stock Publishers
199 W. 8th Ave., Suite 3
Eugene, OR 97401

www.wipfandstock.com

PAPERBACK ISBN: 978-1-7252-6095-5
HARDCOVER ISBN: 978-1-7252-6096-2
EBOOK ISBN: 978-1-7252-6097-9

03/10/22

Contents

Series Foreword | ix

Introduction by Laura Schmidt Roberts | xiii

Part I: On the Global Church and Mission Post-Christendom

1 Churchless Christianity | 3
 PAUL PEACHEY

2 The Search for Guaranteed Survival | 17
 M. H. GRUMM

3 The Christian Mission to the Resurgent Religions | 25
 EDMUND PERRY

4 A Light to the Nations | 36
 JOHN HOWARD YODER

5 The End of Christendom | 42
 PAUL PEACHEY

Part II: On the Charismatic Movement and Gifts of the Spirit: Articles from CONCERN 15 (1967)

6 Marginalia | 51
 JOHN HOWARD YODER

7 Tongues, a Testimony | 55
   JAMES FAIRFIELD

8 You Shall Receive . . . | 60
   HERB KLASSEN AND MAUREEN KLASSEN

9 An Experience in My Life | 74
   S. DJOJODIHARDIJO

10 The Charismatic in East Africa | 84
   DONALD R. JACOBS

11 The Charismatic Aspects of the Work of the Spirit | 88
   MYRON AUGSBURGER

12 A Historical Estimate of the Charismatic Movement | 93
   IRVIN B. HORST

13 The Charismatic Revival: A Survey of the Literature | 99
   GERALD C. STUDER

14 The Prophetic Office in the Church | 124
   WERNER SCHMAUCH

Part III: On Christendom's Christmas: Articles from *Concern* 16 (1968)

15 Nasty Noel | 135
   HENDERSON NYLROD

16 Pious Jingle Bells and the Coming of Christ | 137
   WILLIAM R. MILLER

17 Getting Christ Back Out of Christmas | 142
   MARLIN JESCHKE

18 On the Meaning of Christmas | 147
   JOHN HOWARD YODER

19 Marginalia: The Case Against Christmas | 152
   JOHN HOWARD YODER AND VIRGIL VOGT

Contemporary Responses

20 Global Anabaptist Movement: From Cross-Cultural to Multicultural to Intercultural | 161
   HYUNG JIN KIM SUN

21 Mission and Margin(alization): An Ecumenically-Shaped Anabaptist/Mennonite Approach to Mission | 170
   ANDRÉS PACHECO LOZANO

Appendix: Listing of all CONCERN republication volumes | 187
Bibliography | 195

Series Foreword to the 2022 Edition

In 1952 a group of seven young American Mennonite intellectuals studying in Europe convened for a two-week theological retreat in Amsterdam to discuss the place of Mennonites in what they saw as the modern, "post-Christendom" world. Most all had come to post-war Europe with Canadian or American Mennonite organizations to assist mission, relief, and rebuilding efforts. They are, in the words of one participant, overwhelmed by what they encounter—the theology, imagery, procedures, and practices they bring are inadequate to their work and witness in postwar Europe. They have many questions about what it means to be the church—to be disciples—in that time and place; questions compounded by conversations and studies that open up for them the ideological and philosophical currents sweeping Europe at the time.

What becomes clear in the papers presented in Amsterdam and the subsequently published series *Concern: A Pamphlet Series for Questions of Christian Renewal* (1954–71) is a common concern over a gap between an Anabaptist vision and contemporary Mennonite reality.[1] They view the increasingly hierarchical denominational structure of the Mennonite church in Canada and the United States and its institution-building as inconsistent with an Anabaptist notion of church as community. These structural forms and the accompanying concerns for their perpetuation reflect "Protestantizing" compromise instead of Anabaptist movement-oriented, mission-minded, evangelical zeal. The writers instead call for a more radical and authentic expression of the Christian life. They call for a renewal that would

---

1. Toews, *Mennonites in American Society*, 232. For more on the historical genesis of *Concern* see the front pieces of Vogt, *Roots of CONCERN*, and Hershberger, "Power, Tradition, and Renewal."

realign the mission, leadership, and organization of the church as well as its relationship to broader society in ways more resonant with the tenets of a culturally-engaged Anabaptism; which is to say, they call for a Mennonite response to modernity which is both faithful to their construal of Anabaptist tradition and appropriate to the times.[2]

While *Concern: A Pamphlet Series for Questions of Christian Renewal* and the movement it inspired address the context of the day, the call issued to discern what it means to be a faithful church in and for the times—ever the church's call—is one we face with growing urgency in today's postmodern context. What theology, imagery, and practices are adequate to the work and witness of disciples in this time and place? What is church *for*? Republishing these essays makes more readily available for this task resources shaped by Anabaptist tradition. The themes and issues the essays raise remain relevant: Christian responsibility in and to the "world," the goal of history, critical engagement with political ideologies and economic theories, global mission and the colonial legacy of Christendom, the unavoidably enculturated nature of lived faith, the gifts of the Spirit, desire for renewed (radicalized?) authentic expressions of faith, Anabaptist-shaped church structure and pastoral leadership, the fraught realities of communal authority and discipline.

But the model the pamphlet series provides is equally important. Especially at its inception, *Concern* was intended to be a forum for works in progress versus polished churchly or academic pieces—a place to test ideas, raise questions, challenge practices, even change one's mind. The pamphlets present articles reflecting varying viewpoints intended to promote discussion, critical reflection, and ultimately transformation of understanding, practices, and structured forms of Christian discipleship. This example of dialog across difference as a shared path toward renewal is welcome in the current increasingly polarized context, where disagreement seems more likely to end a conversation than begin one.

Response essays from contemporary Mennonite writers in each volume continue in this vein, critically engaging the contribution and limitations of the historical essays and building out concerns of their own in the current global, ecclesial, and historical climate. One aspect of that climate is especially important to state clearly: the mixed legacy of *Concern* writer

---

2. See Vogt, "Foreword," in *The Roots of CONCERN*. Sawatsky, "Editorial," iii. *The Conrad Grebel Review* 8.2 contains articles on and reflections by participants in the *Concern* movement.

and sometime editor, theologian and ethicist John Howard Yoder, whose sexual abuse must be acknowledged.[3] The depth and breadth of harm Yoder perpetrated, most horrifically on those he abused, and also on the shape and substance of Anabaptist-Mennonite theology and ecclesiology, is difficult to fathom. While significant deconstruction of Yoder's work has been done, grappling with the aftermath and implications continues.[4] Refusing to engage or promote Yoder's work as a whole or selectively is one avenue of response. Such selectivity is evident in this series; most, but not all, of Yoder's essays have been republished here. Some material already widely available, and especially the content or use of which harmed victim-survivors of Yoder's abuse, has not been included. Another avenue of response takes encounters with his thought (in church, in institutions, in print) as an occasion to reframe discussion of it: by first speaking the truth of his serial sexual abuse and then reconsidering his work in light of that context. This series also does some of that work selectively, at the choice of several contemporary response writers and in this acknowledgment prefacing each volume. *Concern* should not be reduced to Yoder's contributions. While persistent, Yoder's voice is but one among many across the original pamphlets. On their own, the other fifty-plus writers give rich, contextualized, and diverse expression to theological, ecclesiological, and missiological explorations in the mid-twentieth century.

A historical republication project such as this is not possible without the expert help of librarians and archivists. I owe such debts in too many places to name but the greatest—to Fresno Pacific University's Hiebert Library Director Kevin Enns-Rempel, archivist Hannah Keeney, and research librarian David Hasegawa—must be mentioned. I have benefitted from the university's support through a sabbatical leave dedicated to this project, multiple Provost's Faculty Research Grants, and the Fresno Pacific Biblical Seminary's Center for Anabaptist Studies donation toward publication costs. I greatly appreciate other contributions toward those costs from the Schafer-Friesen Research Fund (Goshen College), the Gerhard Lohrenz

---

3. See Waltner Goossen, "'Defanging the Beast.'" Waltner Goossen catalogs both Yoder's serial sexual abuse and institutional failure to respond adequately to his victims or Yoder himself.

4. In addition to the many articles in *Mennonite Quarterly Review* 89.1, see for example Anabaptist Mennonite Biblical Seminary, "AMBS Response to Victims"; Cramer et al., "Theology and Misconduct"; "On Teaching John Howard Yoder" collection of essays by Mennonite faculty from various institutions in *Mennonite Life* 68 (2014); Soto Albrecht and Stephens, eds. *Liberating the Politics of Jesus*.

Publication Fund (Canadian Mennonite University), and the Conrad Grebel University College Theological Studies Program. I am especially grateful to the Mennonite Faith and Learning Society (British Columbia), whose work first became known to me through its sponsorship of the Humanitas Anabaptist Centre (Trinity Western University), and whose very generous support of this publication shows concretely their stated commitment to advance education and scholarship from an Anabaptist perspective.

Thanks are due to Fresno Pacific colleagues in the Division of Biblical and Religious Studies, especially Quentin Kinnison, to Rod Janzen, and to Larry Dunn, for unflagging support, probing questions, and insightful feedback along the way. This project would not have come to me without Ched Myers' suggestion and encouragement, and would not have come to completion without the steadfast guidance and input of Ted Lewis at Wipf and Stock. Thank you both for the gift of this work. Finally, I am deeply grateful to the contemporary response writers in each volume of the series whose essays model so well what Paul Ricoeur would call a "refiguring" of tradition. Thank you for grappling with the plurality and ambiguity of tradition in ways that challenge and potentially revitalize it through theology and praxis from and for actual current ecclesial communities, Anabaptist and otherwise.

An appendix in each book in this series lists the contents of the seven total volumes comprising the *Concern* republication project initiated under the editorial direction of Virgil Vogt which this series completes.[5]

Laura Schmidt Roberts

Fresno Pacific University
September 2021

---

5. In addition to this four-volume, thematically organized series, three other volumes complete the Wipf and Stock republication of the *Concern* pamphlets: Vogt, *Roots of CONCERN* and *CONCERN for Education*; Vogt and Roberts, *Concern for Anabaptist Renewal*.

Introduction

Essays in this volume explore the role of culture and context in the church's mission, lived faith, and theological articulation through various avenues of approach: the global church and the ecumenical movement, Christendom's legacy of colonialism and cultural accommodation, critique of rigid and outdated ecclesial structures and forms, the complexities of the unavoidably enculturated nature of faith as proclaimed and lived. The *Concern* writers frequently frame this critical engagement as necessitated by their "post-Christendom" context.[1] While widely used today, the term "post-Christendom" is contested for the ways in which it can mask how Christians still "benefit from the institutional prominence of cultural Christianity as it shapes our society."[2] Such a critique itself resonates with concerns driving the historical essays.

In the first section, "On the Global Church and Mission," writers explore the colonial legacy of Christendom, problematic "exporting" of Western denominationalist structures, loyalties, and theology, and the role of culture in embodying Christian faith. Articles by Paul Peachey (1959) and M. H. Grumm (1960) critique aspects of the Western missionary legacy and demonstrate the felt tension between institutionalization,

---

1. For the origins and context of *Concern: A Pamphlet Series for Questions of Christian Renewal* (1954–71) please see the Series Foreword to this volume.

2. Adams and Villegas, "Post-Christendom or Neo-Christendom?" The authors explain that "Christendom names a social arrangement in which Christianity penetrates the structures of power.... Our argument is that such an era has not ended, that the era of politically powerful Christian institutions is not dying, that we do not live in a 'post' Christendom age. Instead, Christendom is reinventing itself as it mutates into a new form: call it neo-Christendom. This mutation differs from the political system of the Medieval Ages yet retains the same preference for Christian sociopolitical ascendency."

indigenization, and charismatic leadership in Japan and India. Edmund Perry (1961) presses further, calling for a genuine attempt to understand various world religions on their own terms in order to reformulate a theology of and "to" them. John Howard Yoder affirms mission as essential to the nature of the church but asserts "what the church is, is her basic testimony," and in light of "the unfaithfulness of Christendom" calls on the church to repent and be the church.[3] A second article by Peachey reviews the ecumenical movement's hailing the end of Christendom as the liberation of the church but critiques the same for failing to recognize that calling Asian Christians to work toward the "responsible society" in their setting ignores the pre-Christendom/pre-Constantinian nature of their situation.

Yoder's editorial comments ("Marginalia") perhaps best clarify the link between the preceding essays and those from the original *Concern* 15 (1967) which comprise the second section, "On the Charismatic Movement and Gifts of the Spirit." Yoder notes 1) the explosion of growth of charismatic believers in the southern hemisphere, 2) Pentecostalism as transcending denominationalism in mission settings, and 3) that "the genius of the movement is misunderstood when it is seen through its North American forms" because of the class, education, and denominational assumptions governing its analysis and growth. These writings, many from non-Western settings, resonate with the preceding essays in further highlighting questions of culture and context in relation to proclamation and expression of Christian faith, and in critique of Christendom and denominationalist structures and forms in light of the call to a lived faith in the Spirit. Werner Schmauch's essay (1958) concludes this section because, while dating much earlier, it discusses prophecy as a gift needing discernment and contrasts it explicitly to tongues. He argues the prophetic office is central to being the church, because it reflects the Holy Spirit's presence and retains a characteristic of the New Testament church.

In the third section, "On Christendom's Christmas," the contents of original *Concern* 16 (1968) critique Western Christmas observances as syncretist-laden demonstrations of Christendom's cultural accommodation. While one might think consumerism prominent evidence of such accommodation, the articles focus more on 1) the problematic links to pagan observances including an annual (seasonal) cycle versus

---

3. This volume contains work by John Howard Yoder, whose sexual abuse is a well-established fact which must be acknowledged. Please see the Foreword for more about the editor's choice to republish Yoder's work in this series.

a (salvation) history which is "going somewhere"; 2) celebration of the "natural" (vs. the "spiritual") family, and 3) theological emphasis on the cradle (incarnation *doctrine*) without the cross (incarnation *narrative*—"a life"). These pieces resonate with the preceding essays in their critique of Christendom's "Christianizing" legacy and in raising issues surrounding the unavoidably enculturated nature of lived faith.

Two contemporary response essays work to develop aspects of a postcolonial understanding of mission. Arguing that genuine missional encounter yields a mutual transformation of those involved, Hyung Jin Kim Sun approaches the historical writings as critical theological reflections on such experiences. He calls for clearer recognition of the way social and cultural context condition understanding and practice of faith, suggesting the need today for a more robust, *intentionally* intercultural missional theology and ecclesiology which actively engages and integrates diverse, non-Western perspectives. Andrés Pacheco Lozano explores issues of center, margins, and marginalization in mission, using an ecumenical framework to call for a shift to mission *from* (vs. to) the margins. Noting the historical essays and some more contemporary Anabaptist/Mennonite writing exhibit limited critical reflection on the historical alliance between Western missions and the colonial project, Pacheco Lozano sets about constructing an Anabaptist mission from the margins centered in a peace theology for the Missio Dei. These response essays relocate questions of faith, culture, and context in ways that challenge assumptions about center, margins, and the nature of the church's ongoing journey of transformation as the body of Christ.

Part I

On the Global Church and Mission Post-Christendom

1

Churchless Christianity

PAUL PEACHEY

I

One of the most remarkable movements in Christian history is the *Mukyokai Shugi* or "churchless Christianity" of Japan. Arising as a protest to the sectarian and institutional Christianity introduced to Japan by Western missionaries, this movement seeks to "carry Protestantism to its logical conclusion." Today, scarcely three decades after the death of its "founder," *Mukyokai Shugi* numbers ten to fifty thousand adherents and exerts an influence in Japan far beyond its own circles.

No less original was the spiritual progenitor of the movement, Kanzo Uchimura (1861–1930). For nearly half a century this great prophet of God pommeled Japan and the Christian church with the Word of God. Born at the moment when Japan finally opened her doors to the West, his soul became the battleground on which the encounter of East with West was fought out in miniature. Even more important than this, Uchimura telescoped nineteen centuries of Christian development into his own spiritual experience with astounding profundity. For if the Protestant Reformation meant the Germanization of Christianity after centuries of Latin tutelage, in Kanzo Uchimura the "Japanization" of the faith occurred in the lifetime of a single "first-generation" Christian.

Twice Christianity has been introduced to Japan. On the first occasion Francis Xavier, the great sixteenth-century Jesuit missionary, planted the faith here. With great insight into the Japanese mind and culture, the dedicated successors to Xavier won half a million souls to Christ in less than half a century. Then the government, aroused to suspicion by various factors, crushed the movement in a persecution that ranks with the most ruthless in Christian history. For the next two and a half centuries Japan was closed to intercourse with the outside world.

The second influx of the faith came shortly after the middle of the nineteenth century when the doors of Japan were reopened—this time by a "Protestant" power—the United States. (This year, 1959, Japanese Protestants are celebrating their centennial.) When the first Protestant missionaries arrived, conversion was still a punishable crime and real liberty was decades in coming. Simultaneously Catholics were able to resume their work; and, astoundingly enough, remnants of the original Catholic communities came to the surface—after having existed underground without outside contact for more than two centuries.

But meanwhile the progress of the faith in Japan has been slow. The combined Catholic and Protestant faithful in Japan today number fewer than one percent of the population. Why this should be so remains to this day a favorite topic among missionaries and Japanese Christians alike. Though no ultimate answer to this question has been given, several important factors can be noted. One of these is Japan's experience with foreign powers: down through the centuries Japan has always stood under the shadow of the superior power of China which put her on the defensive, both politically and psychologically. It was from the Chinese that Japan took over her higher religions and the arts of civilization, while yet always successfully maintaining her political independence. Japan thus combined an extraordinary capacity to assimilate foreign cultural influences with an equally extraordinary capacity to safeguard the integrity of her own genius.

A further factor was that Japanese folk society and folk religion were already overlaid and in part transformed by a higher civilization and a higher religion. Missionaries were thus confronted, not with the inadequacy of a "primitive" folk society with few resources of its own, but with a sophisticated culture in the light of which Westerners were even considered "barbarians." A final factor we might note is the catastrophe with which the first incursion of Western culture in the sixteenth century ended. The Japanese had ample reason to fear that the interest of Westerners was not altruistic, especially during the century of Western empire building in the Orient.

And yet when Western gunboats hove into sight on their coasts, the Japanese were convinced in terror that they were technologically behind the times. Internal political upheaval combined with external pressure to open the gates of Japan to commerce with the West. True to her own genius, Japan cautiously appropriated the industrial revolution but resisted any encroachments upon her own "soul." As she sent her envoys abroad, these sought to break down the civilization of the West into its component strands and then to appropriate only those elements which would bring their own up to date without destroying its core. In this process Christianity was excluded as an unnecessary and even dangerous element.

Protestant missionaries, therefore, began their work under circumstances which were hardly auspicious. Even apart from the government attitude, which was hostile enough, the first young converts were troubled psychologically with the feeling that somehow they were traitors of their own people. To accept a foreigner's religion in place of one's own value system is indeed always difficult. But where this event is bound up with suspicion of treason the obstacles become well-nigh insurmountable. To accept the foreigner's faith inevitably entailed a kind of submission to a foreigner and to a foreign culture. For the missionary of necessity employed a cultural vehicle, namely his own, to convey the faith. Thus, the missionary brought not only Christ but a visible tradition of organization, sacraments, and creeds.

Fortunately, however, the heroic youths who accepted the faith, often the sons of recently dispossessed warriors (*samurai*), turned on Christianity the same critical faculties that enabled the Japanese to be selective about Western civilization in the first place—they distinguished between Christ and Christianity or Christendom. That is, as the missionary message filtered through the Japanese soul, it was Jesus Christ whom the Japanese believers could espouse, while they rejected the cultural forms in which the faith had expressed itself in the West. It was in Kanzo Uchimura that this process came most sharply into focus, and today it is his living influence that towers, perhaps above that of all other Christians, in Japan.

This filtering of Christianity through the Japanese soul was to have a further result. Not only did these new believers find the Western cultural garb of the faith inappropriate for Japan—and unacceptable in any case as foreign to their own genius, but also beyond this they discovered the inner inconsistencies of Western Christianity. And as they began to "speak back" to their Western tutors from the independent position before Christ and in Christ which they thereby gained; the reaction of missionaries often disclosed these inconsistencies more fully than before. It was the divided state of Christendom that constituted a major stumbling block.

II

How should a non-Christian nation respond to the Christian gospel when it is represented not only by the competing claims of Catholicism and Protestantism but by literally scores of sects? We must ask ourselves bluntly: Is it not scandalous that Japanese Christians should feel themselves as Anglican or Lutheran or Calvinist or Mennonite? How can they feel themselves as such unless these attitudes are artificially cultivated by proponents of these denominations? Is it not a reflection on missionary and national alike that converts and churches should become replicas of Western schisms? Is it reasonable to expect sufficient information and maturity of the young Japanese convert to compare the counter claims of the various denominations and thereby find the one which could truly lay claim to the truth even if such were to exist?

Or is the approach of Uchimura and his "followers" not after all, a sounder one to seek for "essential Christianity" or as a recent *Mukyokai* writer stated, "the most essential element of the Christian faith, without which there can be no Christianity and beside which all other elements can be treated as secondary and nonessential"? That such an approach entails its own perils we must note presently, but before we hasten to note them, we must face the full force of the problem and of the *Mukyokai* reply to it.

We cannot here deal with Kanzo Uchimura biographically, but since he is the clearest expression of the *Mukyokai* genius, we must cite him as an example. Uchimura united with six other students who were baptized with him when he was seventeen years of age to form the Sapporo Independent Church. Receiving some sympathy from the missionary who baptized them, they were soon caught in a competition between Episcopalian and Methodist missionaries. In need of a meeting place, they made plans to erect a church. Their appeal for help to a Methodist missionary brought a loan of $400. To these young Christians this building operation was a step toward full spiritual autonomy. To the missionary making the loan, however, this gesture was viewed as an attempt to hold the group for Methodist affiliation. When the church was completed and the congregation happily declared its independence, the missionary wrote a letter demanding the money back. The young believers rose to the occasion and at great sacrifice were able to repay the debt in full within two years.

This experience proved to be of decisive significance not only for Uchimura personally but for the history of Christianity in Japan. Thoroughly alerted now to the evils of denominationalism and to the necessity of the financial independence of Japanese churches from foreign funds, he went to America soon afterward for a period of study—there to have his illusions about Christendom further shattered. In his spiritual autobiography *How I Became a Christian* he described his trip to America in terms as the following:

> My idea of the Christian America was lofty, religious, Puritanic. I dreamed of its templed hills and rocks that rang with hymns and praises. Hebraisms, I thought to be the prevailing speech of the American commonality, and cherub and cherubim, hallelujahs and amens, the common language of its streets. . . . As my previous acquaintance with the Caucasian race had been mostly with missionaries, the idea stuck close to my mind; and so all the people whom I met in the street appeared to me like so many ministers fraught with high Christian purpose, and I could not but imagine myself as walking among the congregation of the First-born. It was only gradually, very gradually, that I unlearnt this childish notion.[1]

And the unlearning process was well-nigh disastrous. Had he not met in President Julius Seelye of Amherst College an understanding Christian friend, it is doubtful that he would have salvaged his own faith through it. After relating various disappointments, Uchimura continues his account:

> Time fails me to speak of other unchristian features of Christendom. What about legalized lottery which can depend for its stability upon millions in gold and silver, right in face of simple morality clear even to the understanding of a child; of widespread gambling propensities, as witnessed in scenes of cockfights, horse races, and football matches; of pugilism, more inhuman than Spanish bullfights; of lynching, fitted more for Hottentots than for the people of a free republic; of rum traffic, whose magnitude can find no parallel in the trade of the whole world; of demagogism in politics; of denominational jealousies in religion; of capitalists' tyranny and laborers' insolence; of millionaires' fooleries; of men's hypocritical love toward their wives; etc., etc., etc.? Is this the civilization we were taught by missionaries to accept as an evidence of the superiority of Christian religion over other religions?[2]

It is therefore not surprising to find entries in his diary as these: "Feb. 18. Much doubting; not a little troubled. My heart must be fixed on God.

---

1. Uchimura, *How I Became*, 91.
2. Uchimura, *How I Became*, 103.

Men's opinions are various, but God's truth must be one. Unless taught by God Himself, the true knowledge cannot be obtained."[3]

And again, sensing the hollowness and mundane ends of much organized religion:

> I came to my seminary upon an agreement that I should never be licensed. . . . And the fear that I had entertained about the bestowal of this new privilege upon me grew as I observed its benefits talked about within the walls of my seminary. "One thousand dollars with parsonage," "twenty-dollar sermon upon Chicago anarchy," . . . sounded very discordantly to my ears. That sermons have market values, as pork and tomatoes and pumpkins have, is not an Oriental idea at least.
>
> . . . Theology is too big a theme to be comprehended by small men. When small minds find themselves too small for such a gigantic theme, they construct their own theologies fitting their own smallness, and throw anathemas at those who comprehend it better than they. O my soul, do not contract theology to fit thy smallness, but expand thyself to fit its largeness.
>
> . . . I am seeking for a higher type of morality than "must." I am hungering after the morality that cometh from God's grace. But such a morality is denied not only by the majority of mankind, but very little seems to be believed in by the students and professors of theological seminaries. I do not hear anything new and different within these sacred walls than from those which I hear outside. Confucius and Buddha can teach me the largest part of what these theologies are presuming to teach the heathen.[4]

All these experiences were the making of Kanzo Uchimura. Fortunately for him and for the church he was driven back to find an imperishable foundation in Christ alone:

> In forming any right estimate of Christendom, it is essential for us first of all to make a rigid distinction between Christianity pure and simple, and Christianity garnished and dogmatized by its professors. I believe no sane man of this generation dare speak ill of Christianity itself. After reading all the skeptic literature that had come to my hand, I came to the conclusion that Jesus of Nazareth remains untouched after all the furious attacks made upon those who are called by His name. If Christianity is what I now believe it to be, it is as firm and fixed as the Himalayas. . . . Some indeed

3. Uchimura, *How I Became*, 121.
4. Uchimura, *How I Became*, 167, 161, 162.

rush at what they imagine to be Christianity, which is in fact no Christianity, but superstructure over the same, built by some faithless believers who, thinking that the Rock by itself cannot stand all the wear and tear of time, shed it over with shrines, cathedrals, churches, doctrines, Thirty-Nine Articles, and other structures of combustible nature; and some fools of this world, knowing that such are combustible, set fire to them, and rejoice over their conflagration, and think that the Rock itself has also vanished in the flame. Behold, the Rock is there "towering o'er the wrecks of time."

"Christianity is Christ and Christ is a living Person." Again: "Christianity is God's grace to be appropriated by man's faith. Grace and Faith almost exhaust Christianity." Yet another: "Christianity is essentially the religion of the cross. It is not the religion of Christ but the religion of Christ crucified." "Christianity is not an institution, a church, or churches; neither is it creed, nor dogma, nor theology; neither is it a book, the Bible, nor even the words of Christ. Christianity is a Person, a living Person, Lord Jesus Christ, 'the same yesterday, today, and forever.' If Christianity is not this, the ever-present living He, it is nothing. I go directly to Him, not through churches and popes and bishops and other useful and useless officers. 'I in them and they in Me'—so says He of His disciples."

These are the words, not of a careful theologian who has worked out his ideas in a consistent system, but the outbursts of saint wrestling with God amid the realities of life. That there are deficiencies in his statements is not to be denied. But these dare not deter us from seeing his central burden which always comes out with great cogency. Christianity entails the believer's fellowship and walk with Christ and not an authoritative cultural deposit which is to be perpetuated and appropriated externally. If such a conclusion does not answer all the questions that intrude themselves, its authenticity and profundity are not to be gainsaid.

III

When Uchimura returned to Japan, he took an uncompromising stand as a Christian. His association with the Christian movement was constant and intimate, and yet he did not join a denominational group. He first coined the term *Mukyokai*, meaning "no church," in a pamphlet published in 1901. While the word "no church" or "churchless" has a negative connotation, it was meant as a positive affirmation of the church in the true sense and a negation only of institutional Christianity. "*Mukyokai* is a church without a church." Or as a later writer was to say, "*Mukyokai Shugi* is not a mere 'ism' and the 'mu' . . . is not a mere negation; it is a greater or more positive affirmation of the church than that of the churches themselves." That is, since it claims to adhere to the church as "life union with God through Christ," *Mukyokai* stands for a fullness which does not obtain where other limiting principles as creed, sacrament, or office are set up. Another writer states: "*Mukyokai* is not anti-ecclesiastical, but it is working for the kingdom of God where neither Protestantism nor *Mukyokai* (non-church) exist, but where all are one through Jesus Christ and there is one real church which is His body."

Uchimura was opposed not only to institutional Christianity but also to the planting of Western institutions foreign to Japanese soil. That is, he sought both "essential Christianity" and "Japanese Christianity." Says a contemporary writer: "The churches are almost all importations including titles, organizations, methods, and teachings, which in many cases, have nothing to do with the interests and needs of the Japanese." To Uchimura, financial and institutional independence were indispensable to Christianity in Japan. Christianity was to become a "permanent power by the force of its own life."

History has proven the validity of Uchimura's insights. To this day Japanese Protestantism is unable to support the organizational superstructures with which the missionaries endowed it without foreign financial and even managerial help. This is accentuated by a duplication of services due to denominational divisions. (In this respect the Catholics are even more vulnerable, since even the majority of the clergy are still foreign, which is not the case among Protestants.) For this reason Christianity still "smells too much like foreigners," as a student told the writer recently.

These views of Uchimura led to the development of a unique pattern of church life, first evolved by Uchimura himself and then taken up by many others after his death. Believers (and eventual seekers) meet for Bible study under a teacher in a home or rented hall. The meetings include Scripture reading, prayer, and often hymn singing (from the usual Protestant hymnbook); but there are no sacraments. Uchimura published a monthly magazine for a number of years which he entitled *Bible Study*. Devoted chiefly to exegetical studies and certain current topics, he wrote most of his own materials. For a time he had a group loosely organized around his magazine, only to loosen them still further when the impression got abroad that a church was in formation. To ensure that no permanent institution would outlive him, he discharged his assistant and in his will ordered his magazine discontinued after his death.

Bible study in *Mukyokai* is of a high caliber, since many of the teachers are men of high academic standing. Perhaps the most influential *Mukyokai* teacher at the present time retired a year ago from the presidency of Tokyo University, the nation's highest cathedral of learning. Another has supported himself for years as a private scholar, publishing a magazine, leading his weekly meeting, and publishing a commentary of the whole Bible in more than a dozen volumes—some of which have gone through as many as seventeen printings and are widely used by Protestant ministers throughout Japan.

Membership is merely a matter of oral arrangement with the teachers. No lists are kept and absolutely no committees or other organizations occur. The Bible class does not even become a social circle, since visiting before and after is not encouraged. Whatever mutual aid is given, and there is some, is handled by the teacher. A troublesome member of the class may be excluded by the teacher, but this hardly constitutes church discipline in a full sense. Indeed, *Mukyokai Shugi* leaders seem quite Protestant or individualistic in their view that all distinctions between the saved and the unsaved must be left to God. Since membership is almost intangible, whatever discipline obtains is achieved through the individual conscience. But no pressures are exerted on persons to become members. Motivation and ethical response are therefore of a high order.

Perhaps the closest parallel to this pattern of church life to be found in the West is the Society of the Friends. Indeed, Uchimura had some sustained contacts with Friends in Philadelphia. Yet there are important differences. On the one hand the mystic strain is less pronounced, and on the other hand the Bible plays a more central role. True substance of the *Mukyokai* gathering is the study of the Bible, which is the exclusive historical source of divine truth. Yet a fundamentalist view of inspiration is eschewed, and the textual scholars of this movement employ all the resources of critical scholarship. "The Bible is the expression of the life and work of God, and since 'life' is greater than its expression, it cannot be expressed completely in any logical or theological form," says a contemporary *Mukyokai* writer. But likewise, they reject a liberal view of the Scriptures. Concludes the same writer, "apart from both the written Word and the quickening Spirit there is no knowledge of the living Word of God."

It must also be stressed that "churchless Christianity" does not derive from mere quietism or an individualistic view of salvation. While individuals in the movement sometimes do give this kind of impression, certainly many of the leaders are strongly and even radically social in their outlook. Uchimura said at one point, "I learned from Christ and His apostles how to save my soul, but from the prophets, how to save my country." The ethical dimension is expressed in vigorous positions taken on social issues, particularly on the evils of national life such as idolatrous nationalism and militarism. Uchimura sacrificed his academic career by refusing a worshipful act toward an imperial rescript. Prior to and during the late Pacific War, *Mukyokai* leaders were among the most heroic in resisting the demands of the militarists, suffering imprisonment and the suspension of their publications and meetings. In Uchimura, however, an important shift in social attitudes occurred in later life. Where early in his career he became linked to various reform efforts of the Socialists and others, he later abandoned this approach—concluding that only through individual change can social change be affected. But this change in attitude toward history was accompanied by a strong turn to eschatology as the framework of social fulfillment. Thus, even then his view of salvation was not individual escapist.

IV

How is *Mukyokai Shugi* to be assessed, and what attitude should Christians in other movements take toward it? It will be noted first of all that the disavowal of creed and organization as well as the youth and the fluidity of the movement make any assessment difficult. Accordingly, out-group scholars have been extremely cautious in their assertions about *Mukyokai Shugi*, and in-group spokesmen do not give "official" answers. Nonetheless some questions do arise. Perhaps the first thing to stress is that in a very real sense *Mukyokai* stands in the stream of the "left wing" of the Reformation. Said Uchimura fairly early in his career, "The world needs another religious reformation. The sixteenth century ended as an arrested movement. Protestantism upon becoming an organization reverted to Catholicism. If we can carry Protestantism to its logical conclusion, we will have another reformation. The new Protestantism if it is perfectly free cannot remain in churchism."

Seen from this perspective the evil of Catholicism consisted not in the single abuses which the Reformation eliminated, but in the very premises on which it rested—in the attempt to make "an institutional organization the center of the *Ekklesia*—of substituting human service or earthly authority for the activity and authority of the Spirit" in the midst of the believers. The church is seen by Uchimura as a spiritual reality, whose structure and therefore whose unity is found in the experience of the believers. It is the attempt to objectify or incorporate this unity in organizational, creedal, or liturgical structures that leads to disunity. The denominational structure may embrace true Christians, but as such it is of human rather than divine origin.

In the light of this, the ecumenical movement seems, to *Mukyokai* thought, to rest on the same false premises as do the denominations in the first place, even though individual *Mukyokai* leaders manifest a friendly interest in the World Council of Churches. The ecumenical effort is misconceived since it tries to harmonize structures by further structural means, when the real problem is their existence in the first place. Difficulty arises immediately with the shift from the basic reality of "spiritual fellowship with God through Christ" to the stipulating of external criteria, whether creed, sacrament, office, or other institutional means, as essential to the church. There is therefore in the *Mukyokai* a readiness to admit great variety in outward expression, depending on culture and circumstance. Uchimura was willing on rare occasions even to baptize, where circumstances seemed to require it. Rejection of the sacraments is not dogmatic. Basically, since the purpose of theology or dogma is to witness to the reality of the life in Christ rather than to measure faith, uniformity is not an issue. (The possibility of false teaching is nonetheless admitted.)

Perhaps none of the foregoing arguments can be gainsaid, either Scripturally or logically. And yet experience to date has shown that at least procedurally no new approach has been found. For in the perpetual struggle for the meaning of the church, every ecclesiology claims to limit itself to the essential, in a sense, to the minimal. Seen from the "outside," therefore, *Mukyokai Shugi* does what all others do. But since others cannot agree to their definition, they become simply another sect by force of circumstance. The Catholic approach, it must be noted, is the opposite. It seeks for "fullness," where Protestantism is imperfect or fragmentary. For Protestants to return to the "mother church" is not to surrender their own genius but to assimilate it into the fullness of the "Catholic Church." In any case is not the danger great that a movement which comes into existence as a protest and draws deep inspiration from a critique of existing traditions may indeed be deficient or incomplete? This is not to refute the *Mukyokai* argument or to accept the

Catholic dogma (which is not our present subject), but rather to indicate the problems we face even if we accept the *Mukyokai* premises.

Another question to arise at the outset is whether churchlessness is not a form of institution in itself. A contemporary *Mukyokai* writer points out that *Mukyokai Shugi* "is not a denomination, it is a spirit, a character." Nevertheless, a recent scholarly survey of *Mukyokai* beliefs and attitudes seems to detach a second- or third-generation hardening of beliefs—an interest in the precision and preservation of certain formulas rather than the creative openness and flexibility of the "founder." This leads us to ask whether the problem of denomination is exhausted in the question of ecclesiastical institutions, or whether it is not even more profoundly a spiritual or psychological problem. Shared experiences are subject to stereotype in the psychological domain, whether or not there are accompanying institutional structures. Once again this is not to reject the *Mukyokai* argument. There is a biblical view of the church and there are unbiblical views, and *Mukyokai Shugi* has penetrated to the heart of the question. But even a right theology can be falsely held.

A second series of questions, however, is theological in nature. It must be asked, for example, whether a purely spiritual view of the church does justice to the concept of the New Testament in which "sacraments," gifts, and doctrine do play a role, and which provides for visible assemblies of believers. Does not *Mukyokai Shugi* sacrifice something of the concrete reality of the church for the sake of its central valid emphasis? Is it right to say that Jesus did not intend to found the church?

A third series of questions is practical in nature. How does a purely spiritual church actualize herself in history? Does not every actualization define itself in outwardly concrete ways? Must it not be admitted that the regular gathering for Bible study is generically as truly institutional as is the high mass, though, to be sure the two are not to be equated? Or what of the concrete deeds of the Christian fellowship? A young *Mukyokai* adherent told this writer recently that he would like to take up Christian work of rehabilitation in southeast Asia, but there is no organ in his movement whereby he can do so.

One must ask, too, whether, if the shortcoming of Western Christendom derives at least in part from its Westernization, *Mukyokai*'s insistence on being a Japanese "form" of the faith does not lead to the same error here? May *Mukyokai* repeat in Japan the error of the Western church of identifying national culture with Christianity?

A fourth series of questions has to do with the relationship of *Mukyokai* to the denominations. Since *Mukyokai* arose as a corrective, may it therefore be incomplete in itself? One of the most trenchant criticisms of the denominations made by *Mukyokai Shugi* is that "each of them acts as if it were the only body of Christ." And yet *Mukyokai* groups carry on their own work Without necessary reference to other Christians in the locality—and is not that the essence of the denominational sin?

It must be recognized, however, that communication between *Mukyokai* and the denominations is by definition extremely difficult. In communication between the "churches" denominational organ confronts denominational organ. But *Mukyokai Shugi* would destroy itself in the very act of creating an organ to serve as a conversational partner. It is understandable, therefore, that the "churches" should feel frustrated and even resentful in any dealing with *Mukyokai*. And by the same token *Mukyokai* attitudes are often less outgoing than they ought to be. Thus, perhaps the most devastating feature of the denominational pattern of Christianity is that it makes virtually impossible the existence of churches in any form other than sectarian.

Having noted both the substance of *Mukyokai Shugi* and the criticisms to which it gives rise, what conclusions are possible? It has been the purpose of this essay to introduce *Mukyokai Shugi* to readers meeting it for the first time but who are familiar with the problems associated with it. Anything more than some tentative suggestions would require a much fuller study of Kanzo Uchimura and of the movement he inspired than is here possible. In terms of growth, it appears that *Mukyokai Shugi* in Japan far outstrips Protestantism otherwise, proportionately speaking. On the other hand, it is doubtful whether *Mukyokai* alone, or even together with existing churches, will meet the immediate evangelistic needs of the nation. This means, then, the continued existence side by side of *Mukyokai*, the churches, and the missions. What of the Christian witness under these circumstances?

The missions may well feel that the basic task of evangelism and the sharing of the Christian heritage of the centuries justifies their continued presence. But at the same time, it is in *Mukyokai Shugi* that Christianity has really assumed the flesh and blood of Japan. If the missions and the churches are to continue and to prosper, will it not be necessary for them to accept the judgment of *Mukyokai Shugi* and to submit themselves to the resultant transformation? In turn, however, ought this not to open the door for Japanese Christianity to enter more fully into the heritage of the centuries, into the church catholic, lest it be swallowed eventually by the Japanese spirit? Only if the church is truly Japanese can it be truly catholic, and only if it is catholic can it be truly Japanese. However remote and impractical such a suggestion may seem, the gospel itself is the source of this proposal, which postulates unity and holds that "with God all things are possible."

A note on literature: I have mostly not cited sources in the foregoing quotations. They are taken from works by Uchimura, Kurosaki, Jennings, Howes and Cary, and Norman listed in the bibliography. Also consulted were numerous articles in various other works, as well as *Mukyokai* leaders and members. The foregoing is a personal interpretation of a highly tentative nature, since I cannot claim a full understanding of *Mukyokai Shugi*.

2

The Search for Guaranteed Survival[1]

M. H. GRUMM

Wherever the gospel has been preached and a church has been formed, men have been concerned about the conservation and perpetuation of that church. Today in India, where the transfer of responsibility from foreign mission organizations to indigenous church organizations has been going on for some time, this concern has exercised the minds of many in a heightened degree. There has been much talk about the goals of self-support and self-propagation, about the need for the church to stand on its own feet, to sink its roots in indigenous soil, and to find its own leadership. There has been not only much talk but also much effort to find ways of bringing this about.

Problems in the Indian Situation

Puducheri is an Indian village of 800 inhabitants three miles off the trunk road, eight miles from the nearest big town. In the Harijan section there is a modest building with a sign over the door, "Church of India Elementary School." Inside are seventy-seven children, busily engaged by the headmaster and his assistant, who happens to be his wife. On the walls, besides the usual charts and teaching aids and finely scrolled precepts, are hung several pictures illustrating biblical stories and a large picture of Jesus. For on Sundays, by the rearranging of benches and planks, and the transformation of the

---

1. Used by permission from the editors of the *National Christian Council Review*. Mr. Grumm is a missionary in the India Evangelical Lutheran Church, working at Pernambut, South India.

headmaster's desk into an altar through the draping of a freshly laundered *dhoti* and placing thereon a wooden cross and an open Bible, this building doubles as the place of worship for the church of God which is at Puducheri. The church, according to the rolls, consists of 116 members, thirty-six of them communicants, fifty of them children (the remaining adults are still "under instruction"). Except on the second Sunday of every month, when the pastor comes from the nearby town, the services are conducted by the headmaster, who also leads the weekly cottage prayer meeting and conducts the instruction class. His wife leads the ladies of the Mathar Sangam mothers meeting. In days gone by it was the missionary who came twice a month to conduct services, but now since they have their own pastor, who owns only a bicycle and has nine other similar places to take care of, besides the town church, they must be satisfied with seeing him but once a month. But of course, there is always the headmaster.

Always? As it is, the church of God which is at Puducheri worships in a building held in the name of an organization hereafter known as the church. Its teacher-catechist is appointed by the church and is paid with government grant-in-aid. The pastor is appointed by the church and paid by it with the aid of contributions from the churches. Now comes the government, which has been giving grant-in-aid for the running of the school and takes over the building and control of the school. Or it pays the teacher directly, and then transfers teachers at will. Or it directs the management to take a teacher from the government list of waiting candidates. The steps may be gradual, but the end result will be the same: no Christian school, no chapel, no headmaster under shepherd. At the same time the church's subsidy is being reduced and the pastor has to take over more village churches to make the pastorate self-supporting.

Where does that leave the church of God which is at Puducheri? What is it built on? Will it stand? Will the church be able to adjust to the situation and do something to help support the church?

Meanwhile the church is having its own "bigger" problems. It has inherited from the mission a number of general institutions: high schools, boarding schools, teacher-training schools, hospitals and dispensaries, industrial institutes, book depots. As the missionaries turn these over to Indian colleagues, more and more top salaries are included in the church budget. The mission subsidy for that budget, by common consent, is being progressively reduced. Where does that leave the church? What can the church in turn do for the church of God which is at Puducheri?

Perhaps the picture is not quite so bleak in *our* church. Perhaps we have foreseen the problems and have taken some steps to forestall being caught in such a situation. But it can be said with little fear of contradiction that every church in some degree is faced with the problem of the church of God which is at Puducheri. It is also equally certain that only as the church finds a solution for the survival of the church in Puducheri will the church itself survive.

The Question of Continuity

Every church, however it arises, naturally develops, partly from its heritage, partly from its environment and the circumstances of its origin and growth, a distinctive theology, a distinctive tradition and pattern of life and worship, and some type of organization and government. Though all three factors are naturally interrelated, any one or the other of these may predominate over the others in the hierarchy of values of the particular church, and one can think of numerous examples of churches that are characterized by the practical emphasis they place on one or the other of these factors. All three factors in varying degrees exercise a cohesive, conserving influence that makes for the continuity of the church. (They also, incidentally, in varying degrees exercise an influence that keeps the various churches separated from each other—but that is another story.)

It is natural for every church to seek not only self-preservation but self-perpetuation, to find ever surer ways to guarantee continuity. The church is to be built upon the rock against which the gates of hell shall not prevail. And so, each church tends to interpret "the rock" of Matt 16:18 in accordance with its predominant characteristic emphasis. The church that emphasizes theology will speak of the rock as the objective content of Peter's confession, the truth about Christ, the doctrine of Christ. The church that emphasizes Christianity as a distinctive pattern of life will say the rock is Peter's faith in Christ, his direct experience of the revelation of Christ in himself. The church that emphasizes church government will say the rock is Peter as the first in a succession of Christ's representatives to ensure the continuity of the church.

The fact that churches embodying these various emphases have continued for hundreds of years should make us pause in condemning any interpretation not our own. And yet, the rock must manifestly be one, and not many. So here we come to a fundamental question in this fundamental problem. Does a system of theology, or a traditional pattern of faith and life and worship, or a system of church government guarantee the presence and continuity of the church of God? The answer, theologically and empirically considered, must be "No." The Jewish church, reorganized after the Exile by Ezra with a re-established theology and a re-established way of life and a re-established government, furnished a framework within which God preserved his church, but it was that church organization that crucified the Lord of the church and killed Stephen. The most that the firm organization of teaching and life and practice and government in a church can accomplish is to make a framework wherein God can establish and extend his church. "On this rock *I* will build my church." A church can by the grace of God be a help—or it can be a hindrance—to the building of God's church. Insofar as it confuses church and Church and identifies the two, it is a hindrance more than a help. But let none of us start throwing stones at the Roman Catholic Church. They have only had a longer start.

It is a matter of deep significance that in this vital matter of what constitutes the church, in the matter of the interpretation of "the rock," there have been such deep-lying stubborn differences. Those who were waiting for Kittel's *Worterbuch* to reach the Pi's were rewarded with a brilliant study by Oscar Cullmann on *Petros* and *petra*.[2] But the final answer is not there. It is evident that the final answer will not yield to individual scholarship but only to the corporate obedience of faith. That means, certainly not the abandonment of these "necessary evils" of church organizations, but the realization of what they are and what they are not. It means the abandonment, not of the "safeguards" of theology and tradition and government, but of our reliance upon them as guaranteeing the continuity of the church, as being coextensive with "the rock." Whatever can be said positively about "the rock"—and there is much that can be said—it must be recognized negatively that it is not something given to us that we can organize and manage and control and manipulate and sell guaranteed shares in.

What then *can* we do for the continuity of the church, to make it specific, the church of God which is at Puducheri?

The Grand Inquisitor

Dostoyevsky, within his novel *The Brothers Karamazov*, relates a fantasy of a man who thought he had an answer. At the time of the Inquisition

2. Cullman, "Πέτρος, Κηφᾶς."

in Spain the Grand Inquisitor, while going by the steps of the cathedral at Seville, sees Christ, returned to earth and moving among the common people as of old, raise a young girl from the dead. He signals his guards and they lay hold of the Prisoner and take him away to a dungeon. That night the old Grand Inquisitor comes to the cell to talk to the Prisoner. '"Why have you come back?" he says,

> to hinder us, to try to undo the work we have done in your name? We have corrected your great mistake which you have made in the wilderness when you were offered the ways of bread and miracle and authority to win the hearts of men. You spurned them all, for you wanted men to love you in freedom. But the race of men does not want to be free. The responsibility is too great, for they are weak, ever sinful and rebellious. I swear, man is weaker and baser by nature than you have believed him. By showing him so much respect, you as it were ceased to feel for him, for you asked too much of him. And so we have taken upon ourselves this fearful responsibility and we have given men what they want. And men rejoiced that they were again led like sheep. That is the only way of universal happiness.[3]

So eloquent is the old man in his monologue that one wonders for a while on whose side the author stands. But the Prisoner remains quiet with an accusing silence, and at the end he goes over to the old man and softly kisses him on his bloodless aged lips. The old man shudders, goes over to the door, and lets the Prisoner out into the night.

Here again stones are out of place. This is a parable whose application and implications go far beyond a certain church organization deep down into our common human nature. Who of us will claim that he and his church organization have fully resisted the strong temptation in the Indian scene to "give the people what they want"—material things, a good show, strong authority, the subtle temptation to give to them what, it is said, "fits the genius of the Indian people"?

The Foolishness of God

To a church none of whose members had heard the gospel more than five years before, Paul writes a letter, addressed to "the church of God which is at Corinth, to those sanctified in Christ Jesus, called to be saints."

---

3. Dostoyevsky, *Brothers Karamazov*, 133.

He thanks God because of the grace of God which was given to them in Christ Jesus, "that in every way you were enriched in him with all speech and all knowledge . . . so that you are not lacking in any spiritual gift." He assures them that their Lord Jesus Christ will sustain them to the end, and that "God is faithful, by whom you were called into the fellowship of his Son, Jesus Christ our Lord." He acknowledges that "not many of you were wise according to worldly standards, not many were powerful, not many were of noble birth." In almost every chapter he has to take them to task for serious faults. And still, interspersed are statements in the same terms as the opening address: "You are God's field, God's building." "You are God's temple and God's Spirit dwells in you." "You are the body of Christ." Note that he does not say, "You ought to be," or "You should strive to become," but "You *are* . . . "

Then he goes away out to the end of a limb and says to this young group of inexperienced Christians, "All things are yours, whether Paul or Apollos or Cephas or the world or life or death or the present or the future, all are yours; and you are Christ's; and Christ is God's." Enough to make a Grand Inquisitor's hair stand on end! No safeguards, no reservation of veto powers, no mediation of this tremendous power through more experienced fathers in God—in fact, the fathers in God are included in the list of things subordinate to them. Everything on a gold platter. Can they take it? Can they be trusted? Maybe in Corinth, but not in Puducheri! Anyway, they don't want it, this gift of the full responsibility of freedom on a gold platter. It's foolishness. Yes, and "the foolishness of God is wiser than men, and the weakness of God is stronger than men."

We have overlooked a safeguard, God's own built-in safeguard: "All things are yours; and you are Christ's; and Christ is God's." It is enough for God; it ought to be enough for us. For this is not only a built-in safeguard; it is also the built-in power to make them capable, in Christ. If you try to condition the safeguard, you condition the power. Any addition of ours to the safeguard is that much subtraction from the power, so much less built on the Rock; for any human addition is automatically a subtraction from the divine. "For no other foundation can anyone lay than that which is laid, which is Jesus Christ."

Let the theology, the pattern of life, the government serve their proper purpose; let the church which enshrines and guards and promotes them serve its proper purpose: to be a means for the means. Let them not aspire to anything closer than that, lest they inhibit the growth of the body of Christ.

They can get in the way, or they can help; but there is one thing they cannot do: guarantee Christ, who is the Head and the Life of the church.

God's Way

There is only one thing that can: his self-appointed vehicles by which he comes to men, the means by which the life-giving presence flows into the life of the church, the means of grace. This is the Spirit's work. We cannot bind the Spirit to any kind of pattern or plan or means or safeguards of our own. He refuses to be organized. But he binds himself, as far as we are concerned, to his own self-established means; and be they ever so material and prosaic, through them he operates. This is not to deny that the Spirit can and does work as he pleases: "The wind bloweth where it listeth." But as far as we are concerned, in the framework of the pattern of salvation revealed to us, he binds himself to these means, and through the creaturely elements of human nature, human words, water, bread, and wine, the living Christ comes to his church. Here is the only guarantee for the continuity of the church.

By these means the church is constituted and lives; and with them the church proclaims life to the world. For they are given into the church's custody, that "you may shine as lights in the world, holding forth the word of life." But they are given into custody not as its own property, but in stewardship. For they are still God's means, and it is not so much that we are to use them, as they are to use us.

The history of the church is full of examples of how God's means have been misunderstood, misused, and abused. They have been idolized and deified; they have been confused and identified with the reality for which they are the vehicles, the living, eternal Word himself. They have been patronized and deprecated and despised as being merely human and crassly material; they have been spiritualized and bypassed as though they were childlike crutches. They have been treated as private property to be managed and manipulated as men's own means for self-realization and self-preservation. These are lessons for us from church history to teach us to let God be God.

Where the organization of theology, church life, and government is of such a nature that it does not constrict and obscure, but allows, guards, and promotes the free working of the Spirit through his means of grace, there, as far as human endeavor is concerned, we have reached the maximum.

Any other aids, any other safeguards, no matter how well-intentioned, are only hindrances. All the Spirit needs is a chance.

What Can We Do?

Recently a group of workers met for a series of sessions to diagnose the problems of the rural churches for which they were responsible. After all the temperature charts and laboratory test results were in and the group discussed the kind of treatment needed, it boiled down to a rather prosaic answer: a more concentrated, more personalized, more meaningful impact of the means of grace on the members. How that can most effectively be done, by laymen's training, by the extension of the lay ministry, or whatever means can be devised toward that end, is a pressing problem in every church. There is no doubt that after the recent period of organizational activity in the various churches the first priority at this time is the need for promoting the dynamic aspect of church life, the grounding and rooting of the church in the living word of God. It is not merely a matter of Bible study and teaching but doing it in such a way and with such a purpose that the momentum carries over and the thing becomes self-propagating in the church.

The corollary of this is the need for the church in Puducheri, in that word, to learn what is its birthright, its charter, its true constitution, its *raison d' etre*, what it is, how it is, and why it is. "All things are yours; and you are Christ's; and Christ is God's." It is foolish, it is dangerous, it is impossible. But it works.

3

The Christian Mission to the Resurgent Religions

Edmund Perry

The resurgent faiths of Asia present the Christian church today with one of its newest and most demanding tasks. The impact of this resurgence could not be contained in Asia even if the aims of these religions were intentionally limited to Asia. The fact is, however, that Hindus, Buddhists, and Muslims intend to set their respective claims before the entire world as tenable faith alternatives for the whole of mankind.

Given the missionary character of the Christian faith, a full-scale encounter of the church with the other major systems of faith was inevitable. Yet as a pressing task for the church, confrontation by and countermission from these other faiths is really new. As late as 1938 Hendrik Kraemer was telling us that this showdown was yet to come; and most of us continued to assume that such a showdown would pit an offensive Christianity against defensive religions. In 1956 Kraemer could tell us that we were on the brink of the encounter, that the time of the encounter was at hand, and that the offensive mission of the resurgent faiths was going to put Christianity in a defensive stance. Few observers of world affairs in late 1959 will doubt that the encounter has now begun, although it has by no means reached its full proportions.

The very newness of the present situation of the church contributes considerably to the complexity which Christians face in trying to define how they should participate individually and ecclesiastically in the encounter. We of course, are not the first generation to have pondered the problem of the relationship of the many religions to the one Lord Jesus Christ. The early Christian apologists wrestled with this issue as the Christian mission penetrated deeper and deeper into the Graeco-Roman world and became less and less dependent upon the local synagogue as a point of contact and departure for the mission.

As a matter of fact, the two contrasting approaches which have dominated Christian thinking about the other religions were already defined in the early part of the third century of our era. Justin Martyr and Clement and Origen of Alexandria appropriated the Stoic notion of *logos spermatikos*, the Logos seed scattered throughout mankind, to account for those relative proximations of Jesus Christ in pagan philosophies and religions. The germinal Logos lodged in the nature of man, nurtured more by some than by others constitutes an essential unity with the fullness of the Logos incarnate in Jesus Christ. To find good and noble people and ideals elsewhere than in Christianity was no embarrassment to these fathers for they regarded what was found to be the outgrowth of the germinal Logos. With this notion these apologists could be "fair" to other systems of faith without surrendering primacy of Jesus Christ and without modifying their claim that every reasonable man should recognize the full Logos in Jesus Christ and become a Christian.

The contrasting approach was stated by Tertullian, a Latin apologist. "*Quid Athenae Hierosolymis?*" What has Athens to do with Jerusalem? The inevitable choice is that between the redemptive mercy God has offered in Christ and some irreconcilable alternative actualized for Tertullian in the philosophizings of the Greeks. The problem of natural man is not a paucity of knowledge but an impaired will and a plenitude of guilt for disobedience to whatsoever good (or god) he does know. It is not information and enlightenment that such a man desperately needs, but a Savior. Jesus may have peers among the wisemen and teachers, but as a Savior he has no lieutenants and no challengers.

Neither of these approaches was formulated academically by theologians in a detached stance thinking about the problem. Both approaches were formulated in the heat and by the impact of controversy with real flesh and blood challenges from the Graeco-Roman faiths. Neither was addressed primarily to Christians but to Christianity's disputants at the time. Both intended to serve the conviction that all men stand in need of all that God has given in Jesus Christ and that Graeco-Roman piety and philosophy did not and could not offer men Jesus Christ.

How to think of and deal with "other" faiths is thus seen to be not a new or recent concern of the church. It is a problem inevitably coextensive with the church. What is new is the specific "other" faiths which confront us today and the fact that they confront us on their own instigation. But to this day the challenge of all other faiths is being dealt with in the terms presented by the challenge of the Graeco-Roman mentality and religions. Up to the present time Christian theologies of "other religions" have been written in reference to the contrasting poles of continuity and discontinuity, which is to say that even though new challengers have come forth we have continued to define the problem and to formulate answers in characteristically Graeco-Roman terms.

One reason why the continuity-versus-discontinuity debate has persisted, and one of the scandals deriving from it is that, with a few notable exceptions, Christian theologizing about other religions has been carried on by Christians who were talking with each other rather than with prospective disciples. That is our failure—we have been theologizing *about* the religions and not theologizing *to* them. We have been formulating an answer to the problem they constitute and as a reply to their specific and distinctive challenge. A really scandalous amount of our Christian time and energy has been devoted to disputation among ourselves and to reshuffling Christians from the camp of continuity to the camp of discontinuity and back again, with an occasional refreshing pause en route at the comfort station of reconception.

Christians must indeed talk among themselves and seek clarification from each other in their understanding of the world they confront and by which they are confronted. Such conversation in the church appears to the world as Christian soliloquy indicative of senility and loss of contact with reality. And it becomes just that if the Christians do not return actively to engage the world. It is of the nature of the Christian faith to be alternately withdrawn from and involved with the world, to be soliloquizing and dialoging, worshiping and working, being disciplined and going forth to disciple others. A Christian theology of mission regardless of how much sense it may make to Christians themselves, is never fully and genuinely Christian unless and until it is a theology of address to the prospective disciple, relevant though not correlative to his own faith and self-understanding. Christian theology of mission is *Keryg-matio*, proclamatory theology, a proclamation of Christ which challenges men and women not simply where they are but where they understand themselves to be. We do not have a Christian theology of mission that speaks relevantly to our present prospective disciples. We are still talking to ourselves.

The point I want to make is that we simply do not meet the Graeco-Roman mind in the Hindus, Buddhists and Muslims who are presently confronting us. While wisdom in dealing with other faiths will not begin with us, neither did it die with the fathers, let us hope. Certainly, the responsibility for other faiths did not end with the Ante-Nicene fathers. The distinctive character of the other faiths which confront us today and the unique character of their offensive confrontation demand little less than that we begin *de novo* with the Biblical *kerygma* to formulate a theology of these "other" religions. However personally satisfying it may be to us who are heirs of the Graeco-Roman mentality to prolong the continuity-versus-discontinuity debate, the themes of this debate do not speak relevantly to the faith-understanding of the men of resurgent Asian religions. Parenthetically, though not irrelevantly, our internal musings make little or no challenge to the Western secularized, post-Christian man. Consequently, further debate among ourselves using the old terms and references does not promise anything fruitful in fulfilling the demands of our present responsibility.

A new formulation of Christian missionary apologetic issuing from the dynamics of the new situation is demanded of us. At the outset of this task we can readily admit and stoutly maintain that it will hardly be a Christian apologetic unless it issues, as did those apologies of the early church, from the conviction that all men at all times and in all places need all that God has given and is giving in Jesus Christ. The debated and crucial question for Christians at this juncture is this, Has God given and is he giving elsewhere and in other ways what is given in Jesus Christ? Except the Bible be discarded as the normative definition of our faith, we have to hold as Christians that outside the church men are still waiting for God's redemptive act in Christ even though they may have the idea of the Redeemer God and trust utterly in their belief that he is redemptive. The idea of a Redeemer God is not to be identified (i.e., confused), we believe on biblical grounds, with the person of Jesus the Savior. If another religion does not offer Jesus Christ to man, it is not offering what, according to the Bible, God has intended for all men. And when Jesus Christ is offered all that God can give is offered.

Let it be acknowledged that some Christians do not find it necessary to maintain the ultimacy of God's gift in Jesus Christ, or at most they maintain it ambivalently. In his brilliant and lucid chapter contributed to the Joachim Wach memorial volume, *The History of Religions: Essays in Methodology*, Professor Wilfred Cantwell Smith of McGill University states: "I would argue that [exclusivism and proselytism] are (or will become not) obligatory elements of the Christian faith, and indeed my personal view would be that the very value and even the purpose of Christian dialogue with other faiths may well be a Christian learning at last to apprehend one's own faith fully and loyally (and perhaps more truly?) and simultaneously to appreciate the quality and even the ultimate validity (in the eyes of God) of others' [faith].[1] In a footnote Professor Smith asserts further: "those Hindus and Muslims whom I admire, who are my friends (and indeed whom Christians generally must admire, and do take as friends), remain Hindus and Muslims. (And probably it is good that they so remain)."[2]

Professor Smith's firsthand and expert knowledge of Islam and of the Christian mission to Islam and Muslims command us seriously to measure his words. But finally, we have to say that he has abandoned the biblical conviction that God's gift in the person and mission of Jesus Christ is decisive for all men and is intended to constitute a new faith location for all men. We are obligated to ask Professor Smith, "By what canon of authority do you redefine the Christian faith so as to divest it of what has been its distinctive character and its sole reason to exist?"

Unless it can be shown that Jesus Christ has been given to other religions by some other means than the church's mission, Christians who ground their faith in biblical convictions will be compelled by the very nature of their existence as Christians, to continue to preach the gospel of Jesus Christ to all and sundry. The problem is not whether but how to preach this gospel in the present situation. "To serve the present age" is our calling to fulfill. We know we have been brought into the kingdom for just such a task as this.

It is to the faith-understanding of the Hindu, of the Buddhist, and of the Muslim that the good news of Jesus Christ must be preached and related. Apart from the Christians' ignorance of the gospel and its missionary thrust, there is nothing more appalling and discouraging in the present situation than Christians' unfamiliarity with the faith claims of the Hindu, Buddhist, and Muslim and their respective ways of thinking. Until we achieve a Christian understanding of these others' faith-understanding

1. Smith, "Comparative Religion," 49.
2. Smith, "Comparative Religion," 50.

of themselves and the world, we cannot expect a Christian apologetic adequate for this major task now before the church.

To recover the biblical content and basis for the Christian mission, further basic biblical studies like that of Joachim Jeramias' *Jesus' Promise to the Nations*[3] are indispensable. Such studies will enable us to dissociate the languages and thought forms of the West from the gospel. But it is never the gospel of Jesus Christ unless it is related to and through some language in a way that discloses its relevance to a specific framework of thinking. So, the church's present urgent task also demands scholarly studies of the religions with whom we are in encounter.

By scholarly studies we do not mean simply studies in the antiquities of these religions, although this is an essential part of the study. Peoples of the world are finding themselves increasingly free of cultural, economic and political domination. It is a quite natural impulse for these people to search back into their own pre-colonial past and attempt to resuscitate and give contemporary form to a long-smothered glory. But this is only one part of a scholarly study of another religion, and in many instances present-day Christian scholars have a better factual knowledge of this past than the people of the religion in question. What is so much needed just now is a thorough familiarity with the interpretation which the living communities of these faiths are giving to their past—its scriptures, creeds, ideals, rituals, practices, and ethos. Or to repeat, we are confronted by real flesh and blood devotees of these other faiths. In order to understand them as they understand themselves and to relate the recovered gospel to their present self-understanding, we need careful studies by first-rate cultural anthropologists. Professional students of religions have already recognized that the proper study of religions is in considerable degree the study of persons in a specific societal context.

But again, it will not suffice merely to recover the de-Westernized gospel and capture the faith-understanding of the Asian religionists. These two steps are indeed fundamental. Before we can begin to formulate a Christian theology of and to these newly met religions Christians are pressed to ask further, What is Christ doing in these other religions, in the resurgence of their vitality and missionary zeal? We dare not regard either the resurgent religions nor Christ's relationship to them as static. Neither Christ nor the elemental spirals of the universe have been idle since the crucifixion or the resurrection. Assuredly we believe that the

---

3. Jeremias, *Jesus' Promise*.

mighty work of God "under Pontius Pilate" is definitive and that what was done there somehow affected these other religions, but Scripture instructs us to look also for the work that the Risen Christ is doing at this time throughout the world for which he died.

All of us would agree, as Christians, that Christ is operative within the "other" religions, though at this stage of our understanding not all of us would agree that he is the faith-evoking power to which the men of these faiths commit themselves however ignorantly. But to dwell on this is to lapse into a speculative treatment of our problem. At this stage we are compelled by the very renascence of the Asian religions to ask, What can we see Christ doing in the resurgence of these other religions? Later we may be pressed to ask what Christ has been doing in the history of these religions at least apart from if not in the "faith-consciousness" of these other faith-folk.

Many of us interpret the resurgence of these Asian religions to be Christ's judgment upon Christians, first for our failure to carry the gospel to the Asians and secondly for the adulteration of the gospel when we did carry it. Such a statement intends not to condemn so much the faithful servants of Christ who actually went to the mission fields as those of us who determined the conditions under which their mission had to be carried out. Surely Christ is bringing judgment upon us in this present manifestation of revival of religions for our lack of support for his mission and surely he is judging us for the unnecessary scandals of Western culture with which we have saddled the gospel.

In the sense that God's judgment is always his reaction to our provocation, we have to confess that we have brought the present situation of encounter upon ourselves. More than we like to admit we carried the gospel to Asia in close association with Western cultural imperialism and now the religions of Asia revive escorted by nationalism. This is not an unqualified and unwelcomed judgment, however. The freedom in Christ which we have preached has proved itself stronger than our colonialisms and this freedom preached by missionaries is undeniably one of the sources of the Asians' inspiration for national independence and international recognition. For the freedom gained thus far Christians should be as thankful as the politically liberated Asians.

There is another sense in which Christians have brought the present crisis upon themselves and this is in the unplanned for reversals of their missionary work. Significant leadership in the revived religions is the product of Christian missionary schools. Both G. P. Malalasekera, longtime president of the World Fellowship of Buddhists, and Sri Radhakrishnan, Hindu philosopher-missionary and distinguished Indian diplomat, are products of Christian schools. In his essay on "The Spirit in Man," Dr. Radhakrishnan says:

> My training in philosophy, which began in the years 1905 to 1909 in the Madras Christian College, with its atmosphere of Christian thought, aspiration and endeavor, led me to take a special interest in the religious implications of the Hindu religions to which I attributed the political downfall of India.... What is wrong with Hindu religion? How can we make it somewhat more relevant to the intellectual climate and social environment of our time? Such were the questions which roused my interest.[4]

Here is a candid confession that Christian mission provoked a reconsideration and a revitalization of Hinduism among those to whom the church was bringing the gospel of Jesus Christ.

But consider the matter one step further. While the preaching of Christ has helped to inspire the reform and revival of Asian faiths and to encourage social, political and economic liberation, this very liberation is at the same time the occasion for a strong protest from these faiths against the church, against Christians and in some cases against Christ himself. Criticism of Christians and the Christian faith is a theme common to the contemporary polemics of all three of the renascent Asian faiths. Much of this criticism is justified and should bring Christians to repentance. The record of Christians in warmongering has muffled our testimony for the Prince of Peace. Racial segregation in the churches, particularly in the United States, becomes the mocking echo of our witness to man's oneness in Christ. The audience of the Christian missionary ponders the sanity of the spokesmen who speak so freely of Christ breaking down all barriers of separation and yet cannot offer to the world a united Christianity.

If the revival of these religions were only a critique, even an exaggerated critique, of Christianity, we could be thankful, for it becomes Christians to receive judgment and reproof. But the protest against Christianity from these religions comes with a strong positive alternative to as well as criticism of the Christian faiths. We certainly cannot attribute to Christ the creation of faith alternatives which would displace him. Eventually as we understand better the Scriptural teaching about "the powers" and when we are more intimately acquainted with the contending religions, we may

---

4. Radhakrishnan, "Spirit," 475–76.

be able to discern and speak about powers other than Christ operative in the revival of these religions. At the moment let us admit that there are reversals to Christ's mission and ours, which we are not ready to attribute to the work of Christ as Judge and Redeemer.

But not everything in the resurgence of religions of Asia is a repudiation of the Christian message and mission. There are evidences that Christ is being received in some measure, not simply by individuals, but by the "institutions" of these religions as good news to men in their religions. In the Hindu Ramakrishna societies, Jesus is given a place alongside other "founders" of religions. While this provisional acceptance of Jesus is no basis upon which to structure a Christian theology of religions, neither ought we to disparage the fact that the rejection of Jesus here is only a provisional rejection. Remembering that Jesus did not exclude the "outsider" who cast out demons in Jesus's name (Mark 9:38–41), shall we discourage the limited witness to Jesus by the Ramakrishna society? Or, to put it otherwise, are we prepared to declare categorically that Christ is not working in the limited recognition given him by these Hindus? Some Burmese Buddists, as well as Mahayana Buddhists speak of Jesus as the Buddha of the West, and because of the references to him in the Qu'ran many Muslims seemingly regard Jesus more highly as prophet-messenger-and-word of God (but not as Lord and God) than do many Christians who contribute money to support missions to the Muslims.

George Appleton appeals to us[5] to welcome and encourage these partial acceptances, never pretending that the fullness of Christ has been received in such instances as those cited, but receiving these instances as doors which Christ is opening to us for further witness to him and to fuller understanding of him both by us who witness and by those to whom we witness. It is not for us to prescribe how or when Christ will transfigure himself before the missionaries and faithful of Asian religions and before us who already try to worship and serve him as Lord. It is not out of character to expect that when he transfigures himself in relation to Vishnu, Gotama, and Mohammad, Christ will have something to say to Christians as well as to Hindus, Buddhists, and Muslims.

Besides appreciation for Jesus himself, there is in the renascent religions an appropriation of some of the message and mission of the church with reference to responsible citizenship. Although the rebirth of Hinduism has brought some restrictions upon the Christian mission in India it

---

5. Appleton, "Christian Encounter," 138–39.

has also brought and is fostering in some quarters an increasingly sensitive social conscience. In some of the Buddhist countries, Buddhists, stimulated by the precepts and examples of Christian missionaries, are now building up their own social service agencies. But this aspect of the influence of Christianity is rather well known.

Can Christ be seen to be working a more positive grace in the revival of the Asian religions? The Bible instructs us to see Providence reversing the intentions of men in history—all men, that is: Christians, Jews, and others. Joseph says to his brethren who had thought to be done with him forever, "do not be distressed, or angry with yourselves, because you sold me here; for God sent me before you to preserve life." "Ah, Assyria," says God, "Assyria is the rod of my anger and I send him against a godless nation. . . . But (Assyria) does not so intend . . . it is in his mind to destroy" (Isa 10:5, 6). Those who crucified Jesus did so to be rid of him, but God reversed their intention and made the crucifixion the means for saving "many." Paul went in pursuit of Christians only to find himself pursued and made a Christian. Can we not say that while the representatives of the reborn religions come to preach their faith claims, Christ brings them to hear his claims preached even through us?

It needs quickly to be added that Christ brings these others not only that they may hear the unsearchable riches of Christ preached, but also that he may bestow upon us the unsearchable riches he has promised us from all languages, peoples, and cultures. Very few Christians have even begun to appropriate the benefits Christ has to offer in the languages and arts of the peoples of Asia. But best of all he offers us the Asians themselves as brethren for whom with us he died and now lives. They offer themselves to us as brethren in the dignity and on the terms of their own faith-understanding. It becomes us Christians to understand them as nearly as possible as they understand themselves and us, for they are not given to us as Christians, but as Hindus, Buddhists, and Muslims. While we and they were yet sinners Christ died for us all. In Christ we have them as brethren whether or not they become Christian. Neither our responsibility nor our service to them is conditioned by the possibility of their converting to faith in Christ, however much we may desire and work for that. After we have done all, as well as the while we are doing it, we remember that "no man calls Jesus Christ Lord but by the Holy Spirit."

To say that Christ gives the people of the Asian Religions to us as brethren is to say that he gives us to them as servants. They are not our problems, but their problems and their needs are ours and are our responsibilities. Probably no verse in Holy Scripture speaks more relevantly to the task of the church as it meets the religions of the world than this: "You know that those who rule over the Gentiles lord it over them, but it shall not be so among you. . . . He that is greatest among you, shall be the servant of all (Mark 10:42).

Let me suggest only one implication for your consideration. When we Christians begin to identify with the needs of the peoples of the world, and consider ourselves as the servants of those people in those needs, we may have to forego spending $250 million annually in the construction of new tax-exempt buildings and invest that money in the building of men. Buildings are not of the *esse* of the church; but mission in service to human need is. The people of the religions of the world will little note what we build in color, form, and mass, but they will ponder long our investment in the rehabilitation of human lives and the rebirth of the human spirit.

4

A Light to the Nations

John Howard Yoder

One of the more creative recent contributions to the discussion of the Church is a pamphlet by R. Martin-Achard, "*Israel et les Nations.*" The subtitle, "The Missionary Perspective of the Old Testament," poses clearly the author's question. In the framework of the evolutionary view of the history of Israel's religion as shaped by Wellhausen, there was thought to be not only development from "primitive" to "high" religion, from polytheism to monotheism, from taboo to ethics, but also from tribal particularism to missionary universalism. The prophets responsible for texts like Isa 42:1–6, 49:6, Mal 1:11, and the book of Jonah get the credit for drawing from an earlier prophetic monotheism the conclusion that if there is but one God, then the task of the people who know his identity must be to proclaim it to those who worship him without knowing him (Acts 17:23). Thus Israel, or at least the best of the later prophets, had overcome the "chosen-people" particularism and become missionary.

Martin-Achard undertakes to review this by now almost universally accepted theory, not by challenging the philosophy or the view of comparative religion which lies behind it—also a worthy undertaking—but by reading more carefully the texts which are generally understood as "missionary." Taken carefully in their contexts, these prophetic passages are found to promise the vindication, and not the transcending, of Israel's peculiar position as the elect people. "He will establish justice in the Earth" (Isa 42:4) does not mean that the Messiah, or Israel as a whole, will by political expansion or by sending out proselytizing propagandists gain the subjection of all peoples to Mosaic law, but rather that the triumphant rehabilitation of Israel and restoration of Jerusalem will demonstrate to all the world the reliability of God's promises to Abraham. "I will give you as a light to the nations" (Isa 49:6) speaks of the Servant as being visibly blessed in a way that all can see, not of his functioning as an educator. "Proclaiming the Good News of peace" (Isa 52:7) is not the making of converts but the announcing of Zion's restoration. "My salvation shall reach to the end of the earth" refers to the news of God's mighty deeds, not to church expansion.

> Humanity, upon learning of the reversal of the destiny of Israel shall discover the greatness of Israel's God in the face of the Work of Jahweh, the gentiles, overcome, will render Him the Glory which is His due. The ultimate consequences of the reconstitution of Israel is the encounter of the nations with Jahweh . . . In this sense we may speak of the Servant's 'mission.' He does not preach to the distant isles a sort of Gospel . . . He accepts the good news concerning himself and lives before the astonished and convinced world the 'judgment' which Jahweh has pronounced on him. The Elect does not propagandize to win humanity for his God; it is enough that he testify by his very existence, to Jahweh's greatness. Israel's God makes him the light of the world by giving him life.[1]

> The prophet does not invite Israel to roam the globe calling pagans to conversion. The *raison d'etre* of the elect people is simply to exist; its very presence demonstrates the Lordship of Jahweh, its life testifies to what God is, for Israel and for the universe . . . Contemplating the unique destiny of the chosen people, heaven and earth will discover its author.[2]

> God converts the Gentiles by acting in the midst of His people . . . The Church evangelizes insofar as her Lord gives her life . . . The evangelization of the world is not a matter of words or activities, but of presence, presence of God's people in the midst of humanity, presence of God in the midst of His people. It is not without utility that the Old Testament should remind the Church of this.[3]

If this be an accurate reading of the Old Testament, and for present purposes let us assume that it is, it throws light on two kinds of questions. On the one hand, it underlines the originality of the New Testament with respect to the mission of God's people. The Old Testament expected the world

---

1. Martin-Achard, "*Israel et*," 29.
2. Martin-Achard, "*Israel et*," 31.
3. Martin-Achard, "*Israel et*," 72.

to see and to bow to the power of Jahweh, but this was seen as happening in the messianic End-time, and as coming to pass without Israel's taking any active part in bearing the good news. Now that the fullness of time has come, and one of the marks of the New Age is the bringing in of the gentiles, the church is not a passive observer, but God's agency toward this end. The astounded subjection of the nations was not envisaged as meaning their integration into Israel, as has come to pass in the new covenant.

Yet beyond this evident shift between Testaments, there is on the other hand an essential continuity. True enough, the church as Christ's body does God's own work in his name; yet her presence, like that of Israel, is more important than her activity. Not how she seeks to blanket the earth with a message or with her hierarchies, but what the church is, is her basic testimony. For only as her own life as a social entity reflects a reconciling power and a will-to-fellowship which only the pouring out of the Spirit in the last Days can explain, will her proclamation in Jerusalem, Samaria, and to the ends of the earth be testimony instead of bare reporting. Only as the "walk in newness of life" is a visible experience, will the good old phrases about who Jesus was and what he did, be of any evangelistic import. As far as the watching world is concerned, the testimony to the living Christ is a commentary on the visible life of the church, and not the other way around. If the church is not the unconcealable city on the hill, if her presence does not call for an explanation, the commentary will not be read. Being the church is the first and in the broad sense the only task of the church.

This by no means signifies a rejection of the contemporary trend in ecumenical theology to speak of mission as the essence of the church. Yet the reminder is well needed at just this point, that the "mission" which is the essence of the church is not her organizing for delegating people to go to far places, but the simple witness in deed to what God already has done in calling to himself a "peculiar people." The going and the staying of God's people are functions of their being. Two dangers especially may be identified in the light of this reminder. One is the idea that the church's "mission" consists in getting to as many persons as possible as soon as possible with the "gospel" in the most rudimentary verbal form, i.e., with the call to individual conversion, and that any investment of effort in other causes is improper, unless it serve indirectly the same goal (i.e., Christian education is justified if it produces missionaries, relief work if it induces people to listen to preaching, political involvement if it has to do with freedom to travel and preach, local congregations as they provide support in funds, prayer, and personnel).

The Christian and Missionary Alliance and the inter-denominational (in reality non-denominational or crypto-denominational) mission agencies best represent this view. By no means does it follow that other questions are undecided or indifferent; Christians of this conviction in general have very pronounced, and very predictable, views on many issues of ethics and doctrine, and similarly predictable leanings in piety and even in politics; but such matters are not of the essence of the church. Dealing with them is accessory to the real task of evangelism.

The lesson of the example of Israel is that such a narrowing of the essence of the church is a misunderstanding of the way God works and an over-valuing of certain categories of human faithfulness over against others which, less overtly "missionary," might fulfill just as effectively or more so the requirement, "simply to exist; its very presence indicates the Lordship of Jahweh."

Yet an equally profound misapprehension lurks before those churches which stand at the other end of the ecclesiological spectrum. The most obvious conclusion to be drawn from the words of Martin-Achard just repeated would at first thought seem to be that Eastern Orthodoxy, completely self-contained, representing proleptically in her liturgy the transfiguration of all mankind, sitting out the centuries in mystical indifference to the tides of empire while singing the praises of the incarnation, is the ideal pattern for the church whose task is to testify by simply existing.

This would be to misunderstand Martin-Achard and the Israelite hope he has analyzed. The fulfillment of the promise to Israel is not the apotheosis of mankind or of matter, but the establishment of the kingdom, the fulfillment of Jahweh's purposes in politico-social history. The church of those "upon whom the ends of the ages have come" is no company of bystanders, no hitchhiker in the parade of Providence. The church is the motor of history; for good or ill according as she is faithful or apostate, but in either case the motor. The cosmic drama she performs is not the sacramental rehearsal of the ontological mysteries of incarnation and redemption, but the actual defeat of the world rulers of this present darkness in concrete deeds of fellowship and love suffering obedience and faithful witness, in the joyful certainty that the End has begun. With Paul she glories not in her faithfulness to her own past but in being all things to all men; far from celebrating an unshakeable divine privilege, she does not run aimlessly, but beats her body, lest after preaching to others she should herself be disqualified. For the church "simply to exist" is the farthest thing from inactivity; it is for her to be so possessed of a sense of the finality of Christ that her only standards are those of the kingdom to come. This is the church militant whom the Gates of Hell shall not withstand.

There is just one thing wrong with the biblical view of the church which we have been sketching; it does not seem to exist. The definition is fine, but the phenomenon it describes is missing. Joseph Haroutunian has had the honesty to admit this fact in an editorial in *Theology Today*. He asks "why the words of ecclesiastical writers often embarrass us even where they are impeccably Biblical and logical?"[4]

> Israel and Church alike, as we find them in the Bible, are a people hard-pressed by their enemies. They are a little people, a poor and weak people, a people harassed and in peril, having no abiding place in this world. They are a people derided, persecuted and pursued, without recourse to earthly power for redress against wrong and for escape from oppression. When such people are called a "royal nation" or "God's possession," there is a dignity and aptness to the language used, and a man is amazed and encouraged in hearing it. But when the same language is used for the ears and eyes of people whose resemblance to the Israel and Church of the Bible is both remote and blurred, its effect is neither edifying nor joy-giving. It is on the contrary embarrassing, as though it were false.[5]

> We cannot say, "Scripture says" and believe that the Church is in fact the magnificent things theological clerics have been saying about it. It will not do to browbeat us by saying that we do not see the Church described by dogmatic enthusiasts because we have no faith, or that we do not look at the Church from the inside! It will not even do to say that if we believe in God's grace and power, we must believe that the redeemed community is a fact. The Church is not realized by flattering God and "seeing things."[6]

Haroutunian identifies in these last words, and rejects, some of the usual ways of dulling the edge of the problem. It is no answer simply to call for "faith" as some kind of swallowing hard, closing one's eyes, and believing the impossible. There is no way around the fact that the "churches" as we see them cannot simply be equated with the church. Yet the church is visible.

---

4. Haroutunian, "Realization," 138.
5. Haroutunian, "Realization," 139.
6. Haroutunian, "Realization," 141–42.

The clearest and easiest way out has always been that one particular organization, whether an old one with prestigious historical claims or a new one with the right doctrine, practice, or structure, is identified as the true church of God. This we know is no solution in principle, though both some "new starts" and some "valid traditions" have contributed in unchallengeable and indispensable ways to God's Work.

The next clearest answer is that of Darby and his theological heirs among the Plymouth Brethren and dispensational fundamentalists. This is that though a visibly organized, united church was God's intent, that church (the unbroken episcopal tradition) has by its apostasy, i.e., by a fundamental denial of its mission, not only forfeited its own claim to be the church of Christ but has also made it impossible in principle for any other fellowship (lacking universality and apostolic continuity) to take up the torch and restore the true vision of the New Testament Church. Therefore, true Christians must live without full Christian fellowship, meeting but without ministers, praying and praising but with no order of service, sending missionaries and maintaining inter-congregational fellowship but without considering these activities as either ecclesiastical or organizational. This is again no solution.

There can be no solution which accepts as a settled fact the unfaithfulness of Christendom, drawing therefrom the justification for a fundamentally different approach and set of standards from what would apply if the church were what she should be. Necessary adaptation to the present state of things may not imply the resigned admission that they probably can and will not be changed. A smoothly worded description of the relationship (i.e., the difference) between the "visible" and the "invisible" or the "empirical" and the "eschatological" churches, as if things can tolerably (or even somehow should) remain in their present plight, would be such an inadmissible resignation. What is true of an individual is true of the church; the only thing to do about sin is to repent of it. No theory about the unavoidability of sin as a corollary of free will, no description of the paradoxical relation of the empirical self and the real self, no patient explanation that with age, or size, or busyness, or family, or finitude, a certain amount of sin becomes unavoidable, will serve as an excuse. The gospel does not say anything about sin as an unavoidable phenomenon in all human existence; it says "Repent!" which, being interpreted, does not mean "continue in sin, but sorrowfully," but rather "STOP IT!" The churches' not being the church cannot be discussed in the indicative; "Repent and be the church" is the only thing to say.

5

The End of Christendom

Paul Peachey

I

In April 1959, at Kuala Lumpur, Malaya, an assembly of representatives of Asian churches inaugurated the East Asia Christian Conference. The possibility of a regional consultative body in Asia was first discussed during the meeting of the International Missionary Council (IMC) at Tambaram near Madras, India, in 1938. At that time, however, consideration was given to a regional IMC office, rather than to a council of the autonomous church bodies in the area such as has now been established.

The East Asia Christian Conference (EACC), composed as it is of national church bodies usually affiliated also with the World Council of Churches (WCC), was set up as an autonomous agency between the WCC on the one hand, and the national councils and denominations on the other. Its purpose is to express and promote the regional interdependence of the Asian churches. By definition, neither the world body nor the national groupings provide for these functions. The need for more interaction among Asian churches was pointed up graphically by one Asian speaker who noted that in ecumenical gatherings Asian representatives (who for the most part had studied in the West) knew Western churchmen better than they did those from neighboring Asian countries.

One of the first actions of the new Conference was to inaugurate the John R. Mott Memorial Lectures which, by previous arrangement, were presented in conjunction with the Kuala Lumpur convention. Consisting of a total of five addresses, the series was delivered by Lesslie Newbigin,

W. A. Visser 't Hooft, and D. T. Niles, all influential figures in ecumenical circles. These lectures, together with a brief historical introduction to the EACC by Norman Goodall, secretary of the Joint Committee of the IMC and the WCC, have meanwhile been published under the title *A Decisive Hour for the Christian Mission*.[1]

II

While the entire series deserves serious reflection, this article is occasioned by the two lectures of Dr. Visser 't Hooft. As General Secretary of the World Council of Churches, he naturally was deeply interested in the meaning of this step in Asia for world Christianity. This was reflected in the themes which he chose for his lectures, namely, "The Asian Churches in the Ecumenical Movement" and "Asian Issues in the Ecumenical Setting."

These lectures bid fair to open a new chapter in the current discussion regarding the "end of the Constantinian era." The first of these, which had already been published in the "Ecumenical Review" before the present volume appeared,[2] is an attempt to determine the situation in which Christianity finds itself in Asia today. He notes at the outset that only in recent years can one speak of an authentic dialogue between the churches of Asia and those in other parts of the world. Even so, the dialogue has barely begun. To discover why this should be so, Visser 't Hooft places this emerging dialogue into the perspective of ecumenical history. Thus, he comes to compare the present situation with that of a half-century ago at the time of the 1910 Edinburgh missionary conference. Incidentally, it was at that conference that John R. Mott emerged in his mature career as ecumenical "statesman."

The contrasts revealed by this comparison are soberingly instructive. Whereas in 1910, many people expected "that within the foreseeable future . . . a Christendom civilization will spread to all parts of the world," today, quite to the contrary,

> a number of countries have closed their doors to foreign missionaries and . . . in many others the resistance against evangelistic work of any kind has been growing. As it looks out at the world of 1959 the Christian Church does not find, as in 1910, that the stream of world history seems to flow in the same

1. Goodall et al., *Decisive Hour*.
2. Hooft, "Significance."

direction as the stream of the history of the Kingdom of God. On the contrary, the two histories seem to enter into a period of conflict with each other.³

This change in outlook Dr. Visser 't Hooft attributes to the fact that the intervening half century of history has undermined the premises on which the optimism of 1910 had been based. These premises were: 1) The Constantinian "symphony" of church and state (which he indicates, however, was already disappearing in 1910); 2) the "Christendom era" of worldwide interpenetration of Church and Society; and 3) the "'Vasco da Gama era" of Western expansion (an expression borrowed from K. M. Panikkar, *Asia and Western Dominance*) which was still "going strong."⁴ Today these presuppositions have virtually disappeared from historic actualities.

It is the addition of the "Vasco da Gama era" to the discussion of the Constantinian or Christendom problem which gives the whole matter new poignancy. Panikkar sees the Vasco da Gama era as that period of history ushered in by the arrival of the Portuguese explorer at Calicut (S. India) in 1498 and terminated by the withdrawal of the British forces from India in 1947 and of the European navies from China in 1949. This period, he says, was characterized by "the dominance of maritime power over the land masses of Asia; the imposition of a commercial economy over communities whose economic life in the past had been based . . . on agricultural production and internal trade; and thirdly the domination of the peoples of Europe, who held the mastery of the seas, over the affairs of Asia."⁵

Panikkar, and many others like him, regard the missionary enterprise as merely the religious phase of this impingement of the West on Asia. Therefore, when the period of Western expansion ended, so too, by force of circumstances, the progress of missions. Panikkar concludes, therefore, "It will hardly be denied that, in spite of the immense and sustained effort made by the churches with support of the lay public of the European countries and America, the attempt to conquer Asia for Christ has definitely failed."⁶

At this point, however, Visser 't Hooft rightly comes to the defense of the missionary, and says, "There can be little doubt that the vast majority of missionaries desired simply to bring the Gospel to those who had

3. Hooft, "Asian Churches," 53.
4. Hooft, "Asian Churches," 49.
5. Panikkar, *Asia and Western*, 102.
6. Panikkar, *Asia and Western*, 454.

not heard it."[7] Furthermore, the assumption that the cause of missions has failed and ended has the sanction merely of an historical analysis which does not reckon with the intervention of grace. Therefore, verdicts such as that of Panikkar are not the last word in the matter.

But this answer to Panikkar, as it were, does not yet solve our problem. For as Visser 't Hooft points out further, these missionaries nevertheless came "from the 'Christendom' world," and there "nobody had taught them to raise fundamental questions about the 'Christendom' concept."[8] Therefore, in the main, the great Western missionary movement in Asia was not adequately differentiated from the notion of the extension of Western civilization even on the part of the missionaries themselves. But this confusion was an inevitably corollary of the political and cultural "Christendom" which had become the bane of the West. Therefore, while on the one hand many missionaries served heroically and God has honored their labors in raising up the church in Asia, these churches are burdened with a legacy of the misunderstandings of Christendom.

Whatever the motives and achievements of missions and missionaries individually, during the Vasco da Gama era missions were established for the most part where they had the direct or indirect support of Western political power. And in too many instances missionaries became involved in political and colonial intrigues in order to obtain missionary advantages. The harsh conditions of half a century and a century ago, go far to explain certain practices that seem rather incredible today. And lest we be unduly critical we need only to recognize the parallels in our own time. In the present-day relief and mission activities of the churches, we quite typically respect the "iron curtain" when political leaders on either side decide that such a curtain exists. A future generation will surely censure us.

But to return to Dr. Visser 't Hooft's analysis, he appears to accept the passing of "Christendom" (under which term I now included also the Constantinian and the Vasco da Gama eras), and even hails it as the "liberation" of the church. For "the hour of liberation of the Church" is "the hour when it rediscovers how it depends only on God and when it carries on its mission in greater purity and without entangling alliances." The story of the confessing churches under Naziism and of the survival of faith under communism illustrate the power that comes when the false alliances of the churches are broken. In fact, the long close ties between formal Christianity

7. Hooft, "Asian Churches," 51.
8. Hooft, "Asian Churches," 51.

and civilization the West had led the "world . . . to believe that the future of the Church depends on forces outside the life of the Church itself."[9] Thus, the perspective of faith defies the fatalism which informs Panikkar's secular conclusions. The church is indeed affected by social and political factors. But "the Church which is truly the Church, that is, the Church which depends on the Holy Spirit, is not merely the product of historical causality."[10]

III

The "liberation" of the churches, however, confronts them with certain problems or tasks. These the General Secretary treats in his second lecture, "Asian Issues in the Ecumenical Setting." These are: 1. Communicating the Gospel; 2. The search for Christian unity; 3. The responsible society; and 4. Regional cooperation. Of these only the third is pertinent to our present discussion.

The "liberation" of the churches, their coming of age after long dependence on the missions, exposes them to the temptation to accept that "ghetto existence" to which the secular forces now building the new Asia would like to assign them. Precisely because they are a tiny and apparently helpless minority Asian Christians indeed find it all too easy to succumb. To brace them for the fight Dr. Visser 't Hooft places before them the summons of "The Responsible Society": "We are called to witness to the Lordship of Christ over the world by working for a truly responsible society through our service to the needy and through our prophetic ministry to the authorities."[11]

It will be useful at this point to cite the familiar Amsterdam WCC assembly formulation, from which the foregoing naturally stems: "A responsible society is one where freedom is the freedom of men who acknowledge responsibility to justice and public order, and where those who hold political authority or economic power are responsible for its exercise to God and the people whose welfare is affected by it."[12] Striking here is not only the ambiguity of authority, but also the way in which the church and the ethic

---

9. Hooft, "Asian Churches," 56.
10. Hooft, "Asian Churches," 55.
11. Hooft, "Asian Issues," 66.
12. Hooft, *First Assembly*, 77.

of the Christian are bypassed for the sake of general and minimal norms which are without specific Christian content.[13]

It is evident at once that the concept of "the responsible society" represents the ethical legacy of Christendom, namely, the external attempt to somehow Christianize a fallen world order. That Dr. Visser 't Hooft commends it to the Asian churches at this juncture indicates that if Christendom (i.e., also Constantinianism and "Vasco da Gamaism") has been banished from history it has not yet been dissipated from ecumenical theology. And if today someone is able to teach the missionaries "to raise fundamental questions about the 'Christendom' concept," theologians seem less fortunate.

This is said without cynicism, and with high regard for Dr. Visser 't Hooft notwithstanding. Nor is it to say that the goals of the responsible society theology as such are undesirable. It is rather to underscore persistency of the Constantinian legacy of a millennium and a half to which we must now add nearly half a millennium of Vasco de Gama traditions. No Western Christian is free from the blight, and it is to be doubted whether even those alerted to the problem overcome it existentially. And ironically enough, one of the major strongholds of American neo-Constantinism—the all but blind identification of Christianity with national self-interest—are some of the American "free churches" who demand most vociferously the formal separation of church and state.

The Asian churches today are clearly in a pre-Constantinian situation, and precisely this is their opportunity. Quite apart from its biblical inadequacy, the ethic of "the responsible society" is as unsuited for them as was Saul's armor for David. It is as regrettable as the Vasco da Gama era itself, that ecumenical Asian Christians are being burdened with this armor as the price they have to pay for ecumenicity. Our inability to agree on the precise intent of the gospel ethic may call for humility in the attempt to offer the biblical alternative to the Amsterdam formula. Indeed, it may be we shall have to learn it again from Christians who live in a pre-Constantinian world. Quite likely the answer is to be sought in obedience, commitment, and suffering, and this may never yield to neat formulas. And yet this same Lord is waiting in our midst, and it would be unbelief to despair of the possibilities here and now.

W. A. Visser 't Hooft's Kuala Lumpur lectures, if read and assimilated by Western ecumenical Christians, would become a turning point

---

13. See Yoder, "Otherness," 26–29, for fuller critique.

in the whole ecumenical movement. Far more pressing than the questions of intercommunion and of order, which have absorbed so much energy and attention, is the recovery of the pre-Christendom, New Testament ethic for this post-Christendom (and hence anew pre-Christendom) era. Sacrament and order, however important, are matters of symbol, which are meaningful chiefly among ourselves. The question of the gospel ethic, however, is a matter of substance, which has to do with the proclamation of the good news to those who are not among us.

Part II

On the Charismatic Movement and Gifts of the Spirit

Articles from CONCERN 15 (1967)

6

Marginalia

John Howard Yoder

In the opening lines of his article on "renewal" in *Concern* 12, John W. Miller reminded us that the main thrust of biblical prophecy does not promise that it will always, or even usually, be possible to bring back to life a fallen or a dormant church.[1] The Bible speaks far more of judgment and new birth than of resuscitation.

Nonetheless, in God's goodness it may be granted that new life can spring up within the forms and the language of existing traditions, existing congregations, and existing kinds of experience. Most writers and most readers of *Concern* are investing their major spiritual energies in this possibility and probably will continue to do so. But while a minority of people in a minority of churches labor at the vision of renewal within existing forms, most of the nominal membership of most of the churches of Christendom have no concern for that quality of yielded openness which might open the doors for genuine new life. So for most of the church in most of the world most of the time, there is, biblically speaking, no hope this side of judgment; and consequently, no new beginning without new forms.

Where men have closed all the doors, God can open a window. Within or beside apostate churches, he raises up in every age new movements of protest, witness and fellowship. These "free churches" are marked by the duress which gave them birth: socially unbalanced, theologically unbalanced, poor, strangely structured, given to false starts and exaggeration—and of such is the kingdom of heaven. "Not many of you were wise

---

1. Miller, "Renewal," 32.

according to worldly standards, not many were powerful, not many of noble birth." It is too bad that it should need to be so: it would have been better if the wise and noble had seen more clearly and been more obedient; but if they so govern their religious establishments that vital piety, regenerate living, and effective witness can be had only with the sacrifice of scholarly sobriety and socially sensitive statesmanship, that is a price which God has frequently been willing to pay.

Most radical of these new starts in modern times have been the Anabaptism of the sixteenth century and the Quakerism of the seventeenth. Both were overwhelmingly convinced of the doom of conformist religion and of the inadequacy of halfway gestures toward reformation. Less radical in intent, yet formally similar, pietism in the eighteenth century (most activist in its Anglo-Saxon branch, Wesleyanism) and American frontier evangelicalism in the nineteenth propagated a nonconformist, personalist faith so effectively that this type of Protestantism became the new conformism in America's neo-Christendom.

Pentecostalism is in our century the closest parallel to what Anabaptism was in the sixteenth: expanding so vigorously that it bursts the bonds of its own thinking about church order, living from the multiple gifts of the spirit in the total church while holding leaders in great respect, unembarrassed by the language of the layman and the aesthetic tastes of the poor, mobile, zealously single-minded. We can easily note the flaws in Pentecostal theology, organization, or even ethics—very similar, by the way, to the faults of the early Quakers and Anabaptists, or of the apostolic churches—but meanwhile they are out being the church.

Two developments of the last two decades have increased the readiness of "mainstream" Christians to recognize Pentecostalism as a fact and as a hope. Missionary statesmen have recognized the stature of the churches which are growing in Latin America, Southeast Asia, and Africa. One early symbol of this new respect was J. Lesslie Newbigin's identifying as "Pentecostal" one of the three dimensions of the church whose wholeness his *Household of God* portrayed.[2]

The other new development is the transcending of traditional Anglo-Saxon denominational forms by Pentecostal witnesses. Pentecostalism began in the context of denominational pluralisms: or, to be still more precise, in the American southwest, hotbed of pluralism. There was no option visible but to become one more fundamentalist denomination, with all the

---

2. Newbigin, *Household*. See esp. chapter 4.

handicaps—to which we shall return in a moment—which that implied. But in these last two decades new modes of witness have been developed, which others call "neo-Pentecostalism": using the forms not of Anabaptism but of Wesley, "charismatic" groups are formed within mainstream denominations or interdenominationally, propagating an experience without the sectarian structures and strictures.

The intent of this volume of *Concern* (15) is not to propagate nor to evaluate, but to inform. The testimonies we have gathered come from persons who do not represent denominational Pentecostalism. They are Mennonites. Yet these are testimonies. They speak of their own experiences or from firsthand observation.

Aggressive movements of this kind are typically not their own best interpreters; the prophet, the evangelist, the speaker in tongues seldom have the gift of scholarly distance. The task of sympathetic historical-theological interpretation of Pentecostalism has barely begun. John Thomas Nichol's new *Pentecostalism* is the first careful study for the North American movement;[3] for the rest of the world there exists little except for a mammoth Zurich University dissertation in the form of a manuscript handbook of world Pentecostalism, the work of Walter J. Hollenweger, which regrettably will likely not be published except in fragments.

The genius of the movement is misunderstood when it is seen through its North American forms. The unavoidable assumptions of denominational pluralism assigned it a place near the bottom on the class ladder, with the built-in assumption that as members become more educated or more refined, they will move along the denominational cafeteria line to something a little more sober. This vicious circle of cultural selection combined with the theological alignment already dominant in the early decades of the century to link American Pentecostalism with creedal fundamentalism, with its suspicion of biblical scholarship and of intellectual life in general. The use of mass media and competition for the support of voluntary offerings to support ad hoc organizations has contributed to an unwholesome star system replacing other patterns of spiritual leadership. Competition overaccentuates visible distinctives, such as glossolalia. Following the pattern of the late-Wesleyan "Holiness" tradition, Pentecostals are tempted to make one prescribed experience not only a promise or a gift for some but a prerequisite for all who would be recognized as "fully" Christian. Such a normative second experience may draw a person's or a church's sights away from the

---

3. Nichol, *Pentecostalism*.

"more excellent way" of 1 Cor 12:31—14:1. Denominational organization, seen in typical restitutionist-congregationalist terms not as "church" but as a business organization for common concerns, has become powerfully centralized in the larger Assemblies of God groups. All of these traits, clearly present, which have led mainstream churchmen and even fellow fundamentalists to condemn Pentecostalism, are not its distinctive marks but rather the fruits of the warped situation in which the movement came to birth. What the genuinely distinctive marks are it is not easy to say, through the marks of local adaptations, exaggerations, and dilutions. Perhaps the simplest characterization would be that God as Spirit is perceived as working: a) with an immediacy such as to be indubitable even to men aware of the self-deceiving trickiness of the human psyche; b) so as to bring forth the fruits of love, joy, peace, . . . and an unprecedented quality of authority in discernment, leadership, and witness.

It is likewise insufficient to see the movement primarily in the form of the two South American denominations which have joined the World Council of Churches. Being in much of South America not a movement of renewal but a first-generation missionary enterprise, often the largest and sometimes the only predominantly indigenous evangelical church, yet respecting the older "mainstream" denominational missions, some Pentecostal churches which came into being partly by withdrawal from Methodist mission-founded churches have moved rapidly toward the leadership forms of the older groups. This has been read by many as meaning that they outgrew their loose organization, self-supporting ministries, and lively piety by some inner necessity, proving the "mainstream" right after all. All that this proves is that these groups were not very Pentecostal to begin with. Beside them in Brazil the very large, completely indigenous, rapidly growing "Christian Assembly" is in its third generation and still has neither professional ministry nor denominational hierarchy. Africa can show parallel phenomena, where growth is so rapid that the first-generation feel is not outgrown and the "sect cycle" which sociologists consider inevitable never revolves.

7

Tongues, a Testimony

JAMES FAIRFIELD

I "spoke in tongues" February 1964. It's a rather lame way to put it, I suspect. Nevertheless, this is the accepted semantics. Much better to say I prayed in tongues, that first time. And I still do, privately, in my own prayers.

Over the years I had heard much about tongues and "Holy Ghost baptism." Who hasn't? Glossolalia has been featured news in the *Saturday Evening Post* and the staid *National Observer* as well as Christian periodicals of every stripe.

Furthermore, there isn't a church in the country that hasn't worried and wondered about "this tongues business." It has become "the burr in the bishop's shirt" . . . and too often for not so good reasons.

Pentecostals have been congratulating themselves about their notoriety, a little arrogantly, let's admit it. But they can hardly be blamed. For a long time, Pentecostals have suffered the snorts of equally arrogant dissent. The church has preferred to bury the charismatic movement with argument then unload it somewhere. Anywhere. Under heresies, or psychological release, or delusions, emotional, or . . .

Yet Pentecostal-type Protestantism cannot be either unloaded or ignored. Too many genuine Christian converts in every country around the world provide living testimony to God's saving activity through Pentecostal-Protestantism. And something very stimulating is happening elsewhere in the church, in the mainline denominations. Pastors are sharing in the charismatic movement. Many respected members of their congregations, including businessmen and bankers and teachers and advertising men, now speak in tongues and say they are spiritually the better for it. Why? What is actually happening?

Is this burgeoning thing just a fad? Are laymen looking for a sociological kick the pulpit isn't providing? Is that all there is to speaking in tongues?

Or is it the portent of greater spiritual discoveries, and a greater vitality in spiritual living? Is it the whisper of revival? I think it is possible. But I also think that tongues is only a pale beginning...

Frankly I haven't rushed into the circles of those who speak in tongues. I don't want this experience to mean only a change of Christian friends.

I haven't grown another head or climbed another rung above the brotherhood. I'm simply a little more useful to my Lord than I had been before... in one way and one way only.

It hasn't meant a new "experience" with Christ, but only a deeper awareness of his presence, a fresher knowledge of his joy and love, and a better and freer communication with him. To sum up, for me it has meant a new facility in prayer and communion, and a greater expression of praise.

When Reformed Church pastor Ed Barham visited Eastern Mennonite College in February 1964, he spoke to a number of interested students, faculty and local residents. He told us of his personal experience with the Holy Spirit, and the effect on his ministry. His concept of tongues as a factor in communication with God seemed to make sense. As Rom 8:26 reads: "The Spirit comes to the aid of our weakness. We do not even know how we ought to pray, but through our inarticulate groans the Spirit Himself is pleading for us, and God who searches our inmost being knows what the Spirit means."

This was scriptural encouragement for me. I had been praying quietly in tongues in my devotions for about a week before this. I had been thinking much about the scriptural references about tongues and had privately come to the conclusion that tongues was a privilege for the Christian, a privilege I could exercise in prayer and worship whenever I chose. Therefore, I simply determined to pray in tongues.

And that was that. I received emotional confirmation in a deeper sense of the majesty and glory and righteousness of God. My prayers had a lilt of praise a little richer than ever before.

As I prayed in tongues, my heart and mind and understanding expanded a little more in devotional appreciation of the greatness of our great God.

And I laughed, within and without as never before. The apostle Paul speaks to the Corinthians of being hilarious givers (2 Cor 9:7); at least this is a reasonable exegesis of the text. Up until then my imagination had struggled to understand how any form of worship (and giving is worship) could ever be "hilarious."

Now I know what Paul meant. Although I find it very difficult to explain why my praise and worship can be hilarious, nevertheless it often is now. Not foolishly, nor blatantly, but rather, a deeply worshipful joy. Perhaps it is because I have found an uninhibited way that is holy, with which to praise a beloved Lord. And I know many Christian men and women who are filled now with the Holy Spirit (despite the fact they do not "speak in tongues") who ought to step over by faith into this greater facility of joyous praise and communication with our Lord.

I think this is important. Would to God every Christian man, woman, and child would put on all the armor and equipment there is available for the service of Jesus Christ. God knows how we struggle along with our own makeshift dynamics, while the power of the resurrection is ours, for his glory . . . if we will but open up our lives more to his Lordship! If only we had more discernment . . . and spiritually resilient love . . . and "mind of Christ" wisdom . . .

Yet perhaps our Lord can more readily develop these strengths in us, if we are in better, more facile communication with him? And perhaps this is all there is to "tongues?" . . . that it isn't a gimmick or a shibboleth or spiritual green stamps, but simply an enlarging of the channels of communication? I think so.

Further, I am convinced that tongues is a symbol of the greater resources God has for us, rather than—as some insist—the sole evidence of a "second work of grace," or "Holy Spirit baptism." To do so places unwarranted stature upon a very minor spiritual tool. But—and this is an important "but"—tongues can be the evidence of unused spiritual resources, mountains of resources! I am of the opinion that through the charismatic movement God is notifying his people there is a reserve of vitality and ingenuity and expression and understanding that makes Fort Knox look like a piggy bank.

One of my seminary professors who is considerably disturbed about tongues (he sees the dangers all too clearly), made an astute observation. "Instead of seeking tongues," he warned, "we should be seeking—and finding—the gift of discernment."

PART II: ON THE CHARISMATIC MOVEMENT AND GIFTS OF THE SPIRIT

Do you know it, he's right! At least partly. I would like to change his phrasing a little . . . from "instead of" to "as well as seeking tongues we should be seeking—and finding—discernment and wisdom and prophetic preaching and teaching and writing and witnessing and . . ."

Tongues can mean new vistas of service and maturing healthier Christians . . . if we move on. But as so often happens in a revival, people stop in kindergarten, and it could happen with tongues, if too much emphasis-energy is drained off getting people to seek "tongues" and "baptism" at the expense of other spiritual equipment.

How much better it would be if we did go on and clothe ourselves with the whole armor of God . . . and how much more could be accomplished! May I state a "for instance"?

As Mennonites, we have a doctrinal understanding of peacemaking. We say a Christian can heal human situations through love. We say Christ is revealed by love, by nonresistant, redeeming, active love. Yet a doctrine needs more than words to find its expression. It takes Spirit-filled power to turn the other cheek and love an enemy. We cannot genuinely express this sort of love except it be shed abroad in our hearts by the Holy Spirit.

As Christians, yes and as Mennonites, we need an "experience" in our lives to equip us with this quality of love. Soon we may be called upon to prove we can turn our cheek even to bombs and bullets. We'll not do so with just our doctrinal statement on non-resistance.

And we need Spirit-filled help with our Christian witness. We are being called upon now to explode our witness to match the exploding population. We need to be endowed with God's power. We need to be open to his gifting, in every way possible. Even tongues.

I want to testify to spiritually alert Christians that tongues can help them. But I don't want to sidetrack an effective, Spirit-filled Christian by insisting he really hasn't got it, until he has got "it."

Far better to plead and pray for the kind of hungry discipleship which will fill up with all the fullness of God. Far better to call Christians to full-fledged usefulness to the Holy Spirit . . . anointed preaching and teaching and everyday living.

And this seems to be coming. There is a renewed interest in the Holy Spirit, and a larger understanding of His ministry.

And even more, there is infilling with vital life. Men convinced of being lived in by the Spirit and committed to move as he moves them. This is what the rustling in the dry leaves seems to be about, both within

Pentecostal ranks and without. That mystery the prophets longed to see—"that sacred mystery which up till now has been hidden . . . but which is now as clear as daylight to those who love God . . . a vision of the full wonder and splendor of His secret plan for the sons of men. And the secret is simply this: Christ in you! Yes, Christ in you bringing with Him the hope of all the glorious things to come" (Col 1:26, 28).

8

You Shall Receive . . .

Herb Klassen and Maureen Klassen

This is a report from our own personal pilgrimage during the last three years, and, as could be expected, it is subjective, selective, and limited. We have gathered experiences and impressions along the way from what we have seen, heard, and read, and we have been asked to share some of it here. It was about two and a half years ago in England that we had a faith encounter with Jesus, the baptizer in the Holy Spirit. We soon found out that the experience enjoyed by the early Christians is being witnessed in every corner of the world today and in every branch of the Christian Church. Many of God's people are referring to this as a latter-day charismatic revival, in the sense of a continued fulfillment of Joel's prophecy: "It shall come to pass in the last days, saith God, I will pour out my Spirit upon all flesh: and your sons and your daughters shall prophesy" (Joel 2:28–32).

"Charismatic" refers specifically to the gifts of the Holy Spirit that are manifest increasingly today to the edification of the church and the salvation of many souls. The label used to identify this awakening is not significant, but the reality is.

We have encountered a little of these stirrings at first hand in England, Holland, Germany, the United States, and Canada, and have had to evaluate what is happening. This does raise many theological issues and questions of biblical interpretation, but finally, as Jesus said, the way to more knowledge is through obedience: "If any man will do his will, he shall know of the doctrine, whether it be of God" (John 7:17).

What kind of criteria have we applied in trying to determine what belongs to this divinely inspired awakening and what does not?—for as always, there is much that is false mixed in with the true.

Two Criteria

First, do the people involved bear joyful and humble witness in word and deed to the ministry and power of the Holy Spirit? Is Jesus being glorified through the exercise of spiritual gifts? Do the people involved have something to proclaim or are they still questioning, criticizing, and protesting?

Second, is there real evidence that the Great Commission is central in their work and witness? Is the power of the Holy Spirit harnessed first and foremost for witness unto Christ?

To separate these two facets spells spiritual frustration and decline. The two, the "charismatic" and the "evangelistic," are integrally linked in Jesus's personal experience and in the inheritance he left to his disciples. He did not begin to seek and save the lost and cast out evil spirits and heal the sick until the Holy Spirit came upon him at his baptism; and his last command to his disciples is "Wait until you are filled with power from on high," and his last promise is "The Holy Spirit shall come upon you for power to witness." God's law has not changed: when the early Christians met his conditions, his blessing was not lacking—and so it has been ever since.

One place among many where reports of this awakening come flowing in is the monthly newsletter of the *Nights of Prayer for Revival*. An evangelical Anglican missionary who retired in London, England, after years in India, George Ingram, started praying constantly for revival and encouraged others to pray together in groups on the first Friday night of each month. He committed himself to share reports with all who write in. Reports keep coming in from every corner of the world—mission fields and homelands—of men receiving Christ, being revived, being filled with the Spirit, witnessing with new power, and praying with new faith. Many of these outpourings are happening quite independently of one another. Hundreds and thousands of Christians in our day are coming to Christ thirsty and are going away overflowing: filled with the Holy Spirit to work and witness for Christ and to live his praise and glory.

PART II: ON THE CHARISMATIC MOVEMENT AND GIFTS OF THE SPIRIT

In England

In England the movement has tended to find expression in local churches and parishes rather than in the creation of new fellowships and forms of outreach. Michael Harper, for a number of years curate to John R. Stott of All Souls, Langham Place, London, has played an important part from the outset in keeping the movement united and positive. He himself has carried the message and ministry of the Holy Spirit to many denominations and local churches throughout England and Scotland.

One example of the extent of the movement is the fact that over one hundred Anglican ministers testify to a post-conversion experience of being filled with the Holy Spirit. If even one minister is converted and set on fire by the Holy Spirit, it makes the news; but when it happens to over one hundred, the church and the world begin to sit up and take notice. Numerous weekend and weeklong conferences and retreats have been organized for ministers and laymen from all the different branches of the Christian church. They have been a real blessing to many hungry, seeking Christians and have also helped to keep the whole movement biblical, balanced, and focused on Christ and his Great Commission.

When we attended a conference, it was inspiring to see veteran ministers from the large denominations blessed by the rich biblical ministry of two Brethren apostles. And the preaching of the word, when interspersed with quiet praise and worship and gifts of the Spirit, was strongly confirmed and applied to each hungry heart as "edification, encouragement, and consolation." The Fountain Trust has published two popular studies by Michael Harper: a biblical one, *Power for the Body of Christ*, and a historical one, *As at the Beginning*.[1] News from England and other parts of the world is reported in a monthly magazine, *Renewal*, also published by Fountain Trust.

A smaller movement amongst Brethren, many missionaries, and others has developed along parallel yet distinct lines. There has been a great concern in these circles to relate this great contemporary outpouring of the Spirit to the nature of the church as a disciplined missionary brotherhood. Christian Fellowship's *Voice of Faith*, published in Bradford, contains many inspiring theological contributions and gives a representative survey of the concerns of this group.

---

1. Harper, *Power for the Body* and *As at the Beginning*.

In Holland

In Holland the picture looks quite different. About a dozen years ago a strong movement began that has drawn together members from all the different churches (most of them are still members of those churches) into a close missionary fellowship that is actively engaged in evangelistic work in Holland and throughout Europe, especially behind the Iron Curtain. When I was in Amsterdam two years ago there was a group of about seventy university students, teachers, and other young people in their early twenties, doing a courageous and effective job of witness in the tough areas of Amsterdam and towns round about. A testimony to God's blessing were the ex-homosexuals, ex-prostitutes, ex-drug addicts, and ex-alcoholics who have been saved, delivered, and now functioned with them on the streets.

At Driebergen in Holland, a center has come into being around the charismatic ministry of a team of men, where thousands from Holland and all over Europe have found salvation, the fullness of the Spirit, deliverance from various forms of bondage and oppression, and healing. Hundreds have also been baptized in water and many have gone out into the highways and byways of Europe to share the gospel of God's wonderful grace. The work being done behind the Iron Curtain is the most amazing. Reports of underground prayer meetings and revivals come in from most of the Iron Curtain countries—despite increasing opposition. For anyone who can read Dutch, these developments are well covered in their monthly magazine, *Kracht van Omhoog*.

In Germany

In Germany the awakening is not as widespread, but in the diverse places it has taken root it has gone very deep. There is, for example, a kind of evangelical cell group movement amongst Roman Catholics called *Focolarini* which is both charismatic and evangelistic. It is spreading to other parts of the world and God is clearly using it to bring men into his kingdom.

Amongst the freechurchmen, on the other hand, there is the energetic *Rufer* movement. It began among Baptists after World War II and for the first fifteen years teams of young laymen conducted evangelistic weeks in neutral locations and also together with local churches. The work is characterized by a revival of apostolic teamwork, by a new popular hymnody, by new depths in prayer and meditation, and above all by ever creative ways of bringing the gospel to men. It is only in the last few years that the charismatic element has come into its own in the *Rufer* movement. It was in the team that stayed together a whole year (*Jahresmannschaft*) that the gifts of the Spirit began to be manifest as they waited on God every morning (in the afternoons they went out to men and in the evenings they brought men together in various kinds of gatherings). Wilhard Becker, a young Baptist minister, has played a central role in the *Rufer* movement ever since it began. See the *Rufer Rundbriefe*.

Between the Catholic and Freechurch movements is the *Marburger Kreis* that has grown up in the Lutheran State Church. These three movements now function in close working cooperation with one another. Another interesting development in Germany is the *Marienschwesterschaft*, a Protestant order for women, which serves as a very positive example of the charismatic and evangelistic thrusts in the setting of disciplined Christian community life.

In America

In America the work of David Wilkerson and Teen Challenge as described in *The Cross and the Switchblade*[2] has had a very wide hearing and doubtless helped to convince many a defeated Christian that there is more to Christian initiation than just conversion and that the book of Acts in all its manifestations is as relevant today as it ever was. This was our first positive contact with the movement in the US. Teen Challenge has become much more highly institutionalized than, for example, the evangelistic work in Holland, but the Spirit clearly is the same.

The Full Gospel Business Men's Fellowship International (FGBMFI) was started by Demos Shakarian, an Armenian Christian whose family was led in a miraculous way out of sure destruction in southern Russia. It has been a blessing to many laymen in business and other occupations who have found the gospel to come alive at their breakfasts and hotel banquets. Business associates and other friends have often been converted and filled with the Spirit. Their monthly publication from Los Angeles, *The Voice*, is filled with amazing "success" stories that center on the experience of being filled with the Holy Spirit and speaking in a new heavenly language. One sometimes wonders what Saint Paul would make of their colossal airlifts to London and Tokyo, etc., but on the other hand God is doubtless using this

2. Wilkerson, *Cross*.

channel to bring men to Christ (which is more important than having the best and most correct methods without the evident blessing of God).

The Episcopalian church was among the first in America to feel the reverberations of the charismatic awakening in its ranks. There have been outstanding conversions in some quarters with real leaders such as Frank McGuire and Dennis Bennett coming to the fore. The opposition in the church sent Bennett to a small derelict mission in Seattle as a form of ecclesiastical discipline. He has preached the gospel and shared his testimony of the Holy Spirit before thousands in the last seven years. The church is flourishing and a witness going out into the whole Pacific Northwest. The organizational expression of this movement is the Blessed Trinity Society in Van Nuys, California, which has published some fine pamphlets and tracts, as well as a quarterly magazine called *Trinity*.

John Sherrill, journalist, who helped David Wilkerson write up his experience, has published a book tracing his own religious pilgrimage, entitled *They Speak with Other Tongues*.[3] What began as a journalistic assignment led to his own conversion and his own experience of being filled with the Holy Spirit. Along the way he presents a careful study of the Bible and church history on this theme.

Typical American Situation

One rather typical American manifestation that ought also to be mentioned here is the Pentecostal organizations that center around great leaders. Dozens could be named in an ascending order, based on their own traditional measurement of success: city-wide rallies and healing crusades, a monthly magazine, nationwide radio and TV programs, private colleges, etc. These private denominations based on "supporters," not "members," represent a reaction to the larger lukewarm denominations, and for this reason cannot be disregarded.

One outstanding exception to this "big business" pattern is the ministry of David Du Plessis, a South African Pentecostal, who has probably been received in a wider range of historic denominations than any other living Christian. His humble, loving witness to Christ, our Savior, baptizer, and healer, at New Delhi, the Vatican, at universities, at denominational world conferences, and in every other possible church setting is truly amazing. Hundreds of ministers from every possible branch of the

3. Sherrill, *They Speak*.

Christian church have been filled with the Spirit through his ministry. There is nothing imposing about him whatsoever, and he has no denomination or organization or group behind him. He travels as the Spirit directs and as the Lord provides and the blessing of God goes with him. His book, *The Spirit Bade Me Go*, includes the message he gave on Missions at Princeton Theological Seminary.[4]

The last group we would like to mention is Campus Crusade for Christ International. Besides its fruitful ministry among university and college students, it has probably had a wider ministry in evangelical churches and denominations than any other branch of the charismatic movement. On the one hand, this is due to God's blessing on the hundreds of dedicated apostolic staff members; on the other, to the fact that they try to avoid any involvement with the gifts of the Spirit. The motives for the latter position are altogether pure, but the implications are dangerous, for who are we to make the conditions and set aside some Scriptures?

This movement reminds one very much of the Student Volunteer Movement of the late nineteenth century begun by Moody and carried forward by G. T. Studd and John R. Mott. Just as Studd believed that being filled with the Spirit was an experience subsequent to conversion (he prayed with every convert to this end), so Campus Crusade is finding that students converted and filled with the Spirit are most fruitful in leading other students to Christ and to fullness of life in him.

Bill Bright, converted graduate and business executive in California, began the work at the University of California at Los Angeles in 1951. It has grown by leaps and bounds and today the lay division is spreading even more rapidly than the student work—as is also their work in many foreign countries. Quite a few Mennonites have been blessed through the ministry of Campus Crusade in the United States and Canada. *Collegiate Challenge* is their monthly magazine from San Bernardino, California.

History's Experience

Through the charismatic awakening one gains a new appreciation for much that God has been doing in the last two hundred years. There is no doubt about the fact that the ministry of George Fox and John Wesley was charismatic. Both knew what it meant to resist the devil and cast out evil spirits, and both had remarkable experiences in the field of healing.

4. Du Plessis, *Spirit*.

Wesley's "heartwarming" experience at Aldersgate Street some thirteen years after his conversion was a personal Pentecost that set on fire in his heart that which he had known for years in his head. George Fox had a similar experience some four years after his conversion. Madame Guyon, although she always remained within the Catholic church, was also a part of the same movement. She experienced many of the gifts of the Holy Spirit and God blessed her ministry to many.

Moving into the nineteenth century there are men such as Charles Finney who are being rediscovered today. His conversion and baptism with the Spirit, as quoted in V. Raymond Edman's *They Found the Secret*,[5] has become a classic. We might not agree with every aspect of his theology and with all the methods he used, but God obviously had his hand upon him.

Hudson Taylor, William Fraser, and Pastor Hsi were also men who prayed and walked and witnessed in the Spirit. Mrs. Howard Taylor has recorded their experiences. Pastor Hsi, in particular, experienced Christian initiation as did early Christians (first conversion, then baptism in water, then filled with the Holy Spirit, with not much time lost in between). He was then led to cast out evil spirits in the name of Jesus, to lay hands on the sick and see them recover, and to pray opium addicts through to deliverance in Christ. His ministry among drug addicts in China eighty years ago was somewhat similar to that of David Wilkerson and Teen Challenge today.

Norman Grubb has done a real service through his two biographies: C. T. Studd and Rees Howells.[6] The latter deserves to be better known than it is. The fact that the prayers of a few saints in South Wales brought revival to Africa and finally influenced the course and outcome of the second World War is a real antidote to anyone who wonders whether God has made much history since he got our denominations started. In Rees Howells, too, is one example of what a Spirit-filled Bible school or seminary looks like.

Another common text in the charismatic awakening is R. A. Torrey's pamphlet, *The Baptism with the Holy Spirit*, a summary of which makes up the final chapter of his helpful book, *How to Bring Men to Christ*.[7]

---

5. Edman, *They Found*.
6. Grubb, *C. T. Studd* and *Rees Howells*.
7. Torrey, *Baptism* and *How to Lead*.

In Twentieth Century

Two outstanding twentieth century leaders and writers are Watchman Nee and Andrew Murray. Watchman Nee has been in a Chinese Communist prison since 1952. He was converted in 1920 while studying law in China, and in the following two decades exercised a remarkable apostolic ministry, i.e., he was used of God to found more than five hundred congregations all over China. In reading his books on Acts (*The Normal Christian Church Life*), on Romans (*The Normal Christian Life*), and on Ephesians (*Sit, Walk, Stand*),[8] one gets the feeling that he understood Paul better than many expositors because his life was so much more like Paul's. Here are not plausible words of wisdom, but Spirit and power. What God has hidden from the wise and understanding he has chosen to reveal unto babes.

Andrew Murray lived in South Africa and moved in Keswick circles in England. He and Watchman Nee probably never heard of one another, but they exercised similar ministries in quite different surroundings. In *The Full Blessing of Pentecost* and *The Spirit of Christ*, similar themes and a similar approach are evident.[9] The teaching on baptism in the Spirit as an experience with Christ subsequent to conversion is equally clear and wonderfully set out in the context of the total fact of Christ: his mission, his cross, his church, his return.

Other leaders and authors such as Jessie Penn-Lewis in England, Duncan Campbell of the Hebrides revival, and A. W. Tozer (whose booklet, *How to Be Filled with the Holy Spirit*,[10] has been a blessing to many) ought to be mentioned as well. Then there are also the accounts of numerous outpourings of the Spirit on various mission fields: the beginnings of the Ramabi Mukti Mission in India and the great charismatic revival in Argentina (described by Edward Miller in *Thy God Reigneth*[11]) could serve as two outstanding examples.

Evidences of Gifts

In reading the New Testament one is struck with the ministry of Jesus in casting out evil spirits (exorcism) and in healing the sick, and with the integral

---

8. Nee, *Normal Christian Church* and *Sit, Walk*.
9. Murray, *Full Blessing* and *Spirit*.
10. Tozer, *How to Be*.
11. Miller, *Thy God Reigneth*.

part they played in the fulfillment of his mission. One is even more struck by the fact that his disciples carried on this ministry in the early church. Throughout the charismatic awakening today, there is a return to the primitive experience. Apostolic ministry is still confirmed by God, as Paul said: "The signs of a true apostle were performed among you in all patience, with signs and wonders and mighty works" (2 Cor 12:12). Paul knew, too, that these gifts are not given automatically nor forced on unwilling hearts, so he encourages us to "earnestly desire spiritual gifts" (1 Cor 14:1).

Neither for the early Christians nor for us is this an abstract concept, but Christ's compassion at work in us longing to set men free to receive him and to live for him. Just as Christ exercised a gift of the Spirit in ministering salvation to the woman at the well (the gift of a ward of knowledge concerning the woman's so-called husbands), so Peter exercised it in dealing with Ananias and Sapphira and so a garage mechanic in our fellowship has exercised it on a number of occasions in leading teenagers to Christ. A brief word of explanation about exorcism, healing, prophecy, and tongues would probably be in order here.

Exorcism: As Jesus encountered the devil just after the Holy Spirit descended upon him, so Christians filled with the Spirit are very aware of the enemy of their souls. Jesus gave his disciples authority and power to cast out evil spirits in his name and that authority has been exercised down to our own day. Complementary gifts also come into play: the gift of discernment, to determine the source of the problem, and the gift of faith, to step out and act in the name of Jesus. And it is not always a question of demon possession. There are an infinite variety of ways in which the evil one keeps children of God in bondage: through a spirit of fear, or doubt, or confusion, or depression, or bondage to tobacco, or alcohol, or lust. These are all occasions to preach Jesus, the deliverer, and to pray a strong faith-prayer for deliverance. Arthur Wallis, a Brethren evangelist in England, has been led into a wonderful ministry in this field, and many Christians are tasting the glorious liberty of the children of God for the first time.

Healing: Healing has always been a controversial subject in the church: some saying all sickness is of the devil; others saying it is all God's best will for us. Jesus made the promise, "They shall lay hands on the sick and they shall recover" (Mark 16:18), and with this the promise, "Blessed are they which hear the Word of God and do it." Among many Spirit-filled Christians there is a genuine anxiety about large-scale healing campaigns, but in many Christian homes and churches faith is being exercised to pray for, to "lay hands on" the sick, and to "call the elders," and God is vindicating his promise. One of our neighbors in England opened her heart to the Lord but had to experience real deliverance from Spiritism and from chain-smoking and receive strengthening in her body before she could rejoice in the Lord and become a radiant witness for him.

Prophecy: Exorcism and healing many can understand even without ever experiencing them, but what does Paul mean when he speaks of prophesying in the New Testament assembly? It is misleading to see the term paraphrased as "inspired preaching" in recent versions. In both Old Testament and New Testament there is a fairly clear distinction between preaching, no matter how inspired it is, and prophecy. They are both very important, but distinct. What Peter said on the day of Pentecost was inspired preaching of the gospel, but nowhere is it called prophecy.

Prophecy is speaking the mind of Christ under direct inspiration. Paul says that believers hearing it are encouraged, consoled and edified; unbelievers find the secrets of the hearts disclosed and are brought under conviction (1 Cor 14). With a number of ministers present in our home, it has often been the garage mechanic who has spoken prophetically, producing precisely the fruit that Paul describes. It would be difficult, though, to reach any theoretical conclusion about prophecy without hearing it in an actual situation—according to Paul, a common occurrence in every New Testament assembly.

Tongues and Interpretation: The Holy Spirit-inspired gift of tongues has been a headache and a heartache to many a Christian. Some Christians say very sincerely that it is demonic, or just next to it. Others say that unless you have it, you can't possibly be filled with the Holy Spirit. Both positions are wrong because they are unbiblical. It is already a help to some to find out that the word "tongue" in the authorized version is the same as our word "language." It is also a help to notice that Paul describes the same phenomenon as "praying with the spirit." But obviously it is only the Lord himself who can remove all fear and anxiety about his gifts. The same logic applies to conversion and other matters of Christian obedience, as does to tongues; if somebody says you have to be converted, he is wrong, for man is free to choose separation from God. If somebody says you don't have to be converted, he is also wrong. The good news is that you can be converted. The word of God never says that you have to speak in tongues, nor does it say anywhere that you don't have to.

The implication both from Paul's personal testimony of his own experience of tongues and from his description of the meaning of tongues (it is speaking mysteries to God in the Spirit, 1 Cor 14:3) is that the Spirit-filled Christian can by faith speak in tongues. It is his desire, says Paul, that all the Corinthians speak in tongues (the implication being that they all could, but they all won't). No biblical case whatsoever can be made for the position that a Christian should not speak in tongues. But it is just as wrong to demand it as to forbid it. If a Spirit-filled Christian says he cannot speak in tongues he should be asked to give scriptural support for his conviction—in the same way that someone who says he cannot be converted ought to be challenged. (If he says he is too bad, he is wrong; and if he says he is too good, he is also wrong; etc.)

The only way to a solution is through personal experience. Let no man coerce you. Seek the face of God in the word of God and he will open the way. In our own limited experience and that of at least thirty Mennonite ministers and laymen in British Columbia, it has become an enriching part of our prayer life. Praying with the Spirit, it ought to be added, is not an emotional experience, certainly not an ecstatic one (as some New Testament versions mistakenly suggest).

Effect upon Church

We would like to conclude with a few observations about the charismatic awakening and its effect on Christians and churches today:

Being filled with the Spirit, as an experience subsequent to conversion, opens up the subject of New Testament Christian initiation in a new way, and also clarifies a great deal of current confusion on this subject in the church. In the early church, Christian initiation involved three steps: repentance and faith, baptism in water, and being filled with the Spirit—and little time was allowed to elapse between these stages.

The Lord made no mistake when he planned it in this way. Each part of Christian initiation underlines the truth and power of the gospel in a slightly different way. When conversion is isolated it tends to become distorted in one way or another, and when long periods of time are allowed to elapse between these three first steps, the devil is given all kinds of opportunity to do his destructive work. This truth was so important that the Lord allows us to see these steps in his own experience (born of the Spirit at Bethlehem, baptized in water at the Jordan, and immediately

PART II: ON THE CHARISMATIC MOVEMENT AND GIFTS OF THE SPIRIT

anointed of the Holy Spirit for service) and in the lives of his disciples, and in the lives of the early Christians.

When a church becomes charismatic and evangelistic, the concept of "ministry" is broadened and deepened significantly. We've always said that we need one another and that members of the body of Christ are interdependent, but it is another thing to experience this day by day. Here in British Columbia, it is sometimes a medical doctor who exercises real compassion for the lost, a housewife who prays down the blessing of God, a basketball coach who opens the Word, a teacher who visits the sick, and a minister who calls the saints together.

When Christ is being lifted up there is no such thing as a one-man ministry, nor is the exercise of spiritual faith and authority seen to be dependent on theological training and position. It is in direct contact with Jesus that spiritual authority is communicated. Christ alone can train and authorize and commission us. Too often our church meetings are swayed more by good ideas and personal opinions than by promptings of the Holy Spirit and ministry from above. Here also discernment and prophecy are crucial to the spiritual growth and development of the church.

The breadth and depth and spontaneous joy of worship is being rediscovered in all branches of the charismatic awakening. This is refreshing to see. One thing that cannot be forced is spontaneity in prayer and praise. Nowhere is the failure of the historic denominations more evident than in the field of true worship. If we are living to the praise of his glory and rejoicing in his presence, it is because the Lord has sent something down, not because we have worked something up. Each of us knows our need here best. Of Abraham and Moses and Joshua and David and many others it says, "they fell down and worshipped God;" and when we read it we know it was real and that it can be real for us today. Our needs will be met as we wait on God and as we put him first in our lives.

Christianity is not primarily a question of information but of revelation, not of doctrine, but of life. The eyes of many Christians are being opened to see that much current debate on the scriptures and on theological doctrines is missing the point. It is possible to believe in the inspiration and authority of the scriptures and to have all the correct doctrines and still be denying Christ at every step of the way and to be leading an arid, joyless, fruitless Christian life. This does not mean that correct doctrines are not important, but they must grow out of obedience to God and lead back into it. The word must divide us before we can divide the word; we must be experiencing Christ's life in us if we are to "minister life" to others Paul says, "Knowledge puffeth up, love edifieth."

New principles of Christian unity are also being experienced in the charismatic awakening. Denominational lines, both historically and locally, are no longer as distinct and as important as they seemed to be. We cannot offer God the obedience of our parents, nor can we keep God from showing us who all our brothers are round about us. God's grace alone makes it clear, for example, that Watchman Nee's Little Flock is, so to speak, more Anabaptist than the Anabaptists, more Methodist than the Methodists, and more Brethren than the Brethren. Pride in denominational distinctives is at best but a step on the way to all that God has done and to the "new things" that God is doing today.

In closing let us remind ourselves that everything hinges on the ministry of Christ. He has not changed. If we are "in Christ," then the Christ who said and did the following is at work "in us": "The Spirit of the Lord is upon me, because he has anointed me to preach good news to the poor. He has sent me to proclaim release to the captives and recovering of sight to the blind, to set at liberty those who are oppressed, to proclaim the acceptable year of the Lord" (Luke 4:18–9).

Jesus is still crying out: "If anyone thirst, let him come to me and drink; He who believes in me, as the scripture has said, 'Out of his heart shall flow rivers of living water.' Now this he said about the Spirit, which those who believed in him were to receive" (John 7:37–8). The question each one of us faces is not primarily one of "evaluating" and "debating," but of "thirsting," "coming," "drinking," and "overflowing."

9

An Experience in My Life

S. Djojodihardijo

Introduction by Peter Fast

Soehadiweko Djojodihardjo (less complicated and easier on the tongue when simply called Pak Djojo) is really a remarkable person. As leader of the Javanese Mennonite Church in the Muria area in north-central Java, he has seen the church through periods of persecution, suffering, and hardships of various kinds. Although the Javanese Mennonite Church has existed for more than one hundred years, growth was slow and difficult. There were no mass movements toward Christianity in this area. It is a gathered church. Only in the last fifteen to twenty years has the church experienced rapid progress. Indeed, so phenomenal has its growth been that it may well be the fastest growing Mennonite church in the world.

This growth is due in no small measure to the dynamic leadership of Pak Djojo. Having an almost unlimited capacity for work, Pak Djojo has proven himself as a real pastor, counselor, evangelist, and leader, not leader in the sense of skillfully guiding the church through a complex maze of organization and administration, but leader in the sense of being aware of the pulse of the church, applying pressure here, relieving tension there, sensitively gaging the spiritual life of the church, wrestling in prayer to God with the problems and difficulties that face a Christian church in a predominantly Moslem environment and in a country which just recently received its independence, struggling to make a go of it.

Here in Indonesia Pak Djojo's influence extends beyond the boundaries of the Muria area, an area assigned to the Mennonite Church by the Dutch colonial government, in which missionary work could be carried on by the Mennonites. He is a member of the Board of Directors of the newly formed higher Theological Training Institute called "Duta Watjana," the Javanese word for "Ambassadors of the Word." He is also a member of the board of the Christian University at Salatiga in central Java. Furthermore, the Javanese Mennonite Church is a member of the Indonesian Council of Churches.

This spirit of ecumenicity characterizes Pak Djojo. This affects directly the kind of relationship which Pak Djojo seeks with the Mennonite Church as a world brotherhood. He is not interested in seeking relationships with any one brand of Mennonitism. He seeks contact through brotherhood rather than through conference or denomination. This does create problems when seeking foreign personnel to assist in the work of the church here, especially when such personnel come from the United States or Canada. Through what representative body can Pak Djojo work in order to achieve his ideal of brotherhood? Certainly the gift of the World Conference of Mennonites meeting in Kitchener, Ontario, is representative.

One of the most revolutionary events of Pak Djojo's life is his recent experience of the work of the Holy Spirit. This experience of Pak Djojo comes at a time when freedom of religion exists in this land. Never before has the time been so propitious for the church to carry on its missionary activity. Pak Djojo feels this opportunity keenly and is anxious that the church work now. This experience has given Pak Djojo a new zeal to carry on the work of the church.

Pak Djojo has kindly consented to share this experience of his soul with the Mennonite Brotherhood at large, being apologetic on the one hand in knowing that it is a very personal matter, involving him, and admitting that the full import of this experience is not yet known to him. On the other band, he is willing to enter into conversation with the Mennonite Brotherhood on a topic which increasingly engages the attention of the Christian Church, the Holy Spirit. Without him the work of the church must surely come to naught.

In this report it is significant that Pak Djojo does not begin with a theology of the Holy Spirit, but rather with the acts of the Holy Spirit. This indicates that the Holy Spirit is there to be obeyed rather than to be theologized about. What follows is an account of the acts of the Holy Spirit from an active participant in these acts.

PART II: ON THE CHARISMATIC MOVEMENT AND GIFTS OF THE SPIRIT

An Experience in My Life—S. Djojodihardjo

I. Introduction

In the month of August 1963, my wife and I travelled to the city of Malang. I went as a delegate of our church to the Board of Directors' meeting of the theological school STT Duta Watjana. We had the opportunity of staying at the house of the Fast family in Malang.

During our spare time, while the Board was not in session, we met in discussion with the Fasts. At this time I related to them as best I could, the experience of my life which opened my eyes to many things concerning the work of the Holy Spirit in my life and in the life of the church.

I expected criticism and opposition from them. But rather their attention was drawn to this experience of mine and they had a desire to know more about it. Indeed, in their opinion, they deemed it wise that this experience be written up for publication in church papers. My first reaction was negative. I have difficulty stating my religious experience, which is still growing and renewing my whole life, to the public, let alone for publication in a general church paper.

In fact, I am still wrestling about this matter in my own mind. There is something precious and sublime, something powerful and holy working in my life. I don't understand all of it yet. Nor am I able to organize all that happened to me. Because of this I am still unable to explain these things clearly, neither in words nor in writing. What I am able to relate are the simple facts which resulted from this experience of my soul.

Perhaps this material may give opportunity for thought and reflection. For this reason I am writing this to you, to the brothers of the faith. I feel and know and am convinced that the power of the Holy Spirit now works more in my life than it ever did before. But I am not yet able to clarify this whole experience to the public. What I write now is merely a survey of my life after my great experience.

II. What in Fact Did Happen?

The preachers and the evangelists of our church were meeting for several days in order to study the Bible together. This meeting was held in the local church in Pati toward the latter part of July 1963.

According to the decision of the Synod of our church, which had just recently met, the preachers and evangelists were given the task of reviving the spiritual life of the member churches of our synod. At this time the membership of our churches is more than 15,000. Thus, we are beginning to be a large church. The danger that is now threatening our churches is a recession of spiritual life. What tends to be emphasized is all sorts of church organization and church administration. There are many people who want to become Christians. Our churches are always busy giving catechetical instruction to newcomers. This indeed gives us much reason to rejoice. But what about the spiritual life of the older members? Signs of spiritual recession are beginning to be apparent. This problem has disturbed my spirit and mind for a long time. How can the church care for its members so that their faith remains vital in order for the church to become a force which dares to shoulder the responsibility of all things pertaining to the Lord Jesus, the head of the church?

The topic which was discussed at the ministers' and evangelists' conference was, "The Work of the Holy Spirit in the Church." We came to the following conclusion: The Holy Spirit works, controls, leads and determines the direction of the life of the church. This happens whether or not the church is aware of it.

Another viewpoint was that the church which is controlled and led by the Spirit is truly aware of this fact or prepared to submit to the leadership and control of the Holy Spirit. This we were convinced had not as yet happened. Furthermore, want of spiritual control was caused not only by an unwillingness on the part of the church, but also by a lack of knowledge. Because of this the church does not feel or see the power of the Holy Spirit who leads and controls. If we compare the church of the New Testament with our church now, it is apparent that the church lacks power and energy. Our churches now have mostly become promoters of social welfare in the world or merely places for ethical instruction. We feel that we have lost the power of the Most High, a power described in Acts 1:8 and Luke 24:49b. It is as though the church has lost that which is most important, the supply of power from the Almighty. Why is it like this?

The ministers and evangelists at the end of the conference were fully aware of this problem. To end this conference, we invited Rev. Stube from the Episcopal Church in Montana, currently visiting in Indonesia, to speak on the theme, "Baptism with Water and Baptism with the Holy Spirit." He said that the churches received the promise from Jesus to receive the baptism of the Holy Spirit. Whoever had a thirst for the Holy Spirit and a belief in the gift of the Spirit through Jesus Christ, certainly would experience the

PART II: ON THE CHARISMATIC MOVEMENT AND GIFTS OF THE SPIRIT

same thing as that which was experienced by the New Testament church, namely the baptism of the Holy Spirit.

After this talk, Rev. Stube suggested that we hold a group prayer meeting for the purpose of asking for the baptism of the Holy Spirit. At that time many of the ministers and evangelists were only curious to find out what was going to happen. As for myself, I had already sought for more than two years and investigated the Bible concerning the work of the Holy Spirit. Then I committed myself to the Lord. May it happen according to his will.

At this prayer meeting led by Rev. Stube, I suddenly felt that my whole body moved. Then later my tongue and my mouth moved too, slowly at first, then becoming more pronounced and faster. Finally my diaphragm moved, as though it was squeezed, so that sounds came out of my mouth. Strange words came forth forming sentences which I did not understand myself. I continued to speak in tongues for about half an hour. A feeling of tranquility and joy came over me such as I had never experienced in times past. At night when I prayed again, this experience repeated itself. My mouth and my tongue moved. Later words came out as before. Every time I pray now, I can pray in the Spirit, in tongues as the apostle Paul stated in 1 Cor 14:15. Now it is customary for me to pray in the Spirit. But I also pray with the mind.

For more than two years I had continued to feel anxious and worried. This unrest began after I had met with Gerald Derstine, an ex-minister of the (Old) Mennonite Church, in November 1961, and with Rev. Stube, who at this time was visiting Indonesia and held spiritual revival meetings in several churches. He also came to Pati to hold a joint meeting sponsored by some churches in Pati, including ours. I personally could meet with both of them and have a heart to heart conversation. (Both related their own experience, and both were convinced that the Lord Jesus promised to baptize every Christian with the Holy Spirit, whoever asked in faith.) Both Derstine and Stube prayed for me with the laying on of hands. But nothing happened. I felt confused, bewildered and upset.

For two years I continued to study the Bible, to seek to understand clearly what actually is the work of the Holy Spirit, how does he work m the church and in the life of man. Every time someone who claimed to be filled with the Holy Spirit came to hold spiritual revival meetings, I made a special effort to attend. But every time I was not yet able to agree with it. I was still very skeptical about this whole matter. But I had no peace in my heart.

Even earlier I had met with Rev. Doss, an American citizen from India, who also belonged to the Episcopal Church. He was very active and fiery in his preaching and in his manner. After he laid his hands on me, I felt very flexible and pliant. I thought at that time, I had been filled with the Holy Spirit. Later it became clear that I hadn't. I still felt confused and anxious in my innermost being. Finally, all I could do was commit myself to God and to what he willed for me in my life.

Now I thank God that I am able to witness to the fact that the work of the Holy Spirit in the New Testament church is the same as his work now.

III. The "Before" and "After" in My Life

I want to explain the matter of being filled with the Holy Spirit and the change it wrought in my life by the use of several examples in three particular areas: A) in my personal life; B) in my work of serving the church; C) in divine activity (miracles).

A. Changes in my personal life

Although people said that I was by nature a cheerful, happy person, my spirit in fact was often troubled by a feeling of fear and anxiety. I also became angry very easily. Furthermore, a feeling of responsibility pressed down upon me so heavily, that I did not care to live. To me life meant carrying a heavy burden, a burden which I very often was unable to bear. It was as though my life depended upon myself, although I knew that I believed in a Lord who was Almighty and All-loving. I did not know when my own efforts must stop and when I must submit to the power and love of God. I always complained: Supposing I know clearly what the will of God is which he wants me to do in a certain situation, how can I act with firmness, resoluteness and courage? But it's a pity . . . I did not know what the will of God was! Thus, I continually had to wrestle in my spirit. Finally, I could not bear it any longer.

After I had experienced the fullness of the Spirit, this wrestling in my soul abated by itself. A transfer of authority, a change of dynasty occurred. The former feeling of fear and anxiety was displaced by a feeling of serenity and a conviction that God was helping me. This transfer of authority meant that no longer I live but Christ lives in me. These aren't merely words which sound trite. These are facts which came about not as a result of my own efforts. I am not often troubled by my passions and desires any more. It is as though they are gone and don't have the courage to trouble me anymore.

PART II: ON THE CHARISMATIC MOVEMENT AND GIFTS OF THE SPIRIT

These are the changes which I experienced in my personal life. My life is now filled with thankfulness and praise to God. Deep in my innermost being, I always have a feeling of joy. This is how I feel every day in facing my own problems as well as the problems and difficulties of the church.

B. In the work of serving the Church

That which I want to explain here covers only two things: 1) pastoral work, and 2) preaching.

1. Pastoral work: I have always been fond of pastoral work. Many people come to me to express their innermost feelings, their sorrows, and their difficulties. They like to come because, according to them, I am able to listen with patience to what they have to say. Also, they thought that I was capable of giving advice and guidance, which alleviates their sorrows and their difficulties. But in fact is was very difficult for me at that time to know just what were the underlying causes of their sorrows, doubt, depressions, and anxiety.

   After my experience of being filled with the Holy Spirit, it is as though I can quickly understand and feel the causes of their troubles and difficulties. After people relate their various kinds of depressions and problems, and when I later pray with them, suddenly I prophesy or express words of wisdom which affect their inner self. They seem to be freed from their difficulties by the power of God. In fact, I marvel at myself that I have received the gift of expressing words of wisdom like that. All I can do is thank him for his gift of grace.

2. Preaching: Before, when I prepared my sermons, after I had prayed, it was as though I was being led and directed by God. At those times I felt joyful in my heart. But after preparation and delivery of the sermon, gradually my joy left me and a feeling of anxiety, fear and doubt returned. The feeling of heavy responsibility pressed down upon me again. Now I not only feel led and directed by God when I preach, but it is as though my mouth is moved and as though what I say when I preach is entirely controlled by the Holy Spirit. It is not I who preach, but God who uses me. God himself teaches his own church. Furthermore, the feeling of fellowship with God does not cease after I finish preaching, as it did before.

C. In divine acts

Already before this experience of mine I frequently prayed for the sick. It was also clear that my prayers often were answered by God and the sick became well. Thus far I only experienced miracles of healing.

Now I am able to experience other divine acts. I marvel at these myself. May I relate several from among the many miraculous events which I have experienced in the last few months after my spiritual experience.

1. Recently I was called by some young people to come to their conference in Pati. This was a conference of non-Christian youths. Two girls had suddenly become stiff and unconscious. Later they also spoke various and strange words. A medical doctor had already been called. Also, the assistance of a medicine man (*dukun*) had been sought. But to no avail. According to the opinion of some of the young people attending this conference, these two girls were possessed by Satan. I asked one of the girls who she was and where she came from. She answered that she was an old lady and originated from a certain place. Then I requested that the evil spirit leave her. The response was: "I don't like to leave. Even if you use force, I will still stay and continue to possess the girl."

   I began to pray in the Spirit. I had just begun to pray when the girl screamed. It was as if something came out of her. Immediately the girl became conscious again and returned to normal as though nothing had happened, except that she was rather tired.

2. One night I together with another minister and a youth was riding in our car. I invited them to pray asking for God's blessing and grace. Suddenly in the power of the Spirit I began to teach things pertaining to the Christian life. I was conscious and heard everything I said. Besides I continued to drive the vehicle. The speech, or better sermon, lasted for about one half-hour. The beginning of the sermon dealt with the subject: "What is the Christian life?" This was followed by giving instruction and advice to all three of us, one at a time. When the youth's turn came, his life was being analyzed. It was stated that the youth was tottering on the brink of belief and unbelief. Furthermore, his behavior was characterized as being no good. Later he was urged to repent. If he didn't, he would always be troubled.

After an interval of five minutes, the youth suddenly fell face downward and became stiff. He stopped breathing and his pulse was gone. This condition lasted for about fifteen minutes. The minister who accompanied me was caught in fear and began to cry. He called the youth by name. Strange as it may seem, I continued my analysis. After about fifteen minutes my right hand moved and was placed on the neck of the youth. Immediately the youth rose and cried loudly for a long time. Later the youth took something wrapped up in a kind of reddish cloth hidden deep in his clothes. It was a charm which he then gave to me.

This was an amazing and frightening experience. But by means of it, the youth was freed from the power of darkness through the Holy Spirit. This youth repented and now believes only in the Lord Jesus.

3. A woman, a member of our church, was sick with cancer. According to the doctor, this cancer had already developed over a long period of time, since it had already spread to various parts of the body. The doctor was unwilling to operate on her. Furthermore, according to the doctor and the nurse, this woman could not live for more than three months.

One day three ministers from our church and I went to see this woman and to pray for her. While I was praying one of the ministers in a vision saw the cancerous tumor (the size of a duck's egg lodged in her stomach) disappear. After we had finished praying, this minister asked the woman to check whether this sore had actually disappeared. The woman checked and confessed that it was gone! Because of the blessing of God, her sickness is gone and now she is well. She went to the doctor again for her periodic check and was told that she was really healed.

A few days later the woman came to my house to express her thanks and confess her sins which she had committed. She was also willing to confess before God and the whole congregation. She admitted that she had been warned many times by the minister to cease from her evil ways, but till now she had paid no attention to it. This experience moved her deeply because God still loved her although she had committed many sins. This woman repented. It was as though God himself had warned this Christian who had gone astray to return.

Since my spiritual experience, I can testify that several Christians who had forgotten about the church and followed the will and desire of their own heart, were helped by God from their infirmities. They returned and repented.

IV. Praying and Laying on of Hands

About three months after my experience of being filled with the Holy Spirit, there arose a desire in me to pray for the other ministers of our church and to lay hands on them so that they too might be filled with the Holy Spirit. According to Acts 8:17, Peter laid his hands on the brethren which were in Samaria. Then they received the Holy Spirit. Also, according to Acts 19:6, Paul placed his hands on the disciples of John. Later they too received the Holy Spirit.

By prayer and the laying on of hands, the ministers and evangelists of our church were truly filled with the Holy Spirit. Now they rejoice that they have received a gift from God. One of them has received the gift of prophecy, another one the gift of interpreting tongues, some see visions, while others have received the gift of healing. All this happened without the exercise or effort of man. It is God's gift to them. The only thing they must do is pray in the Spirit.

In my opinion this is what the apostle means in 2 Tim 1:6. Timothy is asked to rekindle the gift of God which is in him through praying in the Spirit. The filling of the Spirit is their supply, their equipment which they have received from the Most High, as is written in Luke 24:49: Those who must struggle to become witnesses of Jesus Christ, to them the Lord is eager to give power from heaven as is written in Acts 1:8.

I notice that they are now more willing to carry out their task as servants of the word and shepherds of the flock. Although at this time there are a thousand and one problems which must be faced, especially in the field of economy (lack of food), whereas formerly I heard them moan and complain, now they are more resolute and determined to face their own problems of life.

V. Concluding Remarks

What I have written are facts which took place in my life after I experienced the fullness of the Holy Spirit. I intentionally did not offer an evaluation or write about the work of the Holy Spirit from a theological point of view. My purpose was to let the facts speak for themselves. Evaluations and conclusions may be drawn by the readers.

10

The Charismatic in East Africa

Donald R. Jacobs

as interviewed by
James Fairfield

Fairfield: *It has been suggested that the East African revival shows some of the characteristics claimed for the charismatic movement here in America. Having observed the so-called charismatic movement here, and having participated in the African revival, would you agree to this comparison?*

Jacobs: Before I answer, I want to say that I am not qualified to deal theologically with the charismatic gifts. I will simply talk out of my personal experience with the Holy Spirit's work.

The East African revival has taken a line which is Holy Spirit centered and which honors the Spirit. The object is to allow the Holy Spirit to speak to issues in life thus revealing his activity in a person, rather than any sort of extraordinary "gifts."

We detect the presence of the Spirit in one another by whether we are repenting, you see. If the Lord is touching things in our lives which are not right and is bringing us to repentance—this indicates that the Holy Spirit is actually moving in the brotherhood.

The East African revival is not peculiarly a revival in the context of individual vertical relationships, that is, between an individual and God. Rather it is a revival in *koinonia*. The Spirit, working within the hearts of the people in the group, strengthens the group and gives proof of the fact that the Holy

Spirit is present. Of course, there are the usual evidences of the Holy Spirit expressing himself in joy and in power and in soul winning and this sort of thing. But more specifically, we have thought of the charismatic gifts in terms of those gifts which God is giving within the *koinonia* to increase the effectiveness of the group. One brother will be given a special gift of expounding the word, as the group expects him to be the one who leads out in Bible reading. Another brother has the gift of organization so he will be the person who handles the correspondence and keeps the group in touch with the rest of the brethren in the area. We have some people who are extremely useful and successful in soul winning. This too is seen as a gift.

Fairfield: *Let me press this a little further. All of you identify this as a gifting by the Holy Spirit? And that it isn't just "talent"?*

Jacobs: Of course it is talent, too. For instance, the organizer, the administrator, had the talent for administration before he placed himself and his gifts at the disposal of Christ and the group.

Fairfield: *Then what has convinced you that this is a genuine charismatic thrust?*

Jacobs: Simply because God has miraculously given the full compliment of gifts for the operation of the group. When he brings together a group, the necessary gifts are there. He frees the gifts within the brotherhood by the power of the Spirit, and the group benefits.

Now, if a brother stops repenting; if he hangs up on something and refuses to break; if he grows cold in his spirit; then the effectiveness of his gift diminishes.

It appears there are some talents that you can more or less exercise a little easier without the Spirit than others. However, gifts in the group that deal with revelation and the exposition of scripture are definitely dependent upon the Holy Spirit. A prophet cannot carry on long without the Holy Spirit.

As I said, I feel none of these gifts are really given in a post-conversion experience. Thus, we do not seek for gifts that we don't have. We simply ask God to release the gift that is in us for the sake of Christ.

Fairfield: *Then you credit the Holy Spirit with emphasizing these gifts for the group's benefit?*

PART II: ON THE CHARISMATIC MOVEMENT AND GIFTS OF THE SPIRIT

Jacobs: Yes, this we do constantly, but we don't necessarily separate the Holy Spirit from Christ in our terminology. We often say, "the Lord is releasing that man's gift," and of course it is the work of the Holy Spirit, the Spirit of Christ.

There's one thing that I've never heard in East Africa, and that is the Holy Spirit spoken of as being apart from Christ. Rather, the Holy Spirit is simply Christ's spirit here, working among us. We speak of the Spirit of Christ, rather than "the Spirit," because this has a little different connotation in Swahili than in English. It would be a bit misleading for us to continually talk about "Spirit," because in that connection "Spirit" does come out a little differently. But if the Spirit of Christ is referred to, everybody knows exactly who is being talked about.

So we talk about Christ being in our midst, we talk about Christ helping the brethren, and it is the Lord in the brotherhood rather than the Holy Spirit in the brotherhood, if you know what I mean. Whether this is significant or not, I don't know, it may be our own peculiar semantic problem.

Fairfield: *I think we have a parallel situation here in America among the devotees of the charismatic movement. It seems to be an emphasis on the "Holy Ghost," as if he were somehow different.*

Jacobs: But in East Africa, the way the Lord has been talking to us there, we don't even allow that question to arise. We simply assume that the Spirit at work among us is the Spirit of Christ and refer to him as such.

Fairfield: *What does the East African revival mean in the context of the larger brotherhood? What has it done for the denominational churches?*

Jacobs: This revival is taking place within denominational churches, yet the fellowship is across denominational lines. These fellowships have become the nuclei of revival in all denominations all over East Africa. Through them many have been experiencing Christ in their lives, experiencing the gifts of the Spirit of Christ. Perhaps one might expect more of a dramatic Pentecostal form of charismatic expression. Yet the reality and spiritual power of the revival cannot be denied.

In East Africa there are, however, little pockets of people who do have the extraordinary gifts which are usually characterized as Pentecostal. But generally, the revival in East Africa doesn't see these as authentic, desirable, nor necessary. I have spoken to quite a few of the leaders in the

East African revival, people who are really working in the brotherhood. In speaking about glossolalia and some of these other things, they feel that they tempt a person to seek something other than Christ, "Christ plus." And every time something is added to Christ, they feel that actually a little something is taken away from him.

It has been expressed that in going after a "gift" you are asking for something more than Christ wishes. In a sense you are then belittling Christ. And another thing, we have had a few people in the revival who have gone overseas where "gifts" were actually being sought after, and have come back to us with these gifts, and we found that they were very difficult people to work with! It seemed they had achieved a certain status.

And we have had a few people who simply got hard-hearted through this experience. They were no longer humble and mellow and breakable as they had been in the past. It is really difficult for us to see the value of such gifts at this point. If there are brothers who do have glossolalia, we encourage them to be very private in its use.

We encourage anyone with such gifts to continue to break before God, to have an open heart, then to deal with the gift appropriately, but not to let it come between him and the group. Let it be his, but let it be a blessing, rather than a hurt.

So this is what we've experienced. Speaking generally, I would say that when we think of the Holy Spirit in charisma in East Africa, we have the group in mind, and not an individual. We pray that God will give us all the gifts we need in order to have a fellowship in a group that works in unity and with effectiveness. As the Lord does this, we believe we are then experiencing the charismatic gifts of the Spirit of Christ among us.

11

The Charismatic Aspects of the Work of the Spirit

Myron S. Augsburger

as interviewed by
James Fairfield

Fairfield: *The charismatic movement has implications for the church, theologically, socially, and, of course, personally. Assuming the movement is valid, the question remains: Why? What do you see as its reason-for-being?*

Augsburger: Someone has said every church goes through a three-stage cycle: first, warm enthusiastic acceptance of the gospel; secondly, institutionalization; and thirdly, worship of the past. To interrupt this cycle and to bring persons ever and again to the experiential dimension of sharing with the risen Christ and with the Holy Spirit, God moves upon the church in revival. The present charismatic movement, so-called, is basically an expression of a renewed emphasis upon the experience or existential dimensions of Christian faith.

Fairfield: *In this case, the movement seems to emphasize the distribution of "gifts" by the Holy Spirit. And these gifts seem to be for purposes more than simply the development of personal piety.*

Augsburger: When the Holy Spirit fills a person's life, he also enriches that life and gives that person gifts or endowments according to his will for the advancement of the cause of Christ. This means that the Holy Spirit is always functioning within the church to enrich particular members for the good of the brotherhood. I believe it also follows that persons who sense certain areas of need in the church or in the world and who then seek the Spirit's gifts to meet those needs will find that particular endowments may come to them by prayer which would not happen apart from their own seeking. It is in this sense that the Apostle Paul says, "Covet earnestly the best gifts."

Personally, I hold to the position that the gifts of the Spirit are limited not by time but by God's purpose. In this I am saying that he gifts different individuals in the church, and while not all persons have the same gifts, he sees to it that the church benefits from the full potential of the gifts of the Spirit as outlined in the New Testament. Of these gifts the late A. W. Tozer says there are eighteen distinctive gifts mentioned which are a part of the charismatic expressions of the Holy Spirit. It is significant that the term charismatic relates to *charis* or grace and in the New Testament is to be seen in relation to Jesus Christ. The term *pneumaticos* is associated more directly with the phenomenon of gifts associated with the expressions of the Holy Spirit.

Fairfield: *We hear much in neo-Pentecostal statements of the "baptism of the Spirit," and that this is a unique experience apart from conversion. What are the theological implications here?*

Augsburger: The New Testament speaks of a baptism with the Holy Spirit in which Christ is the one who does the baptizing, and the baptism is the presence of the Holy Spirit in the individual's life. It is my understanding of the New Testament, that while the new birth is the experience in which something happens to my spirit in that it is reborn in relation to Jesus Christ, the baptism with the Holy Spirit is the gift of his Spirit to dwell within my life.

In this sense the baptism of the Spirit is that occasion in which one accepting Christ as Lord receives the Holy Spirit to indwell his person and to become the master of the individual's life. And while he is not limited to or circumscribed by our terms, it is my deep conviction that the New Testament terminology would describe the baptism with the Spirit as an initial experience, a personal Pentecost, in which the Holy Spirit is given by Christ to the individual to dwell in his life.

This means that further expressions of his indwelling in which the Holy Spirit, by his anointing, by his unction or by his infilling or by his endowing the person with gifts, enriches that life for service—these expressions are subsequent manifestations of his work within the individual's life. The church today needs to be praying for a new infilling of the Holy Spirit beyond what we are seeing and experiencing at this moment.

Fairfield: *Of course, in any discussion of the charismatic movement. the subject of glossolalia inevitably comes up. Some have identified "speaking in tongues" with the emotional quotient of the participant. Is this appropriate? For a supposed gift of the Holy Spirit? And does this tend to dichotomize emotions—volition?*

Augsburger: With regard to glossolalia I believe it is true, to quote Sam Shoemaker, that "persons enter in upon the stream of the Spirit at different levels." In my analysis I would say that there are at least three levels—the sensory, the psychical, and the spirit-level. I feel personally that the sensory level is characterized more by that which we commonly describe as glossolalia and that the psychical level is characterized more by other expressions and involvements in emotional release and experience, and that the spirit-level is characterized more by such gifts as discernment, faith, love, and what we commonly call the fruit of the Spirit.

While I feel that glossolalia is a lower level of involvement and thereby is to be identified more with the personal, emotional, and devotional aspects of piety, none of these levels can disqualify the other. As to the volitional aspects of discipleship, it would appear that motivation for action varies with different personalities and temperament and that it would be invalid to say that there is an absence of the volitional in any one of these.

God meets a given individual where he is at any level and then moves him toward maturity in Christ. The most disappointing thing is when individuals use particular experiences as means of satisfying their own egos in claiming a prestigious religious experience which results in a pluralism within a church, manifest in the tensions between groups which claim different levels of spiritual experience.

Fairfield: *There are those who insist the church has overemphasized these concerns, these dangers, at the expense of the gifts.*

Augsburger: I feel the church has underemphasized the importance of the work of the Holy Spirit and personal involvement in his work. On the other hand, I am sure that some of the deeper life experiences always have associated with them the danger of overemphasizing the particulars of the work of the Spirit when the gifts of the Spirit are magnified in a way disproportionate to the fruit of the Spirit or to the presence and dynamic of the Person of the Spirit known in the face of Jesus Christ. The result can only be difficulty, dissension, and division within a given group.

Fairfield: *Why is it that interest in the charismatic has only recently begun to involve the Mennonite Church?*

Augsburger: This current movement of charismatic interest has been slow in entering the Mennonite Church for several reasons. In the first place, the Mennonite Church does have a strong emphasis on the new birth and conversion and the experiential dimensions of the Christian faith. From the Reformation to the present we have been a group which has emphasized strongly the need for an inner baptism with the Holy Spirit and the Spirit-filled life. Our problem is that we have formalized this and sacrificed the matter of motivating individuals to seek this personal involvement for themselves. Consequently, unless we experience a deep spiritual renewal we can anticipate more of the unusual encounters with this movement.

On the other hand, without being judgmental of other groups, it is my calculated opinion from wide sharing that for many persons who have entered into the charismatic experience this is their first basic experiential involvement with the Spirit of the living Christ. While it is easier to speak of this as an added boon to their salvation than to admit that perhaps the conversion prior to this had been formal or merely academic or intellectual, it might be more honest to admit that this becomes the first basic involvement with the Holy Spirit and inner dynamic transformation. This analysis is supported by the evidence that in Protestantism in general there is great hesitancy to enter into the experiential dimensions which are often slanderously referred to as sentimental or mere pietistic involvements.

Fairfield: *Your observation then of the charismatic movement in the so-called mainline churches is that it is a result of a new birth rather than a "second experience" of some nature?*

Augsburger: The New Testament speaks of salvation and sanctification in relationship. It seems to me that it is this relational factor which we need to understand if we are to talk about the various experiences with Christ. As to a "second experience" the basic questions with respect to this have to do with the vagueness as to what has happened in the first experience which should have been a genuine transformation which we describe as regeneration or new birth and not merely some assurance of forgiveness. And a second aspect in which we raise questions is whether the second experience is a final one in complete sanctification. It would appear from the New Testament that we should give adequate recognition of more than one or even two basic experiences with Christ.

From the practical standpoint, within our brotherhood where most of our young people accept Christ as "older children" and are identified with the church, there seems to be a very basic need for a second definite experience of dedication at the level of the mature teenagers where the issues facing more adult life can be met. I see no way of escaping this, but rather believe that we should promote this involvement unashamedly and deliberately.

As to the Anabaptists in the sixteenth century, it is significant that they were criticized for claiming that they had the Holy Spirit. They believed that one is not saved by an outer baptism with water but by an inner baptism with the Holy Spirit. However, in affirming that they had the Holy Spirit when they were charged by Pietists as believing that now they were perfect, the answer was, "I am not infallible, it is simply the Holy Spirit who dwells in me who alone is infallible." One of the basic insights as to their perspective on this is found in their analysis of 1 Cor 12 and 14 in which they insist that the total brotherhood is involved in the dynamic work of the Holy Spirit and that each one has his particular gifts and areas of contribution to be made in the brotherhood. The emphasis here was not on any particular gift but was rather upon the importance of each person as a responsible member in the fellowship where it is needed to accomplish these ends.

12

A Historical Estimate of the Charismatic Movement

Irvin B. Horst

as interviewed by
James Fairfield

Fairfield: *From your historian's viewpoint what do you see as the place of the charismatic movement? Are there identifiable connections for instance with the Anabaptist church? Or even earlier?*

Horst: Some Mennonite historians have tended to try to establish a connection between the early church, particularly the apostolic church, and the Anabaptist movement in the sixteenth century. Intuitively they link these with the most charismatic movements of the Middle Ages and the patristic period. Certainly, one of the most outstanding of the early period is the Montanist movement of which Tertullian was the most important representative. Inevitably the Montanists are considered in these popular histories as an early bridge with the Anabaptist movement.

This is a rather unsophisticated and unreal approach to the actual historical situation. Very often the people who write this kind of history are church leaders, sometimes older church leaders, who sense the need for real spiritual dynamic without thinking through the facts certainly not theologically. They just tend to link up the movements of the past. Their motives are good, but the historical continuity is highly debatable.

Fairfield: *You see the movements not so much as an integrated progression but as isolated situations with little threading together?*

Horst: Yes. The questions of continuity, and of genetic connection are not too important for these movements. You see, in history today we tend to see it scientifically. For this we have to have cause and effect relationships or genetic connections—one historic entity is organically related in some way to a succeeding entity. But this is not the only way the Spirit works. The Spirit does work horizontally, but an even more characteristic work of the Spirit is a vertical injection, a vertical disruption of history. He breaks up the continuities of the secular and the carnal; the human cause and effect tendencies which can pull the church down.

Fairfield: *You are saying that the Holy Spirit works not only in continuity through the church but also directly—then what does this say about our projecting back into the Anabaptist movement some of our current fads? We do this for more than the charismatic, don't we?*

Horst: There is naturally the tendency to identify yourself with what is dynamic and creative. Is it important to say whether or not the charismatic movements are like the Anabaptists? Their own place in contemporary history justifies their existence and not whether or not they are connected to or continue a tradition of the past. I am speaking of bona fide charismatic movements giving some evidence of the Spirit's presence. We have to qualify them, because there are some false charismatic movements.

Fairfield: *What would you identify as a bona fide movement?*

Horst: Well, this is always difficult, because it is a question of degree. You see, you might have a particular movement which is 90 percent an emotional human expression, and very little of the Spirit in it, but still enough to see some signs. But I would say that the Pentecostal movement as a whole is bona fide. Of course, there are various elements to the Pentecostal movement, but I am thinking of the kind of thing that has been happening in recent years in Latin America and even in our own country. If one is open and brings the judgment of Scripture to an understanding of the movement, you can't deny its importance.

Fairfield: *It isn't necessary to vouch for all that the movement encompasses in its spectrum of theological opinion and operation, but simply that we must* recognize that in Pentecostalism there can be and very often is a moving of the Spirit? Do you see in the Anabaptist movement anything to associate with this?*

Horst: Yes—and herein lies an interesting possibility, that Mennonites do stand within a charismatic tradition. You see, in the revival of Anabaptist studies that we have had, particularly through the Goshen school, we have emphasized Anabaptists as Biblicists. This has been helpful, but would it not also be possible to see the early Anabaptists as a movement of the Spirit? There is a lot to commend this approach.

Fairfield: *Charismatic energy in their "brotherhood" and Biblicism, among other things?*

Horst: Yes, decidedly so. Of course, the Goshen school of Anabaptist historiography has seen very clearly—and Franklin Littell also emphasizes this—how that Wesley's revival and the Anabaptist movement have a great deal in common. And of course, in the Methodist movement and the evangelical awakening in general, there was a great outburst of charismatic gifts in an unusual way, in a way that was not characteristic say of Lutheranism or Reformed Christianity. So, in this respect Wesley's revival may have much more in common with the Anabaptists.

Fairfield: *What are the things you see characterizing the Anabaptist charismatic?*

Horst: Primarily the emphasis on the Holy Life and the sanctified life, the work of the Holy Spirit as the indwelling Christ—the new Adam, the transformed man who gives expression to the Christian life and the Christian faith through the work of the Spirit.

Fairfield: *Inevitably the question comes up—is this attributable to a "second work of grace"?*

Horst: Wesley himself had a kind of "second work of grace" in his own experience but he never spoke of it as such. This emphasis on second work of grace, if I understand it correctly, was a bit foreign to original Methodism so that perhaps the original concept was something like the Anabaptist emphasis where justification and sanctification, if not simultaneous with the new birth, were at least related to the original experience. However, Methodism did become identified with a "second work of grace."

PART II: ON THE CHARISMATIC MOVEMENT AND GIFTS OF THE SPIRIT

Fairfield: *And the holiness churches would parallel this? We have near relatives in the holiness group, the Brethren in Christ.*

Horst: Yes, and the United Missionary Church is a good example of an outbreak of charismatic movement in our own circles. Well, it would not matter at all nor would it really be a misinterpretation to link ourselves to the holiness movement in the sense of the Anabaptist concern for the holy life.

Fairfield: *What of the studies a number of brethren have made on the Holy Spirit recently? Are they an attempt to answer the movement? To help it happen?*

Horst: These studies certainly are commendable and have elicited considerable response and interest, yet they tend to be academic. It's like Paul Tillich said of the upsurge of new Reformation studies and Luther studies that they have done practically nothing to make modern-day Lutherans—or to produce Christians who are doing for our generation today what Luther did for his.

I have a concern that when we write books and discuss these things in the classroom, they tend to be quite academic. No one planned for a John Wesley. No one anticipated the Anabaptist movement; it just was an eschatological event. No doubt we need to discuss in the classroom what we do to acquire or have fresh stirrings of the Spirit among us, particularly in the Christian institution. But to ask the question, "What can we do?" seems inappropriate: I don't think we can do very much theologically or historically but this has to be a transcendent work of God among us. There is always something wrong about scheduling a new work of the Spirit.

You had asked about Mennonites and signs or possibilities for a charismatic revival. And I hedged on that because it occurs to me that we are going through a period of "organization." This is my own theory and I have been teaching it to my classes although perhaps it has become too much of a pet theory. But when we get some maturity into our concern about organization, then we might be able to make more place for the typical charismatic movements.

Fairfield: *Are you suggesting that perhaps as Mennonites we are hardly organized enough to respond to charismatic gifts among us? This is a new slant.*

Horst: It is the kind of organization rather than the degree of organization that we need to be concerned about. The type of organization which promotes church unity and working together and cooperation—this is the kind we need. There is a different variety of church organization, which depends on the organization man and is quite mechanistic. Unfortunately, we are not free of the latter.

Mennonites in America today have rediscovered—or discovered for the first time—the power and genius and the resources of organization, and we are capitalizing on this discovery. I doubt whether we have reached the peak of this trend. Now, organization in a certain way is one of the gifts of the Spirit, but that isn't what we mean, I suspect, when we speak of the charismatic gifts.

1 Cor 12 has the expression "governments"—nevertheless the institutional church historically militates against the charismatic church. We should not make a sharp antithesis here, but essentially the organizational church has been antagonistic to the charismatic church. Our church leaders have spent an awful lot of time trying to put out the brush fires, as you might call the outbreaks among individuals, sometimes small groups, concerned about speaking in tongues and the like—when what we really need is a prairie fire. We need to discover how to make organizational room for the Spirit's gifts. In this sense our antagonisms are often misplaced.

We tend to have a rather hard or limited type of organization in our own church, and this would also be true of some of the other Protestant churches. Our view of organization and our attempt at church order is not mature. We are over-defensive about questions of organization and church order. In the long view of church history, it may not be right to stand the organizational-institutional church over against the charismatic church. Because after all, unity and all the Christian traits that we associate with unity, these are also the gifts of the Spirit. A more mature approach to church organization can still make place for charismatic movements. This may seem to be a paradoxical concern here—to keep open our interest in the unity movements and at the same time warm up to some of the more sectarian movements.

Fairfield: *You would see this as your hope for the church?*

Horst: I never thought of it like that but, yes, it seems to stand within the providence of God. It is necessary to emphasize what I said about the current widespread concerns for church unity. This appears to be important and seems to be blessed of the Spirit. Not everything that happens under this rubric is the work of God but in our contemporary scene it does seem that the matter of the churches working together is to some extent the work of God among us, a charismatic work.

Fairfield: *I'm sure some of our more fundamentally inclined brethren will not like you saying that unity movements could be a work of the Holy Spirit, but I find myself agreeing with you.*

Horst: Usually when we speak about the holiness movements and the Pentecostal groups, we immediately go to 1 Cor 12 and other chapters where we think of the gifts. But maybe we should also go to Galatians where you have the fruits of the Spirit. Consider a pragmatic approach to this whole question—you see someone who claims to have the Spirit, or a church or a group, and you ask yourself, now do they really have the fruits of the Spirit? Do they get along with each other, do they get along with other Christians? And it seems to me we have a great deal of Scripture to back this up. So perhaps what we should try to do, if we are Biblicists, is not only be concerned about 1 Cor 12 but also Gal 5. Be concerned for the charismatic possibilities of unity.

13

The Charismatic Revival

A Survey of the Literature

GERALD C. STUDER

The current movement sometimes called "The Charismatic Revival" is also referred to as "Neo-Pentecostalism" or simply "The Tongues Movement." It is necessarily distinguished from the earlier Pentecostalism, which arose in the early 1900s because it differs in several significant ways from the pattern of its predecessor. It is generally agreed that this movement began quietly in suburban St. Mark's Episcopal Church of Van Nuys, California, on Sunday, April 3, 1960. Before that day was over, it was a Passion Sunday in more than the usual sense.

Because the events of that day mark the beginning of this movement, we shall begin our survey with a rather full account of what happened on that occasion. This will be followed by some general observations made after reading widely in the literature of, or about, this movement. Several of the more substantial books will be examined separately, followed by a concluding statement.

The Beginning

At the 7:30 a.m. service on April 3, 1960, the Rev. Dennis J. Bennett calmly related to his Episcopal congregation the story of his "baptism in the Holy Spirit" which had taken place the previous October. He repeated his story at the 9:00 a.m. service and in doing so provoked a drastic response from one of the associate priests, who removed his vestments, publicly resigned and stalked down the aisle and out of the church.

At the 11:00 a.m. service, Father Bennett again told the story of his "baptism" with the accompanying "speaking in tongues." Aware of the explosive nature of his public declaration and moved by a desire for the peace of the church, Bennett shortly thereafter tendered his resignation. By this time the parish of 2,500 members was seething with the news of what had happened, though the majority did not understand its wider significance.

What had brought about Father Bennett's experience the preceding October (1959)? The young rector of the nearby (Episcopal) Church of the Holy Spirit in Monterey Park, California, had come to Father Bennett for counsel. A young couple, nominal members of his parish, had suddenly become active in the church. They claimed that they had been filled with the Holy Spirit and talked with other tongues! The young pastor introduced the couple to the other young couples in the parish in the hope that they might channel their enthusiasm into the conventional church activities. Instead, the other couples also "caught fire" and claimed that they too had been filled with the Holy Spirit.

Bennett informally stepped in to help his fellow clergyman in a situation which seemed out of balance. Again, the unexpected happened and Bennett discovered that instead of his helping these couples return to a more normal (nominal!?) Christian and church life, they had something that he wanted. He was convinced that Jesus Christ was more impressively real to them than to him. Within a few weeks, Bennett himself had also "received" and spoken in other tongues. His personal and ministerial life was transformed as a result and a new joy overwhelmed him. By the time of his public testimony some five months later at St. Mark's Church, some seventy members had also "received" and another six hundred were sympathetically interested.

Bennett has survived the Van Nuys "explosion" to become the tireless advocate of this dynamic "baptism." Following his resignation, he was transferred to the almost-defunct St. Luke's Episcopal Church in Seattle. What happened there also requires some kind of an explanation. From the fifty worshipers who attended the services of that church when Bennett went to it, it grew within the next three years to a congregation of several hundred members with a Friday night prayer meeting regularly drawing from two to four hundred people.

The beginning just described was the major one but there were minor waves to this movement earlier. As early as 1956 there were about twenty ministers representing several major denominations openly involved in a similar experience. In the last days of 1954, a remarkable series of events clearly originating with the Holy Spirit took place in a Mennonite Church in northern Minnesota where Gerald Derstine was pastor. Still earlier, the Full Gospel Business Men's Fellowship International (FGBMFI) was organized in California in 1952. Nevertheless, the Van Nuys incident seems to have marked the beginning of the general outbreak and spread of this movement.

General Observations

The participants in this movement by and large are definitely not factors of divisiveness in their congregations and denominations. On the contrary they become the most faithful and enthusiastic members of their respective churches.

It is frequently months before these participants in the movement make any public acknowledgment of their experience though they begin at once privately to share their new-found joy. There is no particular dissatisfaction on their part with the regular worship services or the other aspects of the congregational program. At most, those having "received," together with others interested in a more vital witness, may begin a weekly weeknight meeting at a private home or in the church. This meeting is usually interdenominational in character and consists primarily of praise and prayer.

In those cases where the participants were professing Christians at the time of their "baptism" they do not doubt for a moment that they had been saved believers before. They rather testify to a life lacking Christian joy, the courage to witness, and a vital faith that benefits them in their daily living. They do not claim perfection after their "baptism," nor do they deny the struggles and temptations that beset them; rather they rejoice now in an overflowing power and joy with which to meet these tests.

They invariably testify also to a new love for reading and studying the Scripture. It is not unusual for one "baptized" spontaneously to begin to spend an hour or more daily in prayer, Bible reading, and meditation.

Those who have "received" are not preoccupied with Christian doctrine though they are decidedly conservative in their Christian beliefs. Their experience leads them to take the Bible far more seriously and to believe and practice it far more literally than before. Yet this literalness is in matters of personal life and practice, not in matters that would add to or subtract from the confessional statements of their respective denominational traditions. In other words, they are not so concerned with whether Methodism, for example, has an explicit place for tongues in its historical statements as they are that Methodists will permit them to believe and witness to their faith as they are led to do. They have no intention of disturbing a worship service or a Sunday School class with tongues speaking but they would like to feel free as occasions arise to quietly interpret the Scriptures to others in the manner they have come to understand.

The "baptized" ones have come to a new appreciation of and desire for, not only tongues but all the gifts of the Spirit. They will generally refer to these as being nine in number and with the variations of terminology found in the New Testament will refer to them as knowledge, wisdom, healing, faith, miracles, prophecy, discerning of spirits, tongues, and interpretation of tongues. They will distinguish also between the fruits and the gifts of the Spirit but will not agree that the gifts are dispensable if the fruits are insufficient evidence. They will certainly not agree either that these gifts, especially tongues, can be adequately explained by reference to psychological laws though they will readily admit that any and all of these gifts may be counterfeited by the Adversary or even by the flesh.

Critics of this movement frequently hold that the gifts of the Spirit ceased with the death of the apostles though they may cautiously grant that Christ may choose upon occasion in his sovereign will to permit, for example, a miracle to be performed or an expression in tongues. They are more inclined, however, to believe that any widespread or continuous evidence of these gifts may be psychologically explained, if not indeed demonically induced.

Both sides frequently give the impression that their minds were made up before they turned to the Scriptures. Yet in all fairness it must be pointed out that the neo-Pentecostal will use the Bible "descriptively" while the critic of neo-Pentecostalism will use it "prescriptively." That is to say, they will not really be "talking the same language" even in English! The traditional non-Pentecostal evangelical goes to the Bible to see what God intends Christians to be and do, while the neo-Pentecostal goes to the Scripture to find words and expressions which describe what God has done. He is utterly convinced that his "baptism" can only have been of God, both because it has led him to believe in, love, and serve Christ more deeply and vitally than ever before, and because it empowers him to love his brothers and his enemies to a degree that before he did not and could not. This is admittedly a generalization with all the risks of over-simplification, but I believe it to be a sufficiently important and accurate characterization to merit taking the risks. No wonder McCandlish Phillips ended his classic report on this movement in *The Saturday Evening Post* with these words: "As the controversy over the resurgence of glossolalia continues, the charismatic himself feels no need to formulate reasoned explanations. He repeats a favorite maxim: 'The man who has an experience is never at the mercy of a man who has an argument.'"[1] (Compare the blind man incident of John 9.)

There are plenty of hermeneutical and theological gymnastics on both sides. Both are equally ingenious and unconvincing. Both are remarkably subjective much of the time. The difference is that for the glossolalist this is admitted and above reproach while the evangelical is less willing to grant subjective proof a legitimate place in his Christian understanding. It is not that the new Pentecostal has less respect or regard for the letter of Scripture than his skeptical brother but rather that the new Pentecostal is less willing to give the objective factors such major, if not sole, priority over the subjective one. Or perhaps to state it another way, the tongues speaker considers present experience to be a factor as valid and objective to a proper understanding as the linguistic, historical, exegetical and theological implications of the biblical record.

Russell T. Hitt seemed to be struggling with just this difference in attitude and interpretation when he wrote in *Eternity* magazine: "In spite of the problem of explaining the current neo-Pentecostal movement in the light of scriptural teaching, it is bringing blessing to many people. Some have come to Christ for the first time. Others have had a real cleansing of their hearts and a filling of the Holy Spirit."[2] He goes on to say that he thinks this could happen without the attendant glossolalia, but he can only rejoice with all who have been so blessed and declares that he feels very close to them in the Lord. He agrees with Dr. John A. Mackay that "crude life is to be preferred to aesthetic death" but Hitt also reminds his reader that there are some perils in the movement.

A striking fact about this movement is the way it has leaped out of its proletarian Pentecostal setting and made a giant arc, passing over the middle-class churches in between to come to rest again at the opposite pole, culturally, economically, and ecclesiastically. Subsequently, as one

---

1. Phillips, "And There Appeared," 43.
2. Hitt, "New Pentecostalism," 10.

has put it, the fallout from this arc has been showering down upon all the churches in between, including all of the historic denominations. But even more than this, the movement has cropped up in the smaller conservative denominational and interdenominational groups such as Inter-Varsity Christian Fellowship, Faith at Work, Wycliffe Bible Translators, Wheaton College, Westmont College, Fuller Theological Seminary, the Evangelical Free Church, and the Plymouth Brethren. It has made its conspicuous appearance on the campuses of major universities.

The procedures used to pass this gift along are widely varied. Generally, it is by the laying on of hands and prayer. Seekers are invited to remain after a service where testimony concerning the value of the gift has been given with perhaps an expression or two of tongues speaking. Occasionally the person leading the after-meeting will suggest that the candidates open their mouths and begin mouthing certain syllables (such as Abba) or the name of Jesus over and over in a sort of pump-priming operation. But on the other hand, there are also prominent leaders in the movement such as David J. Du Plessis who refuse even to lay hands on candidates lest they get a wrong impression as to who the Giver of this gift is. Generally, it is in an atmosphere of quiet teaching and seeking and waiting and there is no great embarrassment to anyone concerned if a candidate does not "receive." Such seekers are urged to remain open to the Lords gifts and to continue to ask for them.

Some participants in this experience testify to having received the baptism without knowing anything about the movement or without having had any contact with one who already was a tongues speaker. It is more typical, however, for persons to have had some specific teaching and deliberate exposure to the fellowship and influence of those who are so gifted.

Critiques of Representative Books

This survey is not comprehensive. No attempt has been made to track down the publications of minor publishers nor to gather the articles that have appeared in the denominational periodicals. Further, this survey will be limited to the literature appearing since 1962. As for magazine articles, we will confine our report to those published in the secular and non-denominational evangelical periodicals. All books or magazine articles included here are written by non-Pentecostals with the exception of three books included either because of their noteworthy ecumenical spirit or of their evident objectivity in report and interpretation. These three items will be indicated in the bibliography to follow by an asterisk. The following items have been used in the writing of this survey. They are listed according to the year of their publication.

Books, Booklets, and Magazines

Voice, a thirty-two-page magazine founded in 1952 and published by the Full Gospel Business Men's Fellowship International of Los Angeles, California. With the July-August issue of 1966 the circulation exceeded half a million copies.

1962

Cate, B. F. *The Nine Gifts of the Spirit Are Not in the Church Today*. Des Plaines: Regular Baptist, 1956. 62pp., $.75.

1963

Jensen, Jerry. *Baptists and the Baptism of the Holy Spirit*. Los Angeles: Full Gospel Business Men's Fellowship International, 1963. 32pp., $.50.
Hitt, Russell T. "The New Pentecostalism: An Appraisal." *Eternity* 14.7 (1963) 10–16.
Jensen, Jerry. *Methodists and the Baptism of the Holy Spirit*. Los Angeles: Full Gospel Business Men's Fellowship International, 1963. 32pp., $.50.
Jensen, Jerry. *Presbyterians and the Baptism of the Holy Spirit*. Los Angeles: Full Gospel Business Men's Fellowship International, 1963. 32pp., $.50.
Stolee, H. J. *Speaking in Tongues*. Minneapolis: Augsburg, 1963. 142pp., $1.95.
*Du Plessis, David. *The Spirit Bade Me Go*. Oakland: self-published, 1963. 122pp.

1964

The Christian Herald 87 (May 1964). Articles by Marcus Bach, John G. Finch, and V. Raymond Edman.
Winter, David. "Charismata Come to Britain." *Christian Life* (March 1964).
Ueyeama, Kahn. "A Physician Looks at the Gifts of the Holy Spirit." *Christian Life* (August 1964).
Jensen, Jerry. *Episcopalians and the Baptism of the Holy Spirit*. Los Angeles: Full Gospel Business Men's Fellowship International, 1964. 32 pp., $.50.
Jones, E. Stanley. "Authentic Proofs of the Spirit." *Faith at Work* (May–June 1964).
Phillips, McCandlish. "And There Appeared to Them Tongues of Fire." *The Saturday Evening Post* 237.19 (1964) 30–43.

*Nickel, Thomas R. *The Shakarian Story*. Los Angeles: Full Gospel Business Men's Fellowship International, 1964. 32pp., $.50.

De Haan, M. R. *Speaking in Tongues*. Grand Rapids: Radio Bible Class Ministries, 1964. 30pp., $.15.

Metz, Donald S. *Speaking in Tongues*. Kansas City: Nazarene, 1964. 115pp., $1.00.

Sherrill, John L. *They Speak with Other Tongues*. New York: McGraw-Hill, 1964. 165pp., $4.50.

Kelsey, Morton T. *Tongue Speaking*. Garden City: Doubleday, 1964. 252pp., $4.50.

View, a twenty-four-page journal issued quarterly, begun in 1964, which seeks to interpret the World-Wide Charismatic Renewal and to relate it to ethics, missions, theology, sociology, psychology, politics, science, medicine, humanities, church history, education, philosophy, and communications. Los Angeles: Full Gospel Business Men's Fellowship International. $2 per year.

1965

Jensen, Jerry. *Attorneys' Evidence on the Baptism of the Holy Spirit*. Full Gospel Business Men's Fellowship International, 1965. 32pp., $.50.

Bergsma, Stuart. *Speaking with Tongues*. Grand Rapids: Baker, 1965. 26pp., $.85.

1966

Sanford, Agnes. *Healing Gifts of the Spirit*. Philadelphia: Lippincott, 1966. 222pp., $3.75.

Criswell, W. A. *The Holy Spirit in Today's World*. Zondervan: Grand Rapids, 1966. 193pp., $2.95.

Jensen, Jerry. *Lutherans and the Baptism in the Holy Spirit*. Full Gospel Business Men's Fellowship International, 1966. 32pp., $.50.

*Nichol, John Thomas. *Pentecostalism*. New York: Harper & Row, 1966. 264pp., $5.95.

Hoekema, Anthony A. *What About Tongue Speaking?* Grand Rapids: Eerdmans, 1966. 161pp., $3.50.

Critique

1962

It is clear from the title, *The Nine Gifts of the Spirit Are Not in the Church Today*, what the conclusion of author-preacher B. F. Cate is on this matter. The booklet was first published in 1956, was reprinted in 1957 and again annually for years 1962, 1963, and 1964. It is subtitled "The Answer to the Modern Tongues and Healing Movements," and Cate spends considerably more pages refuting healing than he does tongues. The author declares dogmatically that tongues have ceased and that what is called tongues today is not the same as that reported in the New Testament. He is not alone in this viewpoint among those producing the recent literature, but he is far more dogmatic about it than most others. He is firmly convinced that his viewpoint is nothing else than the viewpoint of the Scripture provided the New Testament is rightly divided.

1963

Speaking in Tongues by H. J. Stolee is the reprint of a book first published in 1936 by Augsburg Publishing House. O. G. Malmin's Introduction for this recent edition suggests that the significant change in attitude among some within the historic churches in the last few years is the justification for the reprinting of a book written thirty years ago under the title, *Pentecostalism: The Problem of the Modern Tongues Movement*. He proceeds to say that basically there is no discernible difference between these newer manifestations of speaking in tongues and those described by Dr. Stolee, yet he does admit that "a more rational theology of speaking in tongues seems in the process of formulation." Both Stolee and Malmin seem to vacillate between a dogmatic rejection of tongues, on the one hand, and an ultra-cautious allowance for them on the other.

Most fault is to be found with chapter 3, "The Place of Tongues in Scripture." Stolee argues extensively from the silences of Scripture. Other Bible teachings could be similarly "taught away," such as the Virgin Birth, were we to take this approach on other topics. He splits hairs over the fact that Mark calls tongues signs instead of gifts in Mark 16:17. (He doesn't raise the textual problem here since all these evidences but one are reported in Acts.) He defines the purpose of the "signs" Mark speaks of (including healing, etc.) although Mark does not do so, nor does any other inspired writer give this author unshakable ground for his definition. Regarding these signs mentioned in Mark, he summarily says, "But where the Word of God is being preached we know of no conversions caused by signs of this kind"—an irresponsible statement in light of the many well-documented cases of conversion from nominality of Christian experience, if not from outright paganism, which have arisen from an encounter with the spiritual gifts (signs) in this modern charismatic movement. Such cases, for instance, are those of Emily Gardiner Neal in connection with healing and John Sherrill in connection with tongues, to mention only two. Stolee's apparent endorsement of quoted statements by Sir Robert Anderson and Alexander Mackie also indicates a predisposition to reject any possibility of tongues as a valid contemporary Christian experience. He says: "We know, as stated repeatedly, that tongues *have* ceased; that is, such tongues that are from God" (italics his).

In the chapter on "The Modern Tongues Movement," he alludes to story after story of folks carried away by the Pentecostal type of religious enthusiasm and then says: "In nearly every instance it is the same pitiful, sordid, satanic delusion." It is statements like this that reveal the grave inadequacy of this book so far as the present charismatic renewal movement is concerned. Such a generalization is as irresponsible as it would be to check off Anabaptism by a reference to Münster.

Baptists and the Baptism of the Holy Spirit is one of a series of books concerning cases of tongues-speaking people within the historic denominations. We shall speak at this point of the entire series and not only of the three appearing in 1963. Each book is a collection of the testimonies of clergy and laymen from the particular denomination in question as to the who, when, where, what, and why of their baptism with the Holy Spirit and speaking in tongues. The similar pamphlet published in 1965 which collected the testimonies of attorneys is apparently an attempt to point up the reliability and genuineness of the experience by reference to a profession whose primary duty is the ascertainment of facts as against subjective opinions. Many, if not all, of these testimonies appeared first in the pages of *Voice*, the official organ of the FGBMFI, and they are here simply gathered and republished in denominational or vocational groupings.

The common denominator of these testimonies is the evidence of the baptism of the Spirit by speaking in tongues, although the Baptist pamphlet contains a message given by Billy Graham at one of the FGBMFI conventions. Nowhere does Graham indicate a personal experience of tongues. He does, however, very definitely endorse the movement, and undoubtedly his prominence plus this fact was reason enough for including his message. The diversities of attitude and manner of receiving the experience are particularly outstanding in this series, and this is of no concern to the movement. They are concerned about the fact and not about stereotyping a manner.

While the Billy Graham message is the only instance in this published series of a person not testifying to an experience of tongues speaking, it should be said that the possibility of a baptism of the Spirit without tongues is acknowledged otherwise also. Theoretically, every member of the Board of Directors of any official chapter of the FGBMFI must be a "Spirit-filled person" (as they frequently refer to a tongues-speaking Christian). Yet a member of the Board of Directors that founded the Pittsburgh Chapter had not spoken in tongues at the time he served on the Board and has not since. (This man is one of several faithful members of this writer's congregation in Scottdale who have either served on the Board or been active in attending and promoting the local chapter.) Special permission had to be obtained for this man to serve as a Board member but there was no difficulty in obtaining it.

Some whose personal stories are included in these pamphlets testify to an effective ministry of healing through prayer prior to "receiving"; some report bursting forth in tongues before the leader of a seekers' group ever got to them to lay on hands with prayer; some mention the deep significance that this experience has for them now but acknowledge also the time when tongues and prophecies shall be needed no more; some testify to both conversion and "baptism" at the same time though most report months or years in between the two events; some had spoken in tongues years before but had not continued in the practice and resumed it only after becoming acquainted with the FGBMFI; some mention that they had taught and believed for years that this phenomenon was only for the early church. Nearly all who make any attempt to describe the way the experience "feels" compare it to a powerful jolt of electricity.

Testimonies like these abound: "I am a better Presbyterian than ever before, and our church services are more meaningful." "I now have a burning desire to read the Bible, which has become a new book to me. My whole being has been awakened to a sense of gratitude and thankfulness for blessings I took for granted before."

> Out of this experience, I have felt a fuller commitment to the Methodist Church than ever before. . . . I have reread our "Articles of Religion" and am in more complete accord with them than ever! I like my Church. It fits me. . . . The following excerpt from "The Discipline" . . . commands my whole-hearted support: "The Methodist Church believes today, as Methodism has from the first, that the only infallible proof of a true church of Christ is its ability to seek and save the lost, to disseminate the Pentecostal spirit and life, to spread Scriptural holiness, and to transform all peoples and nations through the Gospel of Christ!"

John L. Peters, founder of World Neighbors, says,

> I now find a new and deeper intimacy in the quality of my relationship to my Lord, a new and deeper bond with those who know and love Him. I have found an added and more rewarding method by which to pray and praise. I seem to have discovered a new key to personal worship and edification, a new joy, a new fellowship, a new dimension.

David J. Du Plessis' *The Spirit Bade Me Go* is a collection of articles and speeches by the author and others concerning the amazingly wide and prominent ecumenical contacts of this former Assembly of God minister. He has experienced tongues for more than forty-five years and has the "distinction" of having been "disfellowshipped by the Assemblies of God (USA) for his ecumenical activities." He for years served the earlier Pentecostal movement in the Apostolic Faith Mission of South Africa. A friend of John Mackay, former president of Princeton Theological Seminary, Du Plessis served on the staff of the Second Assembly of the World Council at Evanston, and attended the Third Assembly in New Delhi as an Observer. He has delivered lectures on Pentecostalism at numerous theological seminaries and the Ecumenical Institute of the World Council of Churches. He has served on the planning committee of the Pentecostal World Conferences that began in 1947 and continue to the present. The man has an unusual gift for teaching. This writer participated in a group of about ten persons who sat under his teaching on the Holy Spirit at the International FGBMFI Convention in Chicago several years ago. This unusual gift is evident also in his book, as the following excerpts indicate.

In a speech to the International Missionary Council at Willingen, Germany, in 1952, Du Plessis attempted to explain why the Pentecostals had succeeded in encircling the world with missions in less than fifty years, and that without traditional institutions: "The reason why Pentecostals have been so successful in missions is because they are Pentecostal. I did not say it is because we speak with tongues, for if that was all we had from the experience of the baptism in the Holy Spirit, we would have been a forgotten issue long ago."[3]

Similarly, in a paper prepared for the Commission on Faith and Order of the World Council of Churches, meeting at St. Andrews, Scotland: "The greatest phenomenon has never been the speaking in other tongues but rather the power of the Spirit and the resultant effective witnessing. We are

---

3. Du Plessis, *Spirit*, 14.

great believers in the priesthood of all believers, and we have been far more interested in apostolic power than in apostolic succession."[4]

In all fairness it must also be reported that on one occasion when he was asked whether Pentecostals still teach that tongues is essential to the baptism of the Holy Spirit, Du Plessis answered: "No, unfortunately not, and where this standard is dropped, there the fervency and power of the revival tends to diminish greatly. It seems that we must either accept all the manifestations of the Spirit in Scriptural order or we lose the power that follows the baptism in the Spirit."

In his Missions Lecture given by invitation of the president of Princeton Theological Seminary in 1960, he said: "Many become confused when after great spiritual adventures they discover the enemy is more real than ever. When people tell me they do not know much about the devil and demonism, I must conclude that they do not know the Holy Spirit either." Again, in these lectures he said:

> Once a professor asked me: "Why do you always emphasize tongues?" With a smile I asked him: "Sir, why do you always oppose tongues?" You see, anyone will always defend the issue on which he is attacked. Personally, I encourage no one to seek for a "tongues experience" but rather for a baptism that is true to the Pentecostal pattern.[5]

> Much of the confusion today is a matter of semantics. All too often we hear people talk about the baptism of the Spirit when they mean *in* or *with*. The baptism *of* the Spirit comes at conversion or regeneration. . . . Being baptized by the Spirit into the body is not an encounter with the Church but with the Holy Spirit. Baptism in water is not an encounter with the water but with the Church. The baptism *into* the Holy Spirit is not an encounter with the Spirit but with Christ, the baptizer. This means total surrender and absolute commitment to Jesus. Without this He cannot baptize you in the Spirit. . . . Christians who have never heard the kind of doctrine that says: "This is not for our day, this may be evil, and this is sheer emotion," do not find it difficult to cooperate with the Spirit and to speak as He gives utterance. But those who learned and preach this corrupt doctrine about the manifestations and gifts of the Holy Spirit find tremendous mental blocks in their subconscious mind.[6]

---

4. Du Plessis, *Spirit*, 32.
5. Du Plessis, *Spirit*, 39.
6. Du Plessis, *Spirit*, 70–71.

The Holy Spirit does not give the gift of tongues, or any other gift. He only *manifests* himself through you so that you can give these gifts to the Church for edification (see 1 Cor 12:7).... "But covet earnestly the best gifts: and yet show I unto you a more excellent way [than coveting]" (1 Cor 12:31)—not more excellent than gifts. ... "If I speak with the tongues of men and of angels, and have not love, I am become sounding brass or a clanging cymbal." Therefore, away with tongues, says someone. Is that so? "If I bestow all my goods to feed the poor ... but have not love, it profiteth me nothing." Therefore, away with benevolent societies and charitable associations? Oh, no, that is the very proof of our Christian love. Then why object to tongues?[7]

1964

In this writer's opinion the year 1964 produced the two best books of all those included in this survey. To be sure there is nothing that can take the place of a personal reading of the testimonies to be found in the denominational booklets already commented on, or the book by Du Plessis. But of the books written by non-Pentecostals and initially intended to be written by non-tongues-speakers, those by Morton T. Kelsey and John L. Sherrill are unquestionably outstanding. "Initially intended," mind you, because in the process of gathering the material for his book, Sherrill came into the experience himself, in spite of his original intention.

Kelsey has succeeded as admirably in retaining his critical faculty while writing from without the movement as Nichol has while writing from within it. Yet the fact that Kelsey is so clearly sympathetic to the movement will undoubtedly lead some readers to doubt his objectivity. His qualifications for writing such a book as this rise to his defense, however. He is an Episcopalian clergyman with firsthand acquaintance with the movement in California, where he has been rector of St. Luke's Episcopal Church in Monrovia since 1950. He is a Phi Beta Kappa scholar who graduated with honors from Washington and Lee University and the Episcopal Theological School in Cambridge. He has done graduate work in psychology at Claremont University in California and the C. G. Jung Institute in Switzerland, and in philosophy at Princeton. He is active in the psychological clinic conducted by his church as a facet of the congregational ministry.

---

7. Du Plessis, *Spirit*, 77, 78.

His report is spiced with detailed case histories and personal testimonies from a variety of people, lay and clergy alike. His study has convinced Mr. Kelsey that speaking in tongues is a genuine spiritual experience, more helpful than harmful. Oddly, the Foreword is written by Upton Sinclair and his explanation as to how this came about and what his reactions were to the invitation are interesting, to say the least. The author states in his preface that he originally began to study the subject because it was one of several neglected aspects of Christian experience. The main reason, he believes, that this experience has not been more widely appreciated is simply that most people have had no ground upon which to stand from where they could get a look at it.

A few particularly significant excerpts follow: "It seems to be a physical impossibility to duplicate tongue-speech by deliberate imitation; when gibberish is produced by conscious effort, this also produces muscular tension which soon differentiates the sounds from the effortless flow of glossolalia." Kelsey gives individual treatment to the seven direct passages on tongues speaking in the New Testament but also to eight other New Testament passages in which he says "it could well be that glossolalia was meant. Though the author did not use the precise words, each of these comes from a context suggesting strongly that he had speaking in tongues in mind." To those of us who have long read these passages with the conscious or unconscious conviction that they could mean nothing of the sort, Kelsey's treatment is an eye-opener whether or not we choose to accept it. He closes his discussion of these fifteen passages with the conclusion that this New Testament evidence "is not nearly as extensive as the references to healing, or to dreams and visions, or to the angelic and demonic realm, but it is certainly central to the apostolic narrative."[8]

He later recounts his experience in attending a vesper service held by the Assemblies of God at a campground high in the mountains east of Los Angeles. It was a tent meeting with a nationally known evangelist as leader. There were a variety of talks in a very informal atmosphere. The president of a Bible college spoke on the necessity of education along with the Pentecostal experience. The evangelist preached from Ephesians ("Awake, O sleepers . . . ") and three times in all during the service glossolalia was heard with interpretation. Then Kelsey says: "One remarkable feature . . . was the ability of the leaders to show affection for each other. The men were free enough as they said goodbye, perhaps for years, to

---

8. Kelsey, *Tongue Speaking*, 31.

PART II: ON THE CHARISMATIC MOVEMENT AND GIFTS OF THE SPIRIT

embrace, to demonstrate real Christian affection. Is it possible that Paul was right, and there is *a religious experience which reduces, instead of increases, our need for taboos?*"(emphasis mine).

Chapters 6 and 7 are two of the more provocative chapters in this book in that they demonstrate the discontinuities between tongues and pagan ecstasies. Many authors, ancient and modern, have attempted to demonstrate the similarity, if not the organic connection, between tongues and the condition of the trance medium or some other Hebrew, Greek, or pagan form of ecstatic frenzy. Kelsey's conclusion, easy to reject perhaps until you examine closely his full treatment, is that

> Actually there is nothing to be found in either Hebrew or Greek antecedents comparable to the experience described by Paul's letters and the Book of Acts as speaking in tongues. And if it is suggested that it could not be a new experience but must have been known and not described, we must consider how unlikely this would have been among people who valued such experiences so highly. . . . We forget that even the Greeks were far more cordial to the irrational than our stress on their golden age of reason would make us believe. It almost takes a laboratory study of these elements, such as Dodds has put together, to make us realize how superstitious we often are about the rational Greeks. . . . There is no experience we know of in ancient times which is not clearly differentiated from speaking in tongues, and in several ways. . . . In the light of serious studies about these various phenomena, the New Testament speaking in tongues cannot be put down as simply another occurrence of something that was going on all over the ancient world. The Christian experience was one which was quite different both in kind and in quality from other contemporary experiences to which it has been compared.[9]

Kelsey's conclusion to chapter 6 is worth quoting in full:

> If speaking in tongues is accepted as a Christian phenomenon, in the way the writers of the New Testament saw and described it, the experience is seen as far more complex than many people believe. It is a supernatural gift of a foreign or non-human language given at the time of the breakthrough of the Holy Spirit into an individual life. The speaker, as many have expressed it, has the sense of being filled with a reality beyond himself which speaks through him. Once this experience has been known, one can enter into it at will, and he finds an immediate way of relating to

---

9. Kelsey, *Tongue Speaking*, 141, 143.

God and the Holy Spirit. This language can be interpreted either by the individual or by another person possessed by the Spirit. It indicates that something beyond the human ego is in possession of the human life.

There are difficulties to this interpretation also. It runs counter to the world we live in. Few people even consider seriously the idea that divine powers actually do possess human beings. The rationalistic materialism of our age which is certainly the dominant philosophy of our time can find no place for such an experience. This world which has been so successful in creating antibiotics and atom bombs finds its credulity taxed by the experience of a strange, foreign tongue which purports (for no seeming good purpose) to be given by a divine spirit as a sign of its indwelling. This is simply incomprehensible to many modern men.

The conclusion as to which of these explanations is more plausible depends upon something more than the evidence we have presented. What one can make of this experience will be determined by the world view from which he regards it. Whether tongues is viewed as a psychological anomaly or a religious experience of real worth will depend not so much upon the facts as upon the way we look at the world in which we live, whether our world view has a place for such experiences or not. It is now our task to sketch two Christian world views current in our world today to provide a backdrop against which we can evaluate the experience of tongues.[10]

In the following chapter Kelsey sketches the two different Christian world views alluded to: the basic view of the Western Christian world for the past five centuries is that man gets his knowledge of all reality, God included, through his sense experience and his reason making inferences from it, while the other Christian view which dominated man's understanding for the first thousand years is that man has knowledge of the world in which he lives not only through sense experience and reason, but also through direct experience of the non-physical world. This latter view adds another dimension and introduces a greater complexity to human experience.

Kelsey alludes to many religious movements—from the Lollards through the Anabaptists, the Camisards, the Jansenists, the Methodists down to the modern Pentecostals—as living witnesses to the idea that men still have direct contact with spiritual reality. He says: "In our materialistic world it had to be expressed concretely (materialistically) in an outer

---

10. Kelsey, *Tongue Speaking*, 168.

manifestation or it would not have been heard at all. The present movement is a cry of protest against the materialism and formalism of western Christianity."[11]

Virtually all conservative Protestant theology assumes the worldview of the past five hundred years and follows the track of the basic rationalism of Aristotle and Aquinas and consequently has little place, in contrast to the New Testament, for any direct experience of the spiritual, tongues included. What more common comment is heard in regard to tongues than the question, "But of what use are they!"

Back in 1949 William Sargant, one of the great men of British psychiatry, wrote an article for the *Proceedings of the Royal Society of Medicine* in which he discussed tongues at length. Concluding his article, Dr. Sargant made a plea for open-mindedness in regard to these religious practices. He reminded his readers that

> in psychiatry and religion we must examine facts before condemning theory. In 1743, when England was in an uproar about Wesley's preaching methods, a certain Mr. Thomas Butts recorded this comment: "As to persons crying out and being in fits, I shall not pretend to account exactly for that but only make this observation: it is well known that most of them who have been so exercised ... have peace and joy in believing and are more holy and happy than ever they were before. And if this is so, [it doesn't] matter what remarks are made on their fits." The same might be said today about some of our modern abreactive techniques and shock treatment in therapy.[12]

Or about tongues, and all the more so since even the reactions are far less extreme.[13]

As for the comparison of irrational speech in schizophrenia with Christian tongues, one psychologist familiar with both points out that there is little outward similarity between them, and furthermore that it is surprising how seldom schizophrenic individuals are found who have experienced tongues. Some (e.g., Bergsma) have attempted to explain tongues as a coughing up, so to speak, out of the unconscious of undigested remnants of memory of other languages previously heard but not consciously recalled.

11. Kelsey, *Tongue Speaking*, 183.

12. Sargant, "Some Cultural Group," 374.

13. Incidentally, while the critics of tongues-speaking sometimes mention Wesley as sharing their views, this is not so, as Wesley's reply to Conyers Middleton on this matter clearly proves. See Wesley, "Letter."

But there is no explanation offered by the holders of this theory how it is that the repressed memories of foreign languages happen to consist of such vocabularies for the praise of God and Jesus Christ. There are sufficient documented cases of tongues turning out to be expressions of praise to God in tongues unknown to the speaker but known to other persons in the congregation to underscore the inadequacy of this explanation. Hypnotism is an equally faulty explanation, as Kelsey points out.

If one is set upon finding a psychological explanation for tongues, he will encounter innumerable difficulties in doing so, though tongues-speaking bears some resemblance to dreams and even more to visions. The true vision is like tongues in that it appears to an individual who is perfectly conscious, knows that something beyond his ego is invading his field of consciousness, and is able in most cases by averting his attention to dismiss the experience or to continue it. (See Paul's interesting comment in this connection in 1 Cor 14:32.) In a vision one "dreams" while awake; in tongues-speech he speaks from the unconscious while awake.

There is no question in Kelsey's mind but that tongues can be dangerous in several ways. It can become a shortcut to religious and psychological growth which is more liable to stunt than to give full measure. The experience can be made to displace Christ as the center of Christian experience so that Christian wholeness is lost rather than gained. Our Lord's rule-of-thumb can be helpful here too, namely that "by their fruits ye shall know them." And if such be the case, the classic answer of D. L. Moody to a critic of his evangelistic techniques is appropriate here ("I like the way I am doing it better than the way you are not doing it") in rejoinder to those who see no practical purpose in tongues but who do not themselves exemplify the love, joy, and spontaneous witness that characterizes the lives of so many who have received this experience and who continue in it.

John Sherrill's *They Speak with Other Tongues* is a first-person singular story by a senior editor of *Guideposts* magazine who set out to discover quite matter-of-factly the answers to the question, "What is speaking in tongues?" His research took him across the country into the homes of theologians and day laborers, into musty libraries and hand-clapping church services, and at last to personal adventure as he came face-to-face with a seeming miracle.[14]

---

14. He is the son of the late Lewis J. Sherrill, Professor of Union Theological Seminary, New York, and author of such outstanding books as *Guilt and Redemption*, *Struggle of the Soul*, and *Gift of Power*.

Donald S. Metz's *Speaking in Tongues* has as its thesis that "speaking in unknown tongues is a purely human reaction which may or may not indicate valid spiritual activity, arising from spiritual confusion, spiritual frustration, or spiritual immaturity." It is obvious that the author set out to prove a thesis rather than to examine a phenomenon.

1965

The author of *Speaking with Tongues*, Stuart Bergsma, describes himself as a Christian, a medical man, a psychiatrist, and a common-sense scientist. He begins by listing "three amazing, unique, authentic miraculous phenomena" in the Gospels, Acts, and Epistles.[15] These are tongues, demon possession with exorcism, and healing. The logic of singling these out from a considerably larger list of miraculous phenomena in the New Testament is never made clear. He relegates most, if not all, of the genuine cases of glossolalia to the Apostolic era and declares that modern glossolalia is in "an entirely different category from Pentecost glossolalia and true glossolalia in the Gospel age and the Pauline age." But his explanation for this is exceedingly tenuous and arbitrary: "But for several reasons unknown to us, if we look at what passes for glossolalia in our modern age, it would seem that God very possibly does not choose to act thus through the miraculous in these days. And finally, these manifestations, as they appear today, can be psychologically and physiologically explained."[16]

Bergsma betrays the fact that he is unacquainted with the current tongues movement when he says: "Thus far, to my knowledge, glossolalia has not appeared in the pulpit or church life of any of the churches of the Reformed groups." Harold Bredesen, pastor of the century-old First Reformed Church of Mount Vernon, New York, has been a leading light in the charismatic movement for many years. Bergsma reveals his ignorance further when he says that cases of identifiable languages being spoken are "extremely rare."[17]

He lumps the current movement with the Holy Rollers of his early childhood, the Ouija-board craze of post-World War I days, and spiritualistic seances. He dogmatically asserts: "Obviously nothing can come out of each individual brain that was not once previously stored there" and proceeds

---

15. Bergsma, *Speaking with Tongues*, 5.
16. Bergsma, *Speaking with Tongues*, 7.
17. Bergsma, *Speaking with Tongues*, 9, 10.

to state that the very few cases of modern genuine glossolalia are instances of the repetition of words in another language heard at some time past but not consciously recalled.[18] Of course, this does not account for the fact that these words are so appropriately recalled at the time and place when they are needed and framed by the speaker who doesn't remember ever hearing them into sentences that minister to the needs of others with whom he is worshiping. Bergsma's explanation of tongues-speaking is harder to believe than the miracle itself. He rightly criticizes, just as the apostle Paul does, some of the very real misconceptions concerning tongues-speaking, such as the belief that glossolalia is a means of getting spiritual maturity for nothing, or the craving for a constant diet of sensational experiences. However, he does not have Paul's wisdom when he resorts to disparagement of the gift instead of correction of the abuses.[19]

1966

Hoekema's *What About Tongue-Speaking?* utilizes many of the same arguments and interpretations as the other books. He too strongly pits Scripture against experience and assumes Scripture's priority without seriously weighing the possibility of a balance between the two being a superior and more comprehensive vantage point from which to view and to examine this movement.

He winsomely differs with many views and inclinations commonly found among the Pentecostalists. For example, he reminds the reader that the Pentecostals hold that the baptism in the Holy Spirit must be wrested from the Lord by believers through agonizing prayer and then replies to this with the comment that this was not demanded in the cases of the Samaritans, the household of Cornelius, or the seventy-two Ephesian disciples. Against this however we must also weigh carefully Paul's admonitions to "be filled with the Spirit," "stir up the gift of God within you," etc.

In closing this survey of literature, it will be of profit yet to consider briefly at least the chapter on tongues in a very recent book by the Episcopalian woman, Agnes Sanford. She is the wife of a clergyman and the author of two other significant books: *The Healing Light* and *Behold Your God*. She is in demand as a lecturer and has traveled throughout the world in this work. Her most recent book and the one that concerns us here is *The*

---

18. Bergsma, *Speaking with Tongues*, 13.
19. Bergsma, *Speaking with Tongues*, 17–21.

Healing Gifts of the Spirit. In a chapter entitled "The Gift of Tongues and of Interpretation" she says:

> Now much to the consternation of many people, another truth is emerging concerning the mysterious working of God's Holy Spirit; namely, that He is able to speak both in and through an individual in a language that the person in his conscious mind does not know. ... In the early days it was accepted by simple faith, as just another instance of the marvelous works of God. Then came the age of 'reason' in which it was rejected as gibberish, as hysteria—quite a natural assumption if one does not understand the mental and spiritual laws through which this power works.[20]

She elaborates upon the danger of "laying hands suddenly" upon a person before he is prepared to receive such an experience as tongues. She says that those who in their enthusiasm lay hands on anyone with a minimum of preparation probably do not know that while some are blessed by this, others are thrown into confusion and depression, and she adds, "I do know, for I often pick up the wreckage. After they have been burnt over by such a premature experience it is much more difficult for them to receive the real, deep, life-giving power of the Holy Spirit"[21]—perhaps as difficult for them as for others who have a deep-seated skepticism that such is either desirable, possible, or scriptural! She proceeds:

> Some people teach today that those who speak in tongues have the Holy Spirit and those who do not speak with tongues do not have the Holy Spirit. I cannot agree with this assumption. In the first place the Bible does not teach it . . . "That there may be no schism in the body," says [the Apostle Paul] rather pathetically, considering the fact that the explosion of this gift *without understanding* has caused so much schism and controversy that many people wish it had been left safely wrapped in the napkin of ignorance and buried in the ground, as was the unused talent in our Lord's parable. . . . However, our Lord's remarks to the cautious one who primly buried the talent were not such as to encourage us in turning our backs upon an uncomprehended power. We would do better, as Dr. Henry P. Van Dusen says in his book *Spirit, Son and Father*, to seek the mysterious workings of the Spirit in spite

---

20. Sanford, *Healing Gifts*, 174.
21. Sanford, *Healing Gifts*, 177.

of their occasional eruption into apparent hysteria rather than to reject the Holy Spirit in toto.[22]

Those without understanding ask in response to Paul's word, "He that speaketh in an unknown tongue edifieth himself": "How can a man edify himself if he does not know what he is saying?" And Agnes Sanford replies, the speaker in many cases does know in his unconscious mind and this is why the majority of tongues speakers testify to such an inexpressible satisfaction in the experience.

> He is speaking forth for the first time the deep knowledge of that other part of himself and as he speaks it forth it is raised to a higher level of the unconscious, is grasped in the essence of its feeling . . . and sometimes even emerges into the reasoning mind so that a small peripheral part of it is interpreted in one's own language. . . . I am not against electricity because I may warn a grandchild not to stick a knife in the toaster or touch a hot iron. Those who go berserk over the gift of tongues have stuck a knife in the toaster and it is not the fault of electricity that they have done so.[23]

She explains further: "Tongues when practiced in private prayer are largely a way of silencing the conscious mind so that the spirit may be freed to commune directly with God."[24] She speaks frankly to her neo-Pentecostal friends and warns against making a fetish of holy joy. She reminds them sternly that the purpose of all our Christian walk is not simply the acquiring of joy but the following of Christ as a faithful disciple and soldier in the battle against sin, the world, and the devil.

She asserts that there are two ways of interpreting tongues: one by previous knowledge of the language and the other by direct inspiration of the Spirit. Do such things happen today? she asks, and she answers,

> Yes, they do. . . . I know an instance of a group attended by a seminary professor. He did not profess this gift, but being a teacher of the Bible he was interested in learning whatever he could learn of the operation of the Spirit. . . . It happened that a young woman spoke in tongues, the voice becoming clear and loud, and the words going forth in a tone of authority. The group naturally became silent. When she had ceased, another woman spoke forth in English. The professor said afterwards that the

---

22. Sanford, *Healing Gifts*, 178–79, emphasis in original.
23. Sanford, *Healing Gifts*, 181–82.
24. Sanford, *Healing Gifts*, 184.

first young woman had spoken perfect Hebrew and the second woman had given a very fair interpretation—neither one of them, of course, knowing Hebrew.[25]

Concluding Remarks

With a growing familiarity with this movement both in life and in literature comes the growing conviction that the new Pentecostals have very much the same internal problem with tongues that the historic peace churches have with nonresistance. The clarity of the Scripture on the subject is such for us, and the conviction so deeply rooted in our general understanding of the life and teachings of our Lord, not to mention his redemption by the shedding of his blood, that we can scarcely conceive of any serious Christian not finding the call coming to him loud and clear to embrace nonresistance. We refuse to say that a person must be committed to nonresistance to be truly saved, yet when we come to consider the minimal requirements for membership in the corporate body of Christ, we are loath to leave this facet of discipleship an open option for possible later commitment. Consequently, we hope never to need to declare ourselves finally on this matter, and if we do need to, we live then with an uneasy conscience about it. Our Baptist brethren feel similarly about the mode of baptism. Other traditions also have their deep feelings about, and attachments to, beliefs and practices they consider clearly biblical in origin and essential in Christian experience. Hopefully our conviction that we must love the enemy will permit us to love our brethren also—letting this question remain open to further light. In the meantime, however, we proceed with confidence holding to our belief and sharing it with others at every appropriate opportunity. Just so with those who have in a mature and balanced way entered into a new dimension of experience via the charismatic revival movement.

There are many other facets which even this lengthy survey has reluctantly had to omit. For some undoubtedly the more important facets have been omitted but, if so, it is only because what is crucial varies with each individual.

This writer agrees with those charismatic ministers who argue that the world is as precarious for Christianity right now as it has ever been and that this is why there is a resurgence of this early church phenomenon. The Rev. Dr. John Mackay, President Emeritus of Princeton Seminary, says:

25. Sanford, *Healing Gifts*, 188.

There is a kind of mystic violence abroad in the world today. In my mind this is surging up in the secular realm at the end of an era, and you have got to match that in the religious realm so that religion becomes a very, very exciting thing that absorbs your whole life in the principle of commitment.

In the secular realm we see people like the beatniks and the delinquents who have just got to get their whole emotional being in some direction, even in the wrong direction. But the church is orderly. That hour is over; you could get the historical churches irrelevant to the human situation. One reason is that they're unwilling to face the realities of the kind of relationship to Deity which becomes a very exciting thing. They're scared to death of anything that will get your life.

We are at the end of an era. Revolutionary, volcanic forces are at work, and our people won't face that. We just don't want to look at it, you see, at the very time the volcano is erupting.

The gist of the matter would seem to be that we guard against taking too narrow a view at either end of the question. The individual who has had a particular experience may be too ardent about his discovery; the individual who has not had the experience may be too biased in his views. This has always been religion's dilemma ("I belong to Paul," "I belong to Cephas"). In a very real way this is also religion's challenge to the unity and faith of men in our time as their spiritual adventure affects their relationship to each other and to God.

14

The Prophetic Office in the Church[1]

Werner Schmauch

It is quite literally a dangerous undertaking to speak of prophecy in the church. Simply to formulate the question seems equivalent to separating oneself from the church and moving into the vicinity of the sects. To go farther and affirm that prophecy is a vital expression of the reality of the church, earns one inevitably the annihilating reproach, currently so freely hurled about, of *Schwärmertum* (fanaticism, enthusiasm). Even in those circles where the attempt is made to pattern the ministry of the church directly after the New Testament example, the prophetic office is no longer to be observed. What is at the root of this turning away from prophecy? Is it founded in the knowledge that the series of prophets, channels for the revelation of God's will, has reached the fulfillment of its purpose—and therefore its end—in the Son, as the Epistle to the Hebrews says (1:1)? Or might it be the belief that prophecy is one of the special gifts of the early church (1 Cor 12:28), reserved for that period?

These questions make it all the more urgent that we venture onto this dangerous terrain, formulating the New Testament's position and testing current attitudes by it. Our method shall be to investigate the prophetic office or function in the church and therefore to leave to one side the Seer of Patmos and his "prophetic" work, the book of Revelation, as well as the "prophets" who are mentioned in Acts but whose functions remain unclear (Acts 21:9).

---

1. Paper presented to the Ecclesiastical Brotherhood of Westphalia, Dortmund, January 7, 1958. Translated by John Howard Yoder from the printed version in *Junge Kirche* 19 (1958).

I

If we begin with the fact that the Christian church understands her essential character as stemming from Pentecost, it is immediately obvious that she not only must ever anew take seriously the question of prophecy, but also must recognize the prophetic witness as one of her indispensable—and therefore lasting—marks. The first church itself interpreted the miracle of its coming into being and its essential nature as the fulfillment of the prophecy of Joel:

> And in the last days it shall be, God declares,
> that I will pour out my Spirit upon all flesh,
> and your sons and your daughters shall prophesy,
> and your young men shall see visions,
> and your old men shall dream dreams;
> Yes, and on my menservants and my maidservants,
> in those days I will pour out my Spirit,
> and they shall prophesy. (Acts 2:17–18)

If this is true, the converse must apply as well: To renounce prophecy endangers the connection of the church with its roots in primitive Christianity.

One more thing is already clear: In the early church prophecy is a gift entrusted to the whole church. Since the Holy Ghost is poured out on all flesh, your sons and daughters, my menservants and maidservants shall prophesy. This fundamental fact has immediate and far-reaching consequences. First of all, the nature of Christian prophecy cannot be defined on the basis of the prophets and prophecy previous to Jesus. At the same time early Christian prophetic utterance is not in contradiction to that prophecy which found its fulfillment in the church's Lord. The two are clearly to be distinguished. The prophet of the Old Covenant—to mention only one characteristic difference—stands clearly over against the people, as a chosen individual (Isa 6:9); in the New Covenant he who speaks prophetically stands as an equal within the church, to which as a totality the gift is entrusted (1 Cor 14:31). It may be the universality of the gift that is to blame for the way in which appreciation and understanding of it have been so largely lost. Its sparse appearance in the New Testament is no demonstration of a geographical or temporal limitation of its prevalence, but rather indicates that it is to be assumed everywhere (Acts 2:17) and therefore is only dealt with where the order of the congregation is endangered, as in Corinth (1 Cor 14).

II

Let us pursue one step farther our definition of the essential nature of prophecy in the early church. It has already become evident that it is understood as a gift of the Holy Spirit. Paul lists it among the manifold manifestations of the Spirit, along with healing, speaking in tongues, and speaking knowledge (1 Cor 12:9). Like these gifts, prophecy is imperfect and will pass away when that which is perfect has come (1 Cor 13:9). But this does not mean that it can be held in low esteem in the meantime. Prophecy is one of the greatest, yea, the greatest of the gifts of grace,[2] beyond which there is only room for the extraordinary, the superlative (12:31). A number of observations underline how highly Paul valued this gift. It stands with knowledge at the head of the list of the temporal values contrasted with love's eternity (13:8). The prophets stand in second place after the apostles and before the teachers in the list of God-given ministries (1 Cor 12:28; Eph 4:11; Rom 12:6). Still more weighty is the fact that all can (1 Cor 14:31) and should (14:5) speak prophetically in the worship assembly. After the admonition to seek after love, the first gift recommended as also being valuable is that of prophecy (14:1). The entire literary unit, beginning with 1 Cor 12:1, after having glorified love as the ultimate norm, concludes with the one exhortation: "So, my brethren, earnestly desire to prophesy" (1 Cor 14:39).

We are driven to the thesis: To renounce prophecy would mean nothing less than contesting the presence of the Holy Spirit and the authority of the apostolic word and thereby withdrawing from true continuity of essence with the primal church.

III

Have we drawn the picture of an enthusiastic[3] church, which would seem to justify the reproach of disorderly fanaticism and make the generally recognized reticence toward prophecy appear to be well-founded? Is not

---

2. Translator's note: we follow literally the author's German usage rather than using the transliteration "charismata" or the paraphrase "spiritual gifts."

3. Translator's note: we follow the German in using the word "enthusiasm" in its original, generally pejorative, sense of "God-drunkenness," "ecstasy."

prophetic speech a temporary gift like the power to work miracles, and therefore no longer accessible?

When we read, "earnestly desire to prophesy, and do not forbid speaking in tongues" (1 Cor 14:39), we sense at once the difference in value which the apostle attributes to the two gifts. This order of values is clearly confirmed in the call to seek after the greater gift (14:1) as well as in the listing of the gifts (12:30). But Paul points to still more than a difference in value; there is a difference in character as well. Glossolalia, speaking in tongues, is *given*: it falls upon a person, whose only choice is whether to withstand or not. Glossolalia is not required because it cannot be acquired. Prophecy on the other hand is *granted*. It does not fall upon a person; man's choice is whether to desire and seek after it. This is a deep and essential difference. These two gifts stand at opposite ends of the list; they are contrasted as the highest and lowest, greatest and least (12:28–30).

The order in which the gifts are listed illuminates still further both the difference between prophecy and tongues, and the essential character of prophecy itself. The listing proceeds from the level of the gifts of speech—apostolate, prophecy, teaching—down through miracle-working to healing, through "helping" and "administration" (these two are omitted when the list is repeated) to tongues. The progression goes from the natural to the supernatural, from the normal to the miraculous, in such a way that the highest gift is accessible to all, and the least accessible is the least valuable. Speaking in tongues is the last of all the gifts and at the same time the one farthest removed from the exercise of normal human faculties (1 Cor 14:23). The Christian speaking in tongues has lost control of himself; in prophetic speech he is quite himself. This essential difference is irreducible. Prophecy therefore has nothing to do with enthusiasm, to say nothing of any kind of ecstatic phenomenon. Christian prophecy is an absolutely sober affair. "The spirits of the prophets are subject to the prophets" (14:32).

IV

This sobriety finds its basis in the human faculty which it utilizes and in the activity through which it expresses itself. The comparison and contrasting of prophecy with tongues leaves us with a clear description of prophecy in its own right. Just as sounds must be distinct and languages must be known in order to have meaning, so must prophecy, in contrast to tongues, be understandable (1 Cor 14:11). It is therefore the *nous*, the "mind," which brings forth clear thoughts in communicable form, which is active in prophecy. The word "mind" is used four times in the chapter (vv. 14, 15a, 15b, 19), sufficient indication of its central significance. Not only does he who speaks need his mind in order to be understandable. Not only do those who hear need their minds in order to grasp what he says; they are in fact commanded to weigh "critically" (14:29) what they hear, and toward this end they need no more and no other spiritual qualification than the same mind which the speaker has used. Thus, it is that prophetic speakers and hearers are interchangeable (14:31).

We may note in passing that this description of prophecy gives us a glimpse of a surprisingly mature, articulate, participating local church. Not only does praise or benediction demand the confirmation of the congregation's "Amen," but the functions of prophetic speaking and critical hearing may be exchanged at will. We must ask whether this congregation at Corinth was so much more "mature" than our churches today (hardly, to judge by the rest of the letter), or whether this maturity and articulateness do not come simply from the apostle's having believingly expected it of them.

Be that as it may, the far-reaching function of the mind and its significance for prophecy are evident and may be observed also at another point. For the unbeliever and the stranger to the church the speaker in tongues appears insane, whereas prophetic speech so grasps him that he cannot escape. No further explanation of this effect is given than that, in contrast to tongues, prophecy is understandable (1 Cor 14:23). This means Christian prophecy is a sober matter because it is sensible, clear, convincing discourse (14:9). It is reasonable discourse, which can even make sense to the unbeliever. It must however be noted in this connection that the mind as the organ of prophecy is not autonomous. The exercise of this gift is a ministry of the church, and the mind stands under the same commitment as the church. The mind which functions here is the one which according to Rom 12:2 must constantly be renewed. Yet this subjection of the mind to a higher norm does not hamper it, but rather enables it to test and recognize the will of God.

V

What is the content of prophecy? The fact that the New Testament distinguishes prophetic discourse from apostolic preaching, from teaching, and from speaking of revelation and knowledge, suffices to indicate that it has its own particular function and therefore its own particular content. It may be conjectured from the function of the mind and the duty of the listeners to weigh critically what is said, that prophecy does not have to do with the proclamation of the great acts of God. This is confirmed by the definition, "He who prophesies speaks to men for their upbuilding and encouragement and consolation" (1 Cor 14:3). "Upbuilding, encouragement, and consolation," or in other words, "Learning and being encouraged" (14:31) have to do with human togetherness and believing action. Prophetic speech reveals not primarily what God has done or will do, but rather what men should do. It deals not so much with the realm of faith as with that of love, just as it is love that "edifies" (1 Cor 8:1, note also the place of 1 Cor 13 in the midst of a discussion of prophecy).

Still more may be learned from the case of the unbeliever entering the Christian assembly (1 Cor 14:24). Prophecy does not reveal—at least not in this case—divine mysteries, but rather the concrete situation of man and the action necessary in that situation. Prophecy deals with love, not insofar as love is always and everywhere the same, but rather in its impingement upon the changing situation of man, in which love must prove and affirm itself without possessing detailed instructions. Rengstorf says rightly of the "learning" in 1 Cor 14:31 that "The church needs [thus to 'learn'] when she or one of her members needs a directive in a particular situation and does not find it in Scripture."[4] The fact that Christian prophecy is a ministry of the church by no means signifies that it limits itself to "spiritual" matters, but on the contrary it concerns itself with the events of the day, in the midst of which men need admonition and encouragement and the church and her members need counsel. Christian prophecy is concrete and contemporary.

VI

The thesis just formulated finds support in the apostle's instruction that prophecy should be exercised "according to the analogy of faith" (Rom 12:6). Without analyzing fully this phrase, we may say at the very least that it is no accident that Paul does not say "in faith" or "from faith" but rather "according to the analogy of faith." That confirms that the relation of prophecy to faith is not direct, but indirect. It has to do not immediately with the content of faith and the life which flows directly and necessarily from faith, but mediately with that action demanded by the believer's

---

4. Rengstorf, "μανθάνω," 412.

relationship to the world. The concept of the "analogy of faith" opens to prophecy an illimitable domain of relevance: it addresses man in his concrete situation and determines his behavior. Faith, and love as the external manifestation of faith, give no specific and direct instructions which man could simply pick up and apply. This "lack" justifies both the special place of the mind in connection with prophecy and the necessity of weighing critically all prophetic utterance.

On the other hand, it must be emphasized that the concept of the "analogy of faith" ties prophecy and faith together. The prophet's faith is not immediately demonstrated in his "reasonable" directives for the given situation, but neither is his mind autonomous, nor can the relation of his faith to what he says and does be denied. The statements of the prophet are by no means judgments of purely personal discretion, which could just as well have been quite different. The critical judgment of prophecy, which all the brethren are obligated to exercise, indicates that prophecy in the church must lead to ethical consensus. In the responsibility of faith and driven by love, prophecy uses reason to penetrate a concrete situation in human affairs and to discover the necessary action in that situation.

VII

Christian prophecy has taken on clearer outlines. It is no fanaticism. Nor is it the prediction of events in the dim future. Nevertheless, prophecy is truly *pro-phēteuein*, both "speaking-for" and "speaking-before." In the responsibility of faith and love any one of the circle of equal brethren stands before the church and takes a position for the church (1 Cor 12:7; 14:4), predicting, in the face of a particular need, what should be done. This pre-decision is made without any guarantees. He cannot point to a direct deduction leading irresistibly from the gospel to his decision. He can offer only the decision itself, acquired by his mind and soberly exposed and explained in rational discourse. He must accept being judged by every listener. As he thus places himself and his convictions at the mercy of his hearers, he not only gives them the right but in fact he imposes upon them the duty of testing his prophecy, and thereby involves them all in his cause. We see once again how the speaker falls back into the ranks of the brethren, how the roles of speaking and hearing are interchangeable, in short how prophecy is a gift to the entire church.

The locus of prophecy is thus by definition the church; to be more precise, the assembled congregation (1 Cor 14:23). This prophecy, which deals with the whole realm of human affairs, including the most mundane, takes place in the congregation as it meets for worship. In the exercise of this function the church of New Testament times became a reality; a mature, articulate church, in whose worship the distinction of the sacred from the profane is overcome and the full breadth of human existence including wrestling with contemporary problems has its place beside the liturgy. And today?

The image of early Christian prophecy, which we have sketched, is drawn principally from 1 Cor 14. We have emphasized certain lines which are only brushed lightly in the New Testament text, in order to bring them into sharper focus. If but a fraction of what we have found has been accurately interpreted, it stands in a startling contrast to the evaluation of prophecy in our churches. The church has been more and more willing to forget about the ministry of prophecy; in fact, the word itself has become suspect. This came to be because the church had accustomed herself to a distorted image of the nature of prophecy in the early church. But rejecting prophecy and leaving its exercise to the sects has been as harmful as it seemed respectable. The church gave up not only a distortion and a concept which had become foreign to her interests, but also the reality of a ministry which is essential if she is to be the church. When something of the nature of prophecy does occur, she is generally unable to identify the phenomenon and to recognize in it an indispensable expression of her life. To see its place anew and to desire earnestly the ministry of prophecy, as the apostle directed, would seem therefore to be as necessary today as ever.

―― Part III ――
On Christendom's Christmas
Articles from CONCERN 16 (1968)

15

Nasty Noel

Henderson Nylrod

Angels we have heard on high
    won't you sing us a nice Noel?
    with shepherds and Wise Men
    and holly and ivy
    and a partridge in a pear tree.
O Tannenbaum, King of the Woods,
    evergreen leaves and candles ablaze
    life self-renewing, light returning.
    November's waning sun had warned
    our mortal souls to be afraid
    of cold, of gloomy drizzly dusk
    and stranded cars on slushy back roads . . .
    Tell us spring will soon be here!
Jolly old Saint Nicholas, turn your ear this way,
    tell us what you have for us on this happy day;
    Giver of good and perfect gifts,
        and of the duplicates to take back to the store
        joy of the merchants please give us some more.
        An atom-ray gun or a cowboy suit
        or a Baby-Jesus doll with a halo that really shines in the dark!

PART III: ON CHRISTENDOM'S CHRISTMAS

But the angels didn't have a nice Noel to sing
    They sang about peace on earth
        and sent a bunch of dirty shepherds
        to see a refugee,
        a beggar baby in a barn . . .
No cradle? No bed?
    No, a manger, they said;
No hospital? No clinic?
    No, a shed, they said;
        a smelly old stall where the cattle are fed;
    So the angels didn't have a nice sweet clean Baby Jesus.
And as for the Tree?
    The angels didn't have a pine tree either;
    No French hens, no lords a-leaping, no boars' heads a-flaming,
    His folks did scrape up two turtledoves
        but the priest took them
    And when Jesus got to the Tree it was bare
        only two branches
        and no evergreen needles; only nails.
And what about Ole Nick?
    turned out he was The Other Side.
    Whenever the winter hits bottom
    and the back-to-school buying levels off,
    along comes Mammon with that red-nosed reindeer
    and retail sales go up thirty points.

16

Pious Jingle Bells and the Coming of Christ[1]

William R. Miller

Christmas carols are the oldest form of congregational hymnody. In the days of William the Conqueror church music was reserved to the choir except for the carols, which depicted nativity events in the language of the people. Even after the Reformation they occupied a unique position, for in the English-speaking world it was not till the eighteenth century that songs other than psalms and carols were sung.

The heyday of the English carol was probably the fifteenth century when its cousin, the ballad, came into prominence. But the old favorites that we know today are nearly all nineteenth-century products. "Veni Emmanuel" and "In Dulci Jubilo" come to us in mid-Victorian translations by John Mason Neale. Both words and music for "We Three Kings of Orient Are" and "O Little Town of Bethlehem" date from the 1860s.

Most of the carols we have inherited are pictorial and fall into two basic categories. First, what we might call church school pictures: shepherds, the star of Bethlehem, angels, the cozy manger, the journey of the Magi, the Holy Infant, or newborn king—in short, the elements of a pious fairy tale. The Bible provides us with a slim excuse for this and we inflate it to the proportions of a grand wallow in irrelevant sentimentality.

The transmogrification of the historic Saint Nicholas, bishop of Myra, into the jovial elf with the sleigh is nothing compared with the way in which God, the Son, the Incarnate Word, has been reduced to a cute little doll.

---

1. Reprinted by permission from *United Church Herald* (December 1966).

Why do we show greater respect for George Washington and Abraham Lincoln? We don't commemorate their birthdays by dwelling on the trivia of early infancy. As suckling babes, they are of no interest to mankind, and if this is the sole interest that Jesus has, we are in a bad way.

The second type of carol is secular, typified by "The Holly and the Ivy," "The Twelve Days of Christmas," and these lines from a popular German carol translated by Joseph W. Clokey:

> O tell me, children dear,
> What you like to see
> > Christmas Eve.
> O, a wreath of holly by my bed,
> With its leaves so green and its berries red,
> > Christmas Eve.

Now we are in the world of the yule log, "Tannenbaum," plum puddings, and snowflakes—the world of Tchaikovsky's *Nutcracker* and "Jingle Bells." It is the world, too, of Irving Berlin's "White Christmas," which is far better known to most Americans than many traditional carols and has sold several million records for Bing Crosby, Freddy Martin, and others. Other songs like it, such as the "Merry Christmas" sung by the late Nat King Cole with its "chestnuts roasting on an open fire," or "I'll Be Home for Christmas," one of Bing's 1943 million-sellers with its "snow and mistletoe," evoke a nostalgia for the era of Dickens and Tchaikovsky. The Christmas spirit is reduced to conviviality, the hearty handshake of the genial and generous host.

No, I'm not going to make the usual pitch for putting Christ back into Christmas, at least not in the sense of one more game effort to put over the Christ Child. But I do think it is time to take stock of ourselves and our symbols and images. It is time to take our faith seriously enough to assume responsibility for what has happened—time for us to reject the idea of Jesus Christ as a sort of sectarian Peter Pan, and to ask ourselves what Christmas can mean in the mid-twentieth century.

Instead of clutching at straws, groping for a way to restore the lost world of shepherds and kings and angels, let us accept the fact that this particular brand of religiosity is no better than the pre-Christian trappings of the winter solstice—the holly and mistletoe of the Druids—which are still with us.

"Christmas" means "festival of the Savior." The Savior is not an inarticulate infant but a Man who laid down his life for his fellowmen. Easter is meant to celebrate the final triumph, his victory over sin and death. Pentecost commemorates the founding of the church in his name. In the tradition of Christmas, there are suggestions of the mission and ministry of the living Christ. "Prince of Peace" and the greeting "Peace on earth to men of good will" suggest the man who bade his followers "Love one another as I have loved you."

Why don't we sing about this each December instead of making idols in his name? Most of our Christmas hymns and carols, with their fulsome praise, treat Jesus like a golden calf in which magical powers reside. The stereotype infant king of our Christian fairyland may invite such adulation, but what has he to do with the Word Made Flesh?

For the true miracle of Christmas is far removed from the inanities in which popular piety indulges. It is a miracle beyond magic and angelic geegaws. The incarnation is miraculous in its very simplicity, for in this Man Jesus the whole meaning of human existence was manifested. God is Love, and Jesus is the living proof of what this means.

Christmas is about the coming of Christ, the incarnation of holy love in human history. Here is a basis for joy and hope—let our carols and hymns reflect this. We may feebly defend the attention given by the traditional carols to his place of birth or to his "kingship" at birth, or the importance of his mother's virginity, but what does it profit us? Isn't this like crying, "Lord, Lord"? We might just as well attempt to develop a theology of Santa Claus.

Where did the traditional carols go wrong? Why are they outmoded? We must remember that there was a continuity of human experience from the time of Jesus to the time of Isaac Watts and Charles Wesley which enabled many of the traditional images to endure. Shepherds and kings were metaphors drawn from actual life, and their roles in eighteenth-century England were not vastly different from first-century Palestine or twelfth-century France. The turning point came not in a single generation but in a process of change lasting, say, from the advent of the American and French republics to the invention of the electric light. In less than a century after the latter event (1879), yesterday's Christendom has become a citadel of technology which has little room for shepherds and kings, and to speak of the significance of Christ in terms of the latter is to imply that there is little room for him either.

PART III: ON CHRISTENDOM'S CHRISTMAS

One thing is sure: whatever has happened in theology during the past hundred years, our hymnody remains stalled in the Victorian era. A few tunes or harmonizations of old tunes for Christmas carols date from the turn of the century, but there is no widely sung carol with original words written by the light of an electric lamp. They are all "old-fashioned," all somewhat superannuated specimens of a bygone age.

And the point is that Christ is *not* bygone and should not be treated as if he were. We have to make up our minds: are we committed to him, or to that old-time religion which went out with buttoned shoes?

All right, shall we substitute white-collar workers for shepherds and executives or astronauts for kings? How about the Superego appearing to Mary? Some of the more simple-minded hack writers of hymns would be only too glad to oblige. But there just aren't any modern equivalents for most of the images found in the old carols.

We have to begin anew. Let's not strain for a relevance that will become irrelevant next year but seek out what is central and permanently valid in the incarnation. When modern poets address themselves to this task, they will have little to say about Bethlehem or even about the nativity as such. They will not invent verbal ornaments either for the person of Jesus or for the emotions of the believer. They will try, rather, to speak honestly and pointedly about man's need and the basis of our hope in Christ. Like many of the better popular songs of today, the new Christmas carols will refer not to pictorial themes but to qualities of human relationships. They will be, in a sense, love songs—not sentimental ballads to a Man in the Sky or a divine Daddy Warbucks, but carols celebrating the love which the incarnation represents.

The kind of Christmas carol I have in mind would not be solemn or stern. It would be full of the joy and hope that the incarnation signifies—a serious joy and a real hope, in contrast to the senseless mirth and quaint grandeur of the tunes and lyrics of the old favorites.

Christmas should be celebrated in a song as a time of renewal and futurity—yes, of "joy to the world," to cite one of the most durable of the old Christmas hymns, now 247 years in service. But let us move on from the regal savior of Watts' monarchal age to an image of Christ strong and valid in a world of industrialized republics—not blandly "modernized" or watered down, but convincingly rendered for a world that has come of age.

I am frankly not optimistic about the prospects for the renewal of Christmas carols. Given a choice, I suspect that most people would prefer to fall on their knees before cherished idols than to face the startling fact of Jesus Christ as the incarnation of holy love. Yet Luther, Wesley, and Kierkegaard faced a similar dilemma in their time. With equivalent humility and boldness, and with an even more courageous vision adequate to the present world, the church must proclaim its stance: "We can do no other!"

If we would be faithful to the spirit of Christ without which Christmas is a pagan charade, we must get up off our calloused knees and throw away our Palestinian tourist brochures and sing of the Christ who comes, who has come, and will come—now and forever. Let us sing of the Way and the Truth and the Life, of love everlasting and transforming.

Let us be "fools for Christ" in the wisdom of that love and set it in competition with all the merry gentlemen and red-nosed reindeer and all the rest of the irrelevant folderol, whether ancient or recent. Let us begin not by calculating the consequences but by being true to the reality. We may never make the hit parade, but the integrity we may attain will not be lost in the calculus of eternity.

Who knows? We may strike a nerve in twentieth-century man, touch something alive and real and Christ-shaped in the subconscious of post-religious man. We may even, "good Christian men" that we are, turn from a drowsy and fatigued faith to astonishing newness of life as we confront the spirit of Christ behind the nebulous Victorian "spirit of Christmas."

Our choice, we shall find, is not defined by Bob Cratchit and Ebenezer Scrooge, but by a far larger concept which pits the Incarnate Word against sentimental verbiage.

Our calling as Christians is to discern that word and to proclaim it with joy and gusto. We can do this only as we face Christ with honesty and sing with our own voices as carolers of the 1960s, not the 1860s. Are we ready to make the attempt? The cards are stacked against us, each printed with a grinning "Season's Greetings." There are no easy answers, but we had better come up with something better than "Merry Christmas."

17

Getting Christ Back Out of Christmas

MARLIN JESCHKE

Some churches in Christendom make much of the year, but almost all Christians take for granted that we ought to observe two major religious holidays, Christmas and Easter. Contemporary Christians should be informed that celebration of the birth of Christ does not have a foundation in the early church's tradition. This is worth noting especially if they accept the principle that Scripture should be authoritative for faith and practice. Christmas, as a celebration of December 25, did not begin to be observed until the middle of the fourth century. There is no evidence that it was shaped by the Jewish Hanukkah, or festival of lights (commemorating the Maccabean re-consecration of the desecrated temple in Jerusalem). In fact, it is the other way around. The Jewish celebration has taken impetus from the prevalence of Christmas in Western Christendom.

Christmas is a product of the early medieval church's struggle to Christianize the Roman Empire, to subdue the most boisterous elements that persisted in the Saturnalia and New Year's celebrations. The church tried to replace the popular revelry and indulgence of these dates by reinterpreting the 25th of December as the feast of the nativity of Christ. But the reinterpretation of the date did not suppress the popular pagan elements of celebration. In a sense it legitimized and perpetuated them.

In addition to pagan origins and pagan survivals in the celebration of Christmas there were pagan accretions as Christmas spread northward through Europe. These accretions we can only allude to here—the Yule log, the evergreen tree, the mistletoe from Druid religion, and other customs and practices so submerged in the general welter of traditional activities that moderns no longer consciously notice them.

In short, Christmas is the product of the early medieval church's strategy of syncretism, a practice we are quite ready to recognize and condemn in India or in early Catholic missions in Latin America, but upon which we seem to cast an indulgent eye when it is in our own culture.

We should never underestimate the appeal of the logic of syncretism. It is based upon an old theological tradition that has an honorable history in Western thought. This tradition is natural theology—the view that man apart from revelation already possesses intimations of divine truth which revelation, when it comes along, unfolds in complete light. The danger of syncretism and natural theology is that they open a two-way street. The intention is for Christian truth to supersede the pre-Christian beliefs they supposedly unfold, but inevitably the opposite happens as well. That is, Christian truth is colored by pre-Christian notions, and the net result is a genuine paganization.

This was the danger the church got into by proposing to usurp prime calendar dates from ancient pagan Roman religion. It could contend that December 25 commemorated the birth of Jesus, not the return of the sun. But inevitably the commemoration of the birth of Jesus was informed with meaning derived from the old nature worship.

Before making any hasty judgment about Christmas, however, it is worth noting that Easter too is a celebration in which an ancient pagan festival was displaced by meaning derived from an event in the history of salvation. Easter, of course, comes from and proposes to be the fulfillment of the Old Testament Passover of Israel. This Passover, biblical scholars tell us, was originally a spring festival of the lambs among ancient Near Eastern pastoral peoples. It celebrated the return of spring and the renewal of fertility in field and flock, and betokened thanksgiving to the god of fertility in the act of sacrificing and appropriating his bounty.

But through God's deliverance of Israel from bondage in Egypt the annual spring slaughter of a lamb was invested with entirely new meaning. It no longer signified a recurring natural event, but a unique historic event. Passover no longer meant the ceaseless cycle of the years. It now marked the founding of Israel, and as such a datable event in the past pointed forward to Israel's destiny in the future. Passover became the symbol of Israel's historical and eschatological faith. With the death and resurrection of Christ the Passover hope was fulfilled and became Easter.

A second historic event reinforced the significance of the celebration and added new meaning as well.

We should mark carefully how this successful transformation of a festival of pagan origin came about. Only a divinely ordered event of history effected this change, an epochal event that carried within itself enough meaning and power to shape a people and direct its historical course. In this respect Christmas stands in sharp contrast with Easter and Passover. Instead of having its origin in an act of God that shattered the old meaning of the pagan festival in judgment and replaced it with a new meaning, Christmas had its origin in an artificial human contrivance that reflects the use of apologetics and the technique of syncretism.

But, it may be countered, does not Christmas also originate in a divinely ordered event of salvation history—namely, the birth of Jesus? The answer that must be given to this is that there is a decisive difference. Quite apart from the fact that we do not know just when Jesus was born (whereas we do know when he was crucified), the birth of Jesus is not in itself significant. It becomes significant only because of what the child born at Bethlehem later said and did—or, more exactly, what God did for man's redemption through him. And if the focus is upon his mission, then Easter is reinforced as the appropriate Christian celebration in response to God's salvation.

Often Christmas is justified as a celebration of the incarnation. But strictly speaking, if incarnation means the Word was made flesh, then Bethlehem must not be the focus of this doctrine, but Galilee and Golgotha, where the word is really being spoken in human flesh. When we go to the Gospel records, this is in fact how we see them treating the matter. Only brief space is given to the nativity—about two chapters—and in only two Gospels. The overwhelming attention of the Gospels is given to the public ministry and passion of Christ. The passion itself occupies about one fourth of the space in Matthew and Luke, one third in Mark.

From the Gospels we certainly get no justification for the bloated monster Christmas has become in America today. A man from Mars visiting us would think the Gospels had two chapters on the ministry and passion of Christ, the rest being devoted to his nativity.

What is involved in this issue is more than balance and proportion. At a certain point, difference in degree becomes difference in kind, and thereafter celebration of the nativity ceases to be an act of recalling the eschatological expectation of Mary, Simeon, and the Magi, and becomes instead an idolization of babyhood.

Whether it should be considered coincidental or not, it is significant that Christmas as celebrated in contemporary Christendom is essentially a nature festival. At worst it consists of eating and drinking orgies; at best it represents a celebration of the natural family (in the same fashion as Mother's Day and Father's Day). But even this most favorable way of regarding Christmas conflicts with the Christian concern to make the church, the spiritual family of God, central. Attempts have been made in the past—already in the time of the Puritans—to Christianize this holiday. But in the contemporary Western world it is clear that the trend today in Christmas celebration is away from the church and toward the home.

I think those who count themselves in the believers' church tradition have two very good reasons for reconsidering their involvement in the characteristic Christmas celebrations of Christendom today. First, the believers' church stands for the spiritual community based on regeneration and faith, and this entails opposition to every religious sacramentalizing of natural relationships that tends to undermine the importance of the church. Second, the believers' church insistence on conscious faith as a condition of membership in the spiritual family of God turns our attention to the mission of Jesus in his adult life rather than to his babyhood. This does not rule out normal human sentiments about the beauty of childhood, for Jesus himself shared these sentiments in taking children up in his arms to bless them. But it does mean refusing to make babyhood as such the object of *religious* worship, reverence, or even devotion and adoration.

It can hardly be denied that the creche, the chief religious symbol used in Christmas celebrations, is a symbol of religious devotion to babyhood, or at least to the natural family. We may try to deny this, but we would not accept our own arguments if we heard them from an Indian about the lingam, or from a Buddhist about the image of the Buddha, perhaps even from a Roman Catholic about the crucifix. The fact is that a symbol stands for certain values in a culture whether we admit it or not, and the creche symbol represents the values of the natural family.

I think there is a real connection, whether recognized or not, between traditional Christmas values and the mass church of Christendom. Adoration at the manger leads to infant baptism at the font. Or conversely, infant baptism abets adoration of babyhood as symbolized in the traditional creche. In any case the two go together and reinforce each other. They are part of a total detraction from a view of the Christian calling as discipleship of the crucified Jesus.

PART III: ON CHRISTENDOM'S CHRISTMAS

I would no doubt be considered an iconoclast by most people in American Christendom for voicing this concern. Most well-intentioned Christians would quite readily deplore any, in their view, secularization and commercialization of Christmas, but the answer to this, they would assert, lies in "putting Christ back into Christmas." I must confess to an opposite conviction. On the basis of both theological and practical considerations, I am persuaded that we should take Christ back out of Christmas. Jesus Christ was not present in the origin of this festival and he has never, we can say thankfully, fitted into it in the history of Western civilization.

If our lives are to be ordered according to biblical Christian faith, then the appropriate direction for us to move is away from Christmas. At the very best we can safely say that there is no good reason why we as Christians should not simply contract out of all observation of Christmas as a *religious* celebration. What we do about it as a *secular* holiday in Western culture is a different matter. We have other holidays like this: New Year's Day, Labor Day, Fourth of July (US), First of July (Canada), etc. The appropriate utilization of Christmas as a secular holiday can be discussed on its own merits. But let us get Christ back out of Christmas.

18

On the Meaning of Christmas[1]

John Howard Yoder

If we are to raise the level of our understanding of Christmas from the tastefulness of particular practices, to the appropriateness of spiritual meanings, we will do well to begin by taking our bearings broadly.

Without unjustified oversimplification it can be said that we stand here at the intersection of two competing conceptions of what the Christian faith is all about. These conceptions have their implications for ethics, where they would contrast "discipleship" and "responsibility." They have their implications for the nature of the church as well, in the choice between "established" and "believers' church." But here we see that the difference is still deeper, applying as well to the meaning of worship because it has to do with the very nature of God's intentions among men.

One of these conceptions we may call the "religious" or the "cultic"; it seeks to add depth or meaning to the world as it is, by adding a dimension of transcendence. The annual cycle is transfigured by celebrations of seedtime and harvest, summer and winter solstice. The life cycle is sacralized by sacraments for puberty, marriage, childbirth, and death. One's family, one's class, one's race, one's nation, is celebrated as the matrix of one's God-relation.

The other type of faith we may call "historical" or "covenantal." Here the focus is on events in this world which change it. "Transcendence" means not a dimension "beyond" this world but a power active within it. The cycle of life and of the year are broken through by a history which

---

1. Meditation presented to Mennonite Biblical Seminary Student Fellowship, December 18, 1963.

is linear, which is going somewhere. The given unities of family, class, nation are broken up by two new loyalties: by a visible, voluntary new community of those who respond in faith to what God has done, and by the vision of the stranger, the enemy, the outsider, the ends of the earth as the measure of the extent of that God's purposes.

The history of Israel is the story of the struggle, ultimately successful, of the historical against the religious. Israel accepted the annual cycle of feasts but, despite the parallels to Canaanite celebrations of sowing and harvest, the meanings it reviews and represents are historical: the escape from Egypt, the desert wanderings, the sealing of the covenant at Sinai and Shechem, Jahweh's taking of the land for his people and his choice of Zion for his throne. There is a sacrament of integration into the covenant—circumcision—which applies equally to infant Israelites and adult proselytes; there are no sacramental blessings for birth, puberty, marriage, or death. But the most important institution of Israel is the Sabbath—a cycle so short as to become ordinary, cutting across the sidereal cycle, with no prescribed ceremonies but rest. This "de-ceremonializing" reached its culmination in the new covenant, with the end of the temple and of all seasonal feasts, and with the resurrection being celebrated not once a year but on every Lord's Day. Liberty was left to the "weak" to observe special days without being condemned, but they were forbidden to ask such practices of their brethren.

Only after decades, even centuries, did the annual cycle begin to return. The first step was the reintroduction of the Passover celebration, borrowed from Judaism, and dated with such faithfulness to the Jewish lunar calendar that at first Easter did not necessarily fall on Sunday.

Christmas came much later, first appearing in the fourth century as a replacement for various pagan celebrations of the rebirth of the sun at the winter solstice. Part of the meaning deposited here had been prepared in the gnostic churches which had similarly adopted January 6 (previously celebrated by several Egyptian religions) as the day of "Epiphany," i.e., of the manifestation of deity to men. On this date they had celebrated somehow both the birth and the baptism of Jesus. At this point the subject of celebration was not so much the birth of Jesus as the concept of incarnation. Still later, in the West, Nicholas was moved from December 6, to join the modern complex, Christmas. The manger scene and nativity carols were added much later as a renewed effort to restore historical meaning.

Medieval Christianity went much further in "baptizing" the year. Not only was the life of Jesus distributed through the time from Christmas to ascension; other celebrations with no historical base at all became almost as important (Midsummer, All Saints, national and local saints' days). It was not surprising that the individual's life cycle should have been restored to sacramental centrality. Whereas in Old Israel childbirth, death, and even marriage, were downplayed, being occasions for ritual impurity, they now became sacraments. Baptism, which once meant voluntary entrance into the covenant community, now cleanses all infants from inherited guilt and formalizes the mother's return to society. Puberty is recognized with "confirmation" (whose catechetical and experiential dimensions are late Protestant additions). Sacramentally accompanied from womb to tomb by a religion he did not need to choose, man perceives God more in nature than in history, more as the guarantor of a reliable universe than as the mover of an incomplete story or as the Lord of a yet rebellious creation.

For most churches most of the time, this history of "Christianization" is to be welcomed as a success story. Better a superficial Christianity than none at all. Better a government saying, "in God we trust" and not meaning it, than not even saying it. Better replace the Sun God by the Son of God than let the sun worship go on undiluted.

The Critique

The alternative would be a critique, mild or sweeping, whose strength in the past most Christians ignore. Such critique may proceed on several levels.

- A. There is the simple argument from origins. Because these annual celebrations were borrowed from paganism, they are false. This argument is made most strongly today by groups whom most would call "legalistic" and "sectarian," of which Herbert Armstrong's "Radio Church of God" is probably the strongest example. Some of this thought underlies the traditional Quaker rejection of the pagan names of the months and the days of the week.

- B. One step deeper is the rejection of hypocrisy and dishonest forms. "Let your yea be yea; anything more is of the evil one." If "in God we trust" is not true, then it does more harm than good to say it and print it on our coins and paint it on the walls of our Parliaments. By the same token, any routinized celebration must be hypocritical.

C. Still more basic, perhaps, is the iconoclasm of all biblical reform since Josiah. It begins its modern career with Huldryck Zwingli's attack on "Ceremonies"; it was prevalent in the mainstream Puritanism which runs from him to colonial New England (where Christmas celebration was forbidden) as it was in the otherwise more radical Anabaptism and Quakerism. Here the concern is for the purity of spiritual adoration, the dismantling of idolatry, and the unmasking of unworthy worship. "God is a Spirit: and they that worship him must worship him in spirit and in truth" (John 4:24).

These three strands of the Hebraic-Puritan critique are theologically serious. They could apply as well to the new synthetic religiosities gathered around grandpa's farm ("Jingle Bells") and winter weather ("White Christmas"), reindeer and gifts, as to the genuine old paganisms. They are far more profound than the sporadic efforts of mainstream Christianity to "Get Christ back in Christmas." They recognize that the so easily deplored gluttony, drunkenness, and commercialism are not strange deformations but normal modern expressions of the same cult of fertility and prosperity which celebrated the rebirth of the Sun millennia ago. They already constitute sufficient reason for Christians whose concern for faithfulness goes beyond conformity to seek to get Christmas out of the church rather than trying to squeeze Jesus back in between the holly and the ivy. Their weight is sufficient that we here may pass on to critical considerations on still another level.

Deeper Diagnosis

The idiom of the Hebraic-Puritan critique of cultic ceremony is often legalistic: it discusses whether God ever commanded a given practice. Yet the legalist form covers a deeper theological critique. The issue at stake is far more than verbal authorization or formal mandate.

A. If syncretism is not to be completely forbidden, at least it must be tested. If we do not follow the Hebrew prophets and the Puritans completely, at least we must not accept, without qualification, all pagan forms in the claim to be giving them new content; we must know the difference between success and failure in Christianization, and be honest enough to abandon the failures. The tests would be whether the new historical content can purge and pare off the pagan meanings of the old form. It is not enough to say the pagan meanings should "not get out of hand"; their back must be broken. If this does not succeed, then the pagan form has been legitimized, not displaced, by the new words spoken over it.

This has happened when Christmas is focused on happy childhood and unneeded gifts. A new circularity, living from one Christmas to the next, replaces the linear getting-somewhere of God's causes in the world. The sun reborn will wane yet again; the life we hail as reborn is mortal, a glorification of our own resources and our destiny. The irrepeatable uniqueness of God's past and future are denied again in the wheeling of the Zodiac; the modest week-upon-week of work is laid aside for the annual blow.

B. It is a mirror of this shift when we see the cradle without the cross. The infancy narratives in the Gospels are not about the baby Jesus but about the men and women awaiting the triumphant Messiah, who were promised suffering instead. Rejection at the inn is followed by Simeon's bitter prophecy, "This child is set for the fall and rising of many in Israel; and for a sign which shall be spoken against . . . (yea, a sword shall pierce through thy own soul also)" (Luke 2:34, 25). Herod's menace fulfills for Matthew Jeremiah's word about Rachel weeping for her children. The peasants for whom, legend says, Saint Francis invented the manger scene, knew full well that for a child to be born in a barn means for the mother poverty, stench, and rejection by men, not sweet-smelling hay and cute woolly lambs at play. "Little baby Jesus," clean, chubby, innocent—and in our art usually blond, Aryan—has nothing to do with the Gospel. Not the innocence of the infant but the obedience of the Man, Jesus, saves us.

From here it is but a short step to note that what fourth-century Christendom celebrated was not an event but a doctrine, not a life breaking into the world but the miracle of incarnation transforming it. If in the effort to save Christmas, we bring to it the full weight of the miracle of God-made-infant, we fall into the docetic heresy, affirming the full divine presence apart from the story of the man. Divine sonship is clearly proclaimed first at Jesus's baptism; before that the Gospels only point to its promise. For the sake of the real meaning of incarnation we must, like the Gospels, see the cross behind the cradle. It is because that can no longer be done with the American Christmas that the time may well have come for surgery.

19

Marginalia: The Case Against Christmas

JOHN HOWARD YODER (Part 1)
and VIRGIL VOGT (Part 2)

Part 1

One of the central certainties of the entire left half of the sixteenth-century Reformation—not only of the Anabaptists but also of the Reformed movement from Zwingli's earliest entry on the scene to Calvin and Knox—was the sweeping rejection of what they called "Ceremonies"—all the cultic trappings, signs and gestures, washings and anointings, special utensils and garments, processions and prayers, which gave Catholic worship its sacral aura. Sometimes this iconoclastic thrust was driven by the conviction that these practices were the stronghold of superstition or sorcery; more often it sufficed to argue that they had not been commanded by Christ, and should be stripped away to let the reformed sacraments mean in all simplicity what they were meant by Jesus to convey.

A normal part of this return to the essentials was the abandoning of special feast days and their paraphernalia. Not only the miscellaneous daily saints, but also Saint Nicholas and the Three Kings and Christmas itself were set aside as vestiges of idolatry. This rigor lasted for centuries; Christmas celebrations were forbidden by law in Puritan New England.

Even those contemporary Christians who reread the history of the rigorous wings (Reformed and Anabaptist) of the Reformation, with respect for their voluntarism and their biblicism, do not often catch the meaning of their anti-cultic, anti-ceremonial thrust. Thus, it comes as quite a surprise to many, unacquainted with the same phenomenon in today's radical restitutionisms (Jehovah's Witnesses, Herbert Armstrong, holiness movements), that there could be serious theological objection, not to the abuse or the commercial exploitation of Christmas, but to the day itself.

What were Christians doing when they placed a celebration of their own on the date, and within some of the forms, of a pagan feast? The positive argument says the pagan practices were being displaced, crowded out by a new celebration with the right meanings. The negative critique sees in the same development a selling-out, the acceptance of paganism under a thin veneer of Christian vocabulary. Only within the context of a wider set of theological value presuppositions can one decide between these two interpretations of the same process. What is striking today is the way in which Christians of the free-church traditions, quick to judge the "Constantinian synthesis" for what it did about church membership, religious liberty, the state, war, and empire, have so little question about what it did about feast days. Thus, the challenging of Christmas is left to the Jehovah's Witnesses, Herbert Armstrong, and other barely noticed legalistic sects.

The "displacing" of pagan holidays was no new idea in the fourth century. Israel had done this long before. The regular feasts of Israel were quite parallel in form and in date to Canaanite festivals of seedtime and harvest, but their meaning was transformed. At the cost of great tension and much breakage and slippage, Judaism was able to wrest the forms free of their earlier meaning and make them vehicles of the proclamation of salvation in history.

But if the claim to be able to take over and transform a pagan worship form is made seriously, one must also be honest with the other option; if we cannot bring it off, if the pagan form swamps or swallows the saving substance, if the vehicle destroys its burden, then honesty demands that we admit it. The church has left All Saints to the pranksters and UNICEF; we must ask if it is not time to leave Christmas to the department stores and office parties.

But let us not blame the merchants; if the meaning of the day had not already been less than biblical, they could not have taken it away from us so easily. The root of the distortion was already there before:

Christmas is the family holiday. Biblical faith centers on the pattern of Exodus from the given solidarities of culture. Abram leaves Chaldea, then Haran, then Egypt; Moses leaves Egypt. Marriage is a leaving of father and mother; the disciples' faith may dictate the forsaking of father and mother, houses and lands. Anabaptism rediscovered that the priority of salvation history over Christendom is tested at the point of the sacrament which seals the infant into the faith of the parents. Christmas, with its celebration of infancy, both in the figure of the baby Jesus and in making children the type celebrants of the gift-receiving ritual, reinforces almost sacramentally the child's dependence on the nest-family.

Christmas is the nature holiday. More than any other of the feasts of the annual cycle (except perhaps Halloween), Christmas has maintained from its pagan origins the links with the sun and the stars. Its symbolic centrality in the view of time as cyclical extends even to the economic statisticians. The link which Canaanite religion saw between the "groves" and the stars as donors of prosperity is undergirded by the Nordic equivalents of pine tree and candle. However successful modern man may be in keeping these dimensions of the celebration down in his subconscious, the giving of presents and the feasting are what the anthropologist calls "sympathetic magic," a dramatic symbolizing of abundance in the hope that the universe will get the point and imitate the generosity of the celebrants.

Christmas is typical of a strategy of cultural accommodation. All the dates on the liturgical year have been diluted by an element of accommodation to pre-Christian cult patterns, but only Christmas, of the major feasts recognized by most Christians, has no base either in the early church or in Israel. Easter, Pentecost, and ascension at least reflect datable events. Thus, it is only Christmas which must be explained primarily as an assimilation or displacement of its pagan predecessors in the age of Constantine. It thereby represents in a quintessential way the issue of accommodation versus iconoclasm in Christian cultural strategy. A well-known conservative evangelical churchman, hearing that *Concern* projected a discussion of this question, responded, "I hope you do not give aid and comfort to the Jehovah's Witnesses." But must we not turn the concern around? Is there not a certain loss of moral rigor, a certain trend to respectability, in the desire of Christians to act like the "mainstream," which is responsible for leaving the prophetic-Puritan strain in biblical faith to the sectarian fringes? On this one point, where the religious radicals take the same position as Zwingli and Knox, can we be sure without discussion that their critique has no point, just because it is presented in an unsophisticated way?

Concern's treatment of this theme represents no crusade and no settled opinion. It suffices that we raise the question as one specimen of the many ways in which what claims to be "Christian culture" is less than that, and one of the manifold lines which concern for the rediscovery of spiritual authenticity might take.

Part 2

When the idea of an issue attacking Christmas was first presented to *Concern*'s editors, it met with a mixed response. Is Christmas worth the trouble? Is this an issue sufficiently clear and sufficiently important to command the attention of serious Christians?

Jim Fairfield's first response was negative:

> Perhaps this reveals my paganism, but I can't get excited about an issue, a whole issue, on the paganism of Christmas when I see such other current issues as Vietnam, a long hot summer, the mushrooming city, the disfranchisement of the Indian, the Christian vendetta against communism, the vials of wrath that have been poured out polluting our streams, our air, and our natural resources, so that I am not excited about such a prosaic thing as Christmas.
>
> I suspect that a great many people who spend money at Christmas do so as we do in our family. This is the time when we buy socks for dad and a shirt for son, a new dress pattern and materials for daughter, and a pair of shoes for mother—all items which should have been bought before, because of need, but which were bought with an air of thinking of the other person, and of mutual sharing in a festive occasion. Of course, there is the other side, the extreme materialism and partying and kindred paganisms. But somehow I can't get as upset about it as I can about some of these other issues.

Concern subscribers will have noticed that *Concern* has not published anything recently on either the summer, the city, the Indian, the vendetta, or the vials. This does not mean that these larger issues do not matter to *Concern* editors or readers. Rather, it simply reflects the fact that no one considered *Concern* the best vehicle for his thoughts on these subjects. But now that we come to think of it, is it so sure that pollution, the rush to suburbia, and the mistreatment of minorities are not partly the long-range out-working of the family-centered, acquisition-centered religion of which Christmas is the object lesson and the sacrament? Is Vietnam understandable without the identification of church and world of which the "Christianization" of pagan feasts is the expression?

Enthusiastic support for this venture came, on the other hand, from Lewis Benson, Quaker representative on *Concern*'s Editorial Council. When he heard about our plans, Lewis wrote, "I am very glad to learn that *Concern* is turning its attention to the pagan character of modern Christmas." He went on to say,

> I think the complete rejection and non-observance of Christmas was practiced by Friends for about 200 years. As Christmas festivities have gained momentum during the last 100 years, the Quakers have been carried along. Occasionally an individual Quaker stands out against Christmas but such individuals can be found in many denominations. The original Quaker position concerning Christmas is that Christmas has nothing whatever to do with the gospel and new covenant. On the basis of this original position there can be no such thing as purging Christmas of non-Christian elements.

This Quaker rejection of Christmas goes back to George Fox himself, who objected to all "holy days." According to Fox, "they who are heirs of the gospel, and of Jesus Christ, are redeemed out of the vain observation of days, and out of the Jewish and apostate Christians' holy days, to God by Christ, who made all days, and every good thing, and their eyes are to the supernatural day of Christ; and they are children of this day."[1]

Elsewhere Fox wrote, "And many Friends were imprisoned and had before the magistrates up and down in the cities and nation for opening their shop windows upon holy days and fast days and bearing their testimony against all such observations of days, knowing that the true Christians did not observe the Jews' holy days in the apostles' days. Neither could we observe the heathens' and Papists' holy days. For we were redeemed out of days by Christ Jesus and brought into his day."[2]

Reflecting on his own response to this Quaker position, Lewis Benson writes, "For 35 years I have been a non-observer of Christmas. My wife believes in a quiet, modified 'Quaker' or 'Philadelphia Quaker' Christmas—no gifts, just a quiet family gathering. In my view there is no such thing as a Quaker Christmas. We have managed pretty well,

---

1. Fox, *Works*, 8:81.
2. Fox, *Journals*, 1:315.

however, and this is partly because we had only one child and his birthday is on December 23rd!"

It is obvious, even in this brief summary, that the Quaker protest against Christmas is only one part of a larger position regarding that which God expects of men within the new covenant. It is the broader context which makes the particular issue significant. In a somewhat similar way, Marlin Jeschke and John Howard Yoder put the discussion about Christmas within the larger question of how we understand the working of God in history. Put in such broad context, the discussion about Christmas has important connections to the position that we take on Vietnam, the urban crisis, or communism.

Contemporary Responses

20

Global Anabaptist Movement

From Cross-Cultural to Multicultural
to Intercultural

Hyung Jin Kim Sun[1]

Writings in this volume are tied together under the topic of church mission and spiritual gifts, and the authors touch on diverse interests and issues. Hence, each reader will have different takeaways from this volume. In what follows, I approach the historical essays as critical theological reflections on the mutual transformation the authors experienced through intercultural encounters. I go on to suggest the need today for a more fully developed intercultural missional theology and ecclesiology. But to begin, I explore the texts relating Peter's encounter with Cornelius in Acts 10, 11, and 15 for the relevant themes and issues they raise.

Intercultural Encounters and Mutual Transformation

The texts relating Peter's encounter with Cornelius in Acts 10, 11, and 15 highlight the role of the Holy Spirit and the transformation of Peter, the messenger of the gospel. This conversion experience causes Peter to

1. Rev. Dr. Hyung Jin Kim Sun, aka Pablo, is a Korean-Paraguayan Mennonite who holds a PhD in theological ethics at Emmanuel College from the Toronto School of Theology. He works as Senior Leader for Anti-Racism and Intercultural Conciliation at Christian Reformed Church North America and lives in Mississauga, Ontario with his wife and daughter. Kim Sun became a Mennonite because of his strong conviction in the gospel of peace.

reexamine his theological understanding and praxis, including his assumptions about mission and ecclesiology, which (as portrayed in the Acts narrative) becomes the catalyst for a wider paradigm shift among the early Jewish Christian leaders. Without going too much into the exegetical work of Acts 10 or examining in depth the cultural and historical context of the early church, we know from the text that Cornelius and the people who were present at the house are gentiles, people who were considered as "the other," people who were excluded from the Jewish community because they were perceived as profane. Yet, Cornelius was more than a simple gentile, he was a Roman centurion, one of the people who were on the frontline of oppressing, colonizing, and exploiting the Jewish people through their brutal military power. Although Acts 10:2 describes him as a person who is different from other centurions, it cannot be denied that as a centurion, he played a role in the colonizing work of the empire. However, in a strange way, God led Peter to Cornelius' house and when he began to preach, the most unexpected incident happened: the Holy Spirit fell upon all the gentiles in Cornelius' house. The Jewish Christians, including Peter, were dumbfounded to see these people speaking in tongues and praising God! Even though Peter did not completely understand the situation, he knew that he had no option but to baptize these people with water since they were already baptized by the Spirit.

There is no doubt that this firsthand experience of the Holy Spirit caused Peter to reexamine his theological understanding about God, salvation, baptism, church, and other themes. In Acts 11, we can see Peter sharing this experience with the church in Jerusalem. It seems like he was still processing how to make sense of the baptism of the Holy Spirit. So, instead of offering a full-fledged theological perspective, he retold the incident from his viewpoint at the church of Jerusalem. Later, in Acts 15, at the Council of Jerusalem, Peter was able to articulate more fully what God was trying to teach him through the experience. This experience not only drastically changed Peter's theological view but also profoundly influenced the future direction of the early Christians' mission, their understanding of salvation, and their view of the church's membership. Through Acts 10, we learn that authentic evangelism and mission not only lead toward the conversion of the receivers of the gospel, but also the messengers are transformed by witnessing how God works with and through the new believers. As a result, a genuine missional encounter yields a mutual transformation.

What I note in the texts by these Anabaptist-Mennonite writers in this volume is something like the encounter between Peter and Cornelius. As these writers are hearing and learning about the experiences from Christians in the non-Western world and the new experience of the Holy Spirit among the Anabaptists and Mennonites in Canada and the United States, they are theologizing to make sense of these experiences from their Anabaptist tradition. Through this process, they are reexamining their understanding of God, church, and the world and even becoming more aware of their own social and cultural context. We can see this in multiple examples. Paul Peachey advocates Japanese Christianity be more fully part of the catholic church. Edmund Perry proposes going beyond our Graeco-Roman mentality in trying to understand people from other faiths, including careful study of the social context of people of different faiths so as to understand how Christ is already working among them. John Howard Yoder makes a connection between the early Anabaptist movement and Pentecostalism, explaining how both movements are quite similar. After analyzing various works of the Holy Spirit that occurred in several contexts, based on their Anabaptist and Christocentric perspective, Herb and Maureen Klassen suggest two criteria for discerning whether a spiritual phenomenon is the work of the Holy Spirit or not. The conversation between Myron Augsburger and James Fairfield explores how to make sense of the work of the Holy Spirit in relation to Mennonite theology as well as the Mennonite Church's slowness to show interest in the charismatic movement. All these proposals, conversations, and insights emerged from these writers' critical reflections about God, church, and the world in light of their Anabaptist tradition as they listened to Christian voices from different parts of the world. Subsequently, their theological endeavors led them to deepen and broaden their Anabaptist faith and practices, informed by new learnings and discoveries.[2]

Through this mutual learning, these Anabaptist-Mennonite writers also became more aware of and attentive to their social and cultural context. As Christians living in Canada and the US, two major issues these authors name and problematize from their context are the assumption that Western denominationalist structures are the only or best way to do church and the colonial legacy of Christendom, as we can see in the

---

2. Authors in this volume reflect other limitations and blind spots, such as their limited understanding of missions as "sender and receiver" mentality and their inability to recognize how Mennonite missionaries implicitly participated in Western colonialism. The scope and length of this essay do not permit me to engage these issues.

writings of Paul Peachey in "Churchless Christianity" and "The End of Christendom." During this time, many Christian churches in Canada and the US did not consider these issues as problematic and some even approved of them. Yet, as Christians who belonged to a historically marginalized Christian community that from its beginning critiqued Christendom and advocated for the early church model, they were able to clearly name and problematize these issues. Additionally, by being part of a marginalized community they intentionally sought to listen to the voices of other marginalized groups within the global church, namely, Asian, African, and South American Christians.

These two issues, presumptive, uncritical export of Western denominationalist structures and the colonial legacy of Christendom, not only distort our essential understanding of Christianity but, as Yoder says, can lead us to misinterpret the genius of the Pentecostal movement.[3] This means that we may misunderstand both the work of the Holy Spirit and the authentic expression of Christianity in Latin America, Asia, and Africa as a result. When we have our rigid understanding of how churches should be organized and structured, and when our theology is built upon a Christendom perspective, we will inevitably end up misinterpreting the works of the Holy Spirit that do not align our way of doing church and condemning radical faith movements that do not reflect Christendom's compromise with the state or government. Going back to the Acts 10 story, if Peter insisted on his theological framework which excluded the gentiles when the Holy Spirit manifested over Cornelius and his household, he could have demonized the work of the Spirit or misunderstood it, assuming for example that the people drank too much wine. These issues also interfere with our ability to learn from the experiences of our brothers and sisters from non-Western countries because we fail to see their expression of Christian faith as genuine. Thus, these writers problematize these issues, instead encouraging readers to learn from brothers and sisters outside of the Western world how to fully embrace the gifts of the Holy Spirit and how to be differently (less) structured churches. Through them, we can learn what Christianity not marked by Christendom looks like.

This mode of reexamining God, church, world, and one's social and cultural context in a missional and intercultural encounter is, in fact, nothing new. For this reason, Theo Sundermeier, a well-known German missiologist, asserts that mission studies can be termed as xenology, "the study

---

3. Yoder, "Marginalia," essay in this volume, 53.

of the encounter of the church with those who are strangers to it."[4] Another missiologist, Klaus Hock, frames it as the study that focuses "on the analysis of the transformation of Christian discourse in the processes of crossing borders."[5] Throughout Anabaptist-Mennonite history, there have been extensive missional and intercultural encounters as well. Three renowned Mennonite scholars, S. F. Pannabecker, Wilbert Shenk, and Calvin Redekop agree that the early Anabaptists actively engaged in missions work and that sharing the gospel was one of the core values of the Mennonites.[6] However, the religious persecution suppressed them, and they were forced to scatter in remote areas. Consequently, Edmund Kauffman states that due to "continued isolation, at first caused by outside suppression and opposition but later maintained as an ideal, Mennonites were not much affected by, and took little interest in, what was going on in the world about them."[7] Yet, the suppressed spirit of the mission was revived, according to T. D. Regehr and Shenk, when revival movements from the Protestant churches swept through Europe, Canada, and the United States in the mid-nineteenth century.[8] These movements helped Mennonites to rediscover the missional nature of their faith tradition. The church's renewed commitment to mission brought various Mennonite groups to work together. They began to see the missions work as the highest calling of the church. These missional and intercultural engagements caused them to reexamine their theologies and their social and cultural context; the writings from this volume are a few examples of that endeavor which has a much longer history.

The Need for an Intercultural Church

Sixty years later, what insights can be gleaned from these *Concern* essays? I believe that readers in the Anabaptist-Mennonite tradition who reside in Canada and the United States should embrace the attitude and the approach of these writers' theologizing: we should reflect critically on our Anabaptist faith, theologies, and practices as we listen carefully to Christian voices outside of the Western world and to marginalized groups. And this critical reflection should be done as we seriously consider our current

---

4. Sundermeier, "Begegnung mit dem Fremden," 397.
5. Hock, "Grenzziehung und Grenzüberschreitung," 254.
6. Pannabecker et al., "Mission (Missiology)"; Redekop, *Mennonite Society*, 233.
7. Kaufman, *Development*, 56.
8. Regehr, *Mennonites in Canada*, 328; Shenk, "'Great Century,'" 162–77.

social and cultural context. This theological approach should look different today because we are now living in a whole new context. For example, the statistic gathered in 2015 by the Global Anabaptist Profile shows that the Mennonite church has become much more global.[9] Though the proportions doubtless differ by region and conference, people from different cultural backgrounds and faith traditions are joining Mennonite churches in Canada and the United States, and immigrant churches are emerging and flourishing within our denominations. Decades ago, Edmund Perry alerted his readers that Asian religions would move beyond their continent, but now our context is more clearly marked by people from many religions, including several well-established Asian religions that actively share their faith in Canada and the US. Furthermore, more than ever before, there is a massive scale of migration occurring worldwide. For instance, if we observe the forced migration alone, the United Nation High Commissioner for Refugees (UNHCR) reports that in 2017, every two seconds, an average of one person is being displaced.[10] In this global crisis, Canada and the US have been accepting large numbers of migrants and refugees. All these social factors, from micro to macro level, are shaping some major cities in Canada and the United States to be a much more pluralistic, multicultural, and multi-faith society. This is the context in which we reflect on our faith and listen to non-Western and marginalized voices.

Another shift is that many Mennonite churches—particularly white Mennonite churches—are no longer marginalized communities. In the past, white Mennonite communities had limited socio-political and economic power but in the present, they are much more influential, stable, and wealthy. Of course, compared to other Mainline Protestant churches, they are smaller in number, size, and finances, and in some places, they might be in a more challenging situation. Yet, seen from a global perspective and from more marginalized communities (racialized, immigrant, and Indigenous communities, for example), these churches are powerful and affluent communities. Thus, our critical theological reflection should be done with awareness of this significant shift in social location for many white Mennonite communities in Canada and the United States.

Through critical social theories and cultural studies, we are learning that contexts are much more complex and the people in the same community can have different experiences due to other contextual factors.

9. Kanagy et al., *Global Anabaptist Profile*, 29.
10. UNHCR, *Global Trends*.

Some of these contextual factors are geography, gender, ethnic affiliations, culturally constructed power, class, economy, ecology, generation, education, and place.[11] This means that even though a white German Mennonite man and a Colombian woman who both came to Canada as refugees are attending the same Mennonite church where the church leadership is predominantly white and male, what they experience from the church can be drastically different.

I propose that in the current social and cultural context an appropriate way of living out our Anabaptist faith and practices as we intentionally integrate voices and experiences from diverse people is by becoming an intercultural church. Though the term might sound novel to many, the core concept is nothing new from a biblical perspective. After the early Jewish Christian leaders started to welcome gentile Christians, the early churches began to become more heterogeneous and diverse. Slaves and masters, men and women, Jews and gentiles, rich and poor, royal families and lower-class people gathered in one place to worship God. They were the first people to live out the vision of becoming an intercultural church. In Gal 3:28, we see the apostle Paul encouraging the churches in Galatia to be communities that fully embrace diversity and differences when he states, "There is no longer Jew or Greek, there is no longer slave or free, there is no longer male and female; for all of you are one in Christ Jesus." Paul is not saying that these social, ethnic, and cultural factors do not exist but rather that these differences cannot and should not divide our oneness in Christ. Church unity must be pursued out of and not in spite of difference. Diversity and differences are not sources of division but rather gifts that can enrich our community to understand God, church, and the world much better. As a result, differences should be respected, celebrated, and embraced in our global and pluralistic society.

Here it is important to note that there is a huge difference between a multicultural and intercultural approach. To explain briefly, a multicultural approach seeks to tolerate, recognize, and respect different cultural and ethnic groups. Like a mosaic, each group exists within their own boundaries and contributes to some larger whole; but there is only a minimal interaction among the groups. However, an intercultural model seeks to promote active engagement among different cultural and ethnic groups in settings where each group is present in their full identity and dignity. This approach envisions all cultural and social groups are equally

---

11. Bergmann, *God in Context*, 44.

ready to learn from each other and shape each other, even as they maintain their own identity.

Another helpful way to explain an intercultural church is by describing it as "radically welcoming" church, a concept coined by Stephanie Spellers. Spellers differentiates among an inviting, inclusive, and radically welcoming church. An inviting church is a church that invites people who have different backgrounds. While the newcomers are invited, the church requires them to assimilate to the existing culture, practices, and to adopt the dominant identity of the congregation. An inclusive church is a church that takes more seriously its responsibility to incorporate marginalized groups and so they make statements and preach about the importance of being an inclusive congregation. It sees the need to embrace the others. Nonetheless, the effort to make the change is mostly focused at an individual level and does not examine closely how the church system and power dynamic are structured in the church. Different from these models, a "radically welcoming church" seeks a truly mutual relationship with different groups. It perceives the others as gifts from God and wants the church to express the full range of voices. In order to make this a reality, churches make an intentional effort to invite and welcome people and include those from the margins. They also share power so that together, they can shape the church's identity, theology, mission, and leadership in mutual respect.[12]

What does it mean then to be an intercultural church, particularly for the Mennonite churches in the United States and Canada? In another paper, I argued that for Mennonite churches to become intercultural, we should be ethnically and theologically intercultural. To be ethnically intercultural requires us to move from our ethnocentric to ethnorelative church identity. In other words, our churches should move away from our dominant ethnic identities, Dutch-Russian and Swiss-German, and embrace other diverse ethnicities that are part of our church community. To be theologically intercultural, we should actively engage and integrate theological perspectives from diverse perspectives and from the non-Western world. If we have mostly been reading theological works by Western white males and based on their thoughts and experiences, it is about time to learn from and listen to theological perspectives from different social groups.[13]

Reading these historical essays from our present context, there is much to critique. But through this response essay, I have chosen instead to focus

12. Spellers, *Radical Welcome*, 63–74.
13. Kim Sun, "Forging an Intercultural," 201–5.

on the high value of the attitude and approach of these writers' theologizing. Like they did, I would like to urge contemporary Anabaptist-Mennonite sisters and brothers to reflect critically on our theologies as we engage in intercultural relationships within and outside of our communities. And in this engagement, let us be careful not to impose our dominant view, whether it is a Western, male, or white perspective, but rather mutually learn from each other as we respect the worldview and the struggles of the people from different social and cultural groups. Moreover, as we discover new ways the Holy Spirit works through these intercultural encounters, let us be willing to change our heart, mind, theology, and even our church structure as Peter and the early Jewish Christian leaders did.

Seeking to become an intercultural church is a joyful work because it will bring new discoveries about God, church, and the world, and it will continually surprise us. Nonetheless, it is also a difficult and messy task because of our human inclination toward egoism and ethnocentrism. As we try to fully embrace the other, we will not only encounter their gifts but also their foreign cultural practices, struggles, and pains. This engagement will take us to uncharted territories and make us ask new sets of questions. It will also expose us to new realities of oppression and violence previously unknown to us when we lived and related only among our small and limited social groups. Yet, if we seek to model the early church and to be a missional church, if we seek to be an alternative community that shows how to live the way God desires us and the whole world to live—in our global, pluralistic, and multicultural society where injustice and exclusion are prevalent—should we not then strive to become an intercultural church?

21

Mission and Margin(alization)

An Ecumenically-Shaped Anabaptist/Mennonite Approach to Mission

ANDRÉS PACHECO LOZANO[1]

In recent times in the Mennonite global communion (not unlike other global communions and ecumenical spaces) conversations over controversial and potentially church-dividing issues—such as the discussions over same-sex relations—have raised concerns about a renewed neocolonialism. An argument in this regard has been that issues exclusively of concern to the Global North are being imposed on the Global South—that just as past missionizing efforts brought culturally shaped theology and ecclesiology, so contested social issues prominent in the Global North are being exported to the Global South. Among many other things, this argument unveils the current need to revisit the relationship between colonialism, mission and margin(alization), even as the historical essays in this volume demonstrate such questions are a longstanding concern among Anabaptist/Mennonites.

In what follows, I reflect on how these questions of mission, margins, and marginalization are relevant for (a renewed) Anabaptist/Mennonite understanding and practice of mission today. This exploration will be facilitated through analyzing one particular approach to mission in the

1. Andrés Pacheco Lozano, PhD, originally from Colombia, now lives in the Netherlands where he is Lecturer and Researcher at Mennonite Seminary in Amsterdam/The Netherlands and Research Assistant of the chair of (Peace-) Theology and Ethics at Vrije Universiteit Amsterdam/The Netherlands.

ecumenical movement, namely the World Council of Churches' (WCC) statement *Together Towards Life: Mission and Evangelism in Changing Landscapes* which articulates a "mission from the margins."[2] This approach will enable us to (1) recognize key aspects of mission and margin(alization) and identify how they are reflected in the historical essays of *Concern*; (2) assert the reality and necessity of the ecumenical context for Anabaptist/Mennonite understanding of mission; and (3) be challenged to reflect critically on our Anabaptist/Mennonite theology and practice of mission. As will be seen, of special interest will be reflecting on how a self-critical peace theology could be central to a renewed vision of Mennonite mission as mission from the margins governed by a mission spirituality.

WCC Mission from the Margins: An Ecumenical Approach

Recently I have been involved in the WCC program "Pilgrimage of Justice and Peace" (PJP), launched during the tenth WCC Assembly in Busan, 2013. It has represented an entry point for me to gain a sense of the global ecumenical fellowship and theology. The questions the *Concern* essays in this volume raise regarding mission and margin(alization) led me to re-read another important document adopted at the WCC Assembly in 2013, the statement *Together Towards Life: Mission and Evangelism in Changing Landscapes*. This ecumenical approach to mission presents several elements that we[3] in the Anabaptist/Mennonite family can learn from and be challenged by, especially its view of mission as from the margins.

> 2. WCC, *Together Towards Life*.
>
> 3. As the reader will see, my use of "we" and "us" might seem ambiguous or blur at times. For instance, I use "we" to refer to the global Mennonite communion; to the Anabaptist/Mennonite tradition; and to the Mennonites in Colombia. This blurred use of "we" and "us" is intentional. As the following lines will demonstrate, my attempt is to avoid "us-them" dichotomies, seeking to escape dualisms that I perceive are imposed through colonialism. Yet, the use of "we" here is not to say that being Anabaptist/Mennonite signifies the same regardless of the context or time, or that the experiences regarding mission are equal around the world. Such a generalizing approach can be a way to ignore or suppress existing differences and particularities within the Anabaptist/Mennonite communities and histories. Such generalizations can also reflect a colonial approach that assumes there is only one story or approach to Anabaptist/Mennonite history, and with it only one understanding and practice of mission. The aim here is instead to point to some of possible threads in terms of the understanding and practicing of mission—how some patterns of mission have been appropriated and are continued in different contexts and spaces. Whether this attempt is helpful or not is subject to the reader's analysis.

This dialogue between an ecumenical missiological approach and Anabaptist/Mennonite understandings is based on two assumptions. First, there has been a history of exchange between Mennonites and the ecumenical movement (particularly the WCC) that has shaped both regarding the peace vocation. As Fernando Enns argues, the Historic Peace Church (HPC) (including Anabaptist churches) vocation for peace would not be the same without ecumenical relations; and in return, the life of the ecumenical movement in terms of the peace vocation (particularly the WCC) would not be the same without the HPC's contribution. Thus, by looking at the ecumenical family we are not simply looking at how "other churches do theology"; we also see glimpses of our own Anabaptist (peace) theology represented and renewed.[4] Second, I contend that, following Jeremy Bergen, Anabaptist identity becomes intelligible in dialogue with other traditions; Anabaptist/Mennonite identity "has integrity only to the extent that [we are] . . . engaged in genuine dialogue with other Christians about Christian faithfulness and mission. As Christians, our mission is to the world; as Anabaptist, our mission is in relation to other Christians."[5] It is based on these two assumptions that I see the importance of exploring the ecumenical *Together Towards Life: Mission and Evangelism in Changing Landscapes* document and its mission from the margins approach not merely as another statement for illustration or comparison, but as an approach that can enable us Anabaptist/Mennonites to revisit our own missiological approaches.

The *Together Towards Life* of 2013,[6] the first full mission statement made by the WCC since 1982, reflects a need to discern how "to seek vision, concepts and directions for a renewed understanding and practice of mission."[7] In this renewed vision, mission is seen as expression of the love of the Triune God that overflows and embraces God's creation. God's

---

4. See Enns, *Peace Church*.

5. See Bergen, "Ecumenical Vocation," 103.

6. Two clarifications are needed here. First, this statement is but one way of articulating a vision for mission within the ecumenical fellowship rather than the norm or the only way in which mission is understood in different ecumenical spaces. And second, rather than compromising its value for not being the only vision on mission, the value of this statement resides in it how it presents a path to be walked by the churches themselves: it is a horizon that enables churches to look critically to their own missiological approaches and be guided by this new framework of mission as they seek to witness to the *Missio Dei*.

7. WCC, *Together Towards Life*, 3.

mission (*Missio Dei*) begins with creation and continues in re-creation enabled by the power of the Holy Spirit. Although not reduced to human beings—God's mission aims at the renewal of the whole of creation—we humans are invited to participate in God's mission through the action of the Spirit.[8] The statement insists that the purpose of God's mission, "fullness of life (John 10:10)" is also "the criterion for discernment in mission."[9] "Fullness of life," "wholeness of life," or "*shalom*" (a term more often used by us Mennonites) all signal God's will for creation.

"Fullness of life" as the purpose of the *Missio Dei* seems to correspond to the ecumenical understanding of Just Peace.[10] In using this phrase, the ecumenical movement offers an alternative vision of mission that self-critically confronts colonial understandings whereby mission is framed as the sending of missionaries from different "centers" of the world to "unexplored" territories—that is, the margins. Furthermore, by asserting "fullness of life" as criterion for discernment in mission, this approach also offers a way to overcome superficial separations between mission and peace. Mission is not reduced to proselytism and disconnected from peace (more on this later); and peace is not reduced to a "program" or "initiative" of the church. Rather peace is part of the very essence of the *Missio Dei*. Mission and peace are, therefore, deeply interrelated.

As Christians, our participation in God's mission is reflected in our witness to God's purpose of fullness of life, which brings to the fore the question of the responsibility of the church in society in light of social, economic and political injustices that are life-harming or "shalom-breaking." At the same time, it is key to recognize that this witnessing can be and has been compromised and thwarted inasmuch as some of the "shalom-breaking" patterns have been legitimized by certain problematic understandings, theologies, and practices of mission. As will be seen, it is precisely here that a mission from the margins approach offers not only a distinctive vision of

---

8. While the *Mission Dei* is open to the whole of creation, I want to focus particularly on some of the features of human participation.

9. WCC, *Together Towards Life*, 37.

10. Framing the *Missio Dei* in these terms seems, therefore, to be the result of the consolidation of the Just Peace paradigm within the WCC—a paradigm that emerged as one of the learnings from the WCC's Decade to Overcome Violence 2001–11 initiative. Within this framework, Just Peace is understood as: "a collective and dynamic yet grounded process of freeing human beings from fear and want, of overcoming enmity, discrimination and oppression, and of establishing conditions for just relationships that privilege the experience of the most vulnerable and respect the integrity of creation." WCC, *Just Peace Companion*, 4.

mission, framed as mission *from* the margins, but also a self-critical stance regarding the relation between mission and marginalization—which will be described as a constitutive aspect of a "mission spirituality."[11]

Mission and Margin(alization)

The WCC mission from the margins approach highlights the tension that has existed regarding "center" and "margins"; *center* often being the "senders" and "saviors," and *margins* often depicted as "receivers" and "saved." Historically, mission has been understood as a geographical expansion from a Christian center to the margins, that is, to the "unreached territories" of the earth. Today, the "landscape" has changed, as more Christians live in the Global South and Asia (previously seen as missionary spaces) than in the Global North. This should cause us to reconsider the center-margins relation.

To speak of the center-margins relation implies focusing on factors that have shaped and perpetuated dynamics such as power relations and imbalances. Exploring such dynamics helps clarify the interrelation between Christian mission and the colonial project.[12] It means acknowledging that wounds created or supported by missionary work exist in the margins and need to be addressed, wounds such as the dislocation of bodies (identities) and communities from the land, racism, poverty, discrimination, and silencing. Such acknowledgment further calls churches to seek to heal these wounds and to transform the structures and institutions (including churches) that have caused such wounds.

At the center of this missiological ecumenical framework is a shift in approach, from "mission *to* the margins" to "mission *from* the margins." This shift affirms that the marginalized are agents of God's mission.[13] The

---

11. It is important to say that the WCC *Together Towards Life* statement is not necessarily a reflection of how all member churches understand mission. It is instead, in my reading, a renewed vision of mission building on the history of the WCC and the new (critical) understandings of mission and Just Peace, among other things. My point here is also not to present this as "the vision" on mission, but rather to seek key elements that aid critical reading of the historical *Concern* essays and that challenge our Anabaptist/Mennonite understandings and theologies of mission.

12. For a more detailed analysis of Christianity (and especially Christian theology) and colonialism, see Jennings, *Christian Imagination*.

13. The statement reads "We affirm that marginalized people are agents of mission and exercise a prophetic role which emphasizes that fullness of life is for all." WCC, *Together Towards Life*, 39.

emphasis intends not to idealize suffering or the status of marginalization but to recognize two fundamental aspects. First, it stresses a call for Christians to discern and witness to God's presence with those who are marginalized, moving away from assumptions that the sharing of the good news with others is what brings about or secures God's presence.[14] Rather, God's presence in the margins and with the marginalized precedes human action. This acknowledgment leads the WCC mission from the margins approach to a critical view of mission as proselytism,[15] opting to speak instead of *evangelism* as communication of and witnessing to God's mission, that is, fullness of life.

Second, a "mission *from* the margins" approach insists that commitment to God's life-giving mission requires discernment of what is life-affirming and life-destroying, and that such discernment comes only by listening to the voices of the marginalized. In this sense, this shift also expands understanding of the center-margins dynamic from being primarily a geographical one (for instance, Global North and Global South) to a socio-political one.[16] It does so by highlighting the different forms of marginalization within our societies across class, gender, racial and ethnic lines, not just geographical lines. Life-harming phenomena such as racism, gender injustices, poverty, exclusion (to name but a few) are not realities confined to a specific territory. They are rather transversal human-made oppressive realities, operating interdependently, reflecting an intersectionality, placing people in specific spaces/locations along a center-margins spectrum globally, within each society, and also within the church. To recognize the marginalized as agents of God's mission implies, then, recognizing their existence—addressing the question *who are the marginalized in this context?*—and listening carefully to their voices in order to assess

---

14. In this regard, WCC, *Together Towards Life* states "Among the surprises of the Spirit are the ways in which God works from locations which appear to be on the margins and through people who appear to be excluded," 14.

15. "Today's world is marked by excessive assertion of religious identities and persuasions that seem to break and brutalize in the name of God rather than heal and nurture communities. In such a context, it is important to recognize that proselytism is not a legitimate way of practicing evangelism." WCC, *Together Towards Life*, 30.

16. A key theological challenge embedded in this understanding of colonialism—i.e., seeing how it has transcended geographical and historical dimensions—means then to recognize that colonialism has set a trajectory which has been articulated, supported and further developed *theologically*. Key here for a renewed exploration of Anabaptist/Mennonite understandings and practices of mission is to look critically at how and to what extent our theologies have related and continue to relate to the colonial theological legacy.

critically our own participation in these life-harming realities, acknowledge the wounds caused, and seek to heal them.

Traces of and critiques of the relation between mission and marginalization can be seen in various of the *Concern* articles. Paul Peachey's study of the *Mukyokai Shugi*, or "churchless Christianity," in Japan offers a good example. Peachey reflects on how the *Mukyokai* movement emerged as a protest to the "institutional Christianity" that was introduced to Japan by Western missionaries; it sought to distinguish "between Christ and Christianity or Christendom." The movement confronted the particular Western embodiment of Christian faith brought to Japan—the beliefs, practices, and structures as articulated by the different denominations and expected to be continued by the "newly-converted" (from the center *to* the margins). In doing so, Peachey explains, the movement spoke "back to their Western tutors" (*from* the margins to the center), exposing not only the inconsistencies of Western institutional Christianity but also affirming and building on their own faith in Christ. They sought to find their own path as Christians within the Japanese context—a context in which they, as a movement, were also in the margins.[17]

Although such a critical historical approach to mission and margin(nalization) is helpful, it focuses more on other denominations and less on the Anabaptist/Mennonite tradition and its missionary approach. For instance, I was particularly confronted by Peter Fast's introduction to S. Djojodihardijo's testimony. In addition to the fact that Pak Djojo's own account is framed (as if his testimony would require validation), there is no critical reflection on the relation between Mennonite mission and the Dutch colonial project in Indonesia, despite the latter assigning an area in Indonesia to the former in order to carry out missionary work.[18] Pak Djojo's narrative of his journey of walking in the Spirit and his experiencing of the Spirit's gifts, with all the persecution and suffering it implied, is challenging and inspiring. Yet, as I read it today, it can be misinterpreted as an expression of missionary "success." We focus only on the gifts of the Spirit and how people lived them in that context, thereby dismissing or bypassing a critical reflection on the relation between Mennonites and the Dutch colonial project. These complex dynamics present within our own history of

17. Peachey, "Churchless Christianity," essay in this volume, 3, 5, 6, 10–12.

18. Peter Fast comments: "Pak Djojo's influence extends beyond the boundaries of the Muria area, an area assigned to the Mennonite Church by the Dutch colonial government, in which missionary work could be carried on by the Mennonites." See Djojodihardijo, "Experience," essay in this volume, 74–75.

mission and colonialism should lead us to reconsider our understandings and framing of Anabaptist/Mennonite mission.

As has become clearer in different Mennonite circles over time, one factor that limits critical exploration of the relation between Mennonites and colonialism is our own history of marginalization. Articles from the "On the Charismatic Movement and Gifts of the Spirit" section of this volume reflect an analysis of the gifts of the Spirit and the "new" charismatic movements that make associations with the sixteenth-century Anabaptist movement, including a shared marginal status and shared emphasis on the central role of the Spirit. This demonstrates how the history of marginalization and persecution have become central elements of our Mennonite identity, enabling us to identify with other marginalized movements. But it also limits our self-critical assessment regarding our own role in marginalizing others. This challenges us to reconsider the center-margins perspective not as a simple dualism (as if one could only be either oppressor or marginalized) but rather as a lens that helps us discern critically what is life-destroying and life-giving *within* our history, identity, theology, understandings of mission, and missional practices.

This challenge is evident, for example, in the recent Mennonite World Conference publication *God's People in Mission: An Anabaptist Perspective*.[19] This collection of diverse articles provides a view of historical and contemporary approaches to mission, seeking to guide and inspire the reflections and actions of the global Mennonite family. The book recognizes the shift of landscape in mission, and there is a careful exercise to root mission biblically and theologically from an Anabaptist/Mennonite perspective. Yet, even though the historical alliance between Western missions and the colonial project is mentioned in the introduction, it is barely explored throughout the book. It only affirms that "some members" of the Anabaptist family bought in to the colonial discourse of superiority-inferiority of peoples.[20] Aspects such as settlements on Indigenous lands, the relation with governments and colonial powers, and

---

19. Green and Zaracho, *God's People in Mission*.

20. The introduction acknowledges how the Western mission allied with the colonial project, causing "unfortunate and tragic outcomes," which are not described further. Anabaptist/Mennonite mission is seen as one that, in general, struggles against the imperialistic powers in its missionary engagement; "Members of our Anabaptist family, socialized within a Western milieu, also shared with the others shaped by that milieu a perception that saw people from the South as primitive, infantile, and weak." See Green and Zaracho, *God's People in Mission*, 7.

discrimination, are not further discussed. This shows the need to further analyze critically the connection between Mennonite mission and colonialism and the relationship between the center and margins. It also demonstrates the urgency and possibility of doing so as global communion.[21] Without such a careful exploration of these intersections there will be no renewed understanding of Anabaptist/Mennonite mission.

A central issue here is that an inadequate engagement with the colonial legacy and the violence of the past could lead to a misguided understanding of unity that is built on the silencing of different voices—a silencing of the past. Another danger is how such a view might maintain the narrative that the current number of churches and members are (univocally) an expression of God's reassurance of our missionary practices, regardless of the harm some of these have caused. The key point here is not an assumption that all Anabaptist/Mennonite missionary approaches and experiences have been or are the same, but the need to develop a self-critical assessment that seeks to discern life-giving versus life-harming practices within all approaches.[22] Without incorporating these elements critically, the wounds caused remain unhealed and we risk perpetuating the colonial and violent past in different and new forms.

Mission Spirituality: Self-reflexive Gift

The renewed ecumenical vision of mission from the margins recognizes that the Holy Spirit is the dynamic power of mission who enables and empowers our participation in the *Missio Dei*. Articles in this volume explore another way to experience the action of the Spirit in mission, and that is through the Spirit's gifts. In James Fairfield's "Tongues, A Testimony" and Herb Klassen and Maureen Klassen's "You Shall Receive . . . " we see an

---

21. Approaching these critical questions as an Anabaptist/Mennonite global communion will allow us to learn about life-giving and life-harming mission practices in our different contexts, identifying attempts to silence the wounds created by practices that have been framed as mission, as well as recognizing attempts that have sought to address—to heal—such wounds may enable learning from experiences which could be seen as examples of mission from the margins.

22. While in some cases how missionary approaches and practices have been life-destroying is easily recognizable, for instance those based on the perceived "superiority" and "inferiority" of peoples, in other cases this discernment is more complex and difficult. Yet it is precisely in the apparently "less violent" or "peaceful" approaches where this discernment is all the more needed, in order to avoid producing new forms of colonialism and oppression.

important attempt to recognize the Spirit's gifts (particularly speaking in tongues) and validate the personal experience and renewed faith of the believer. Werner Schmauch offers a different account, focusing on prophecy instead of tongues as a personal and communitarian gift and office.

Alternatively, the WCC's mission from the margins highlights the Spirit's gift of *discernment* as central to what I will call a "mission spirituality."[23] Discernment is expressed in the constant challenge to recognize the presence and action of the Spirit, which can be identified "wherever life in its fullness is affirmed in all its dimensions, including liberation of the oppressed, healing and reconciliation of broken communities, and the restoration of creation"[24] Central to such a spirituality is the differentiation of the life-affirming presence and action of the Spirit from that of life-harming evil spirits, identifiable wherever death, exclusion, oppression, and destruction prevail. Through the work of the Spirit, such self-reflexive discernment is a gift that connects the personal experience of God with the communal, social, and ecological aspects of God's mission. Self-critical discernment is key as we seek to witness to the *Missio Dei*, for the ecumenical approach of mission from the margins locates *fullness of life* as the purpose of and as criterion for discernment of the *Missio Dei*. In so doing it reframes the center-margins dichotomy, envisioning a new understanding of mission whereby the voice of the marginalized becomes fundamental and the recognition of God's presence in the margins becomes a central aspect. A mission from the margins approach stresses the need for a mission spirituality characterized by discernment that can lead us to seek transformation in the world even as we ourselves are also transformed in witnessing to God's mission.

Aspects for Further Exploration: Anabaptist/Mennonite Mission from the Margins?

In light of this discussion of the ecumenical approach and the questions raised or implied by the historical essays in this volume, I would like to focus on two possible implications for Anabaptist/Mennonite Mission: (1) What

23. The different *Concern* articles on the gifts of the Holy Spirit in this volume emphasize how the experience of these gifts goes beyond (and sometimes even can overcome) denominational lines or borders. It is interesting to note that the ecumenical family also identifies and speaks about the gift of discernment, which could be interpreted precisely as a way to focus on the work of the Spirit across and beyond our denominational lines.

24. WCC, *Together Towards Life*, 11.

might a mission from the margins approach grounded in a self-critical mission spirituality mean for Anabaptist/Mennonite theology, especially our peace theology? and (2) How might a mission spirituality begin to address Mennonite dual-identity as both marginalized and marginalizing?

Peace Theology for the Missio Dei

Theology shaped by a mission spirituality as described above includes critical self-assessment. This challenges Mennonite mission theologies (1) to discern how expressions of colonialism and marginalization have marked or shaped our theologies; (2) to explore to what extent theologies so shaped, including theologies of peace, have been appropriated and continued by the people who were once the focus of missionary work; and (3) identify to what extent such theologies still inform our missiological practices today. None of these questions can be answered in isolation, that is, disconnected from the experiences and wounds of the marginalized and excluded, or from other Christian denominations.

Given its insistence that mission and peace are interconnected, a mission from the margins approach provides a lens through which to trace and critically reflect on the intersections between mission and margin(alization) in Anabaptist/Mennonite peace theology. It also challenges us to embrace a recast a peace theology for the *Missio Dei* as central to reframing mission from an Anabaptist/Mennonite perspective.

As a Mennonite from Colombia, I have seen how central peace has been in the history and theology of our church, particularly in light of the long-term armed confrontation that our country has experienced. The peace orientation of the church results from a long journey of seeking to witness to God's will for the fullness of life. It has been nurtured by Mennonite missionaries, and further inspired by our understanding of the sixteenth-century Anabaptist movement and its emphasis on nonviolence as an expression of discipleship. This peace approach has been recognized, reinforced, supported, and accompanied by different brothers and sisters, churches, and institutions internationally.

Yet I have also seen how our understanding of and theological reflection on peace as Colombian Mennonites has focused predominantly on the armed confrontation, restricting the options to see other forms of marginalization as questions relevant to our peace theology. For instance, topics such as women serving in leadership, gender-based violence, patriarchalism, racism, and same-sex relationships have been framed as "less-pressing issues" compared to armed-violence. Responses to these topics are delayed or addressed "simply" as hermeneutical or cultural issues, rather than as central questions that can lead us to challenge and renew our peace theology and a broader peace witness.[25]

If rooted in a mission spirituality and in the gift of discernment, the theological task at hand implies a careful self-critical stance. In the Colombian case, it requires us to differentiate life-affirming from life-harming aspects of this distinctive peace theology. It requires us to discern how these aspects have been shaped by Colombian culture(s) and particular context(s), what the result of the concrete expression of the Christian faith in Colombia has been, to what extent they have been inherited from missionaries and agencies coming from abroad, and how they have been reinforced by the different Mennonite institutions present in the country. This task of identifying life-giving *and* life-harming aspects present in our own peace theology is key as we reconstruct our peace theology, as we seek to be receptive to God's Spirit and to be witnesses to God's mission of "fullness of life." Such self-critical peace theology is thus key in the renewal of our understanding, theology, and practices of mission.

Dual Identity and Repentance

Seeking to nurture a mission spirituality rooted in God's mission implies engaging with our Mennonite "dual identity," that is, acknowledging that both the stories of our own marginalization and suffering as well as the situations where we have harmed or marginalized others have become part of our identity(ies).[26] How do we deal with the double nature of our own

---

25. My point here is not to deny that some of these issues have been discussed or addressed, at least to some extent, by churches in Colombia. What I am arguing here is that we have not discerned deeply and self-critically enough 1) how these different topics and forms of oppression operate interdependently in marginalizing peoples, groups, and entire communities; 2) how these are interconnected with the armed violence and rooted in the colonial past; 3) how we as church have reproduced and supported these forms of marginalization; and 4) how our limited peace understanding and focus might have led us to bypass or ignore some of these, thereby compromising our peace witness.

26. Reflecting on the Anabaptist/Mennonite identities, Bergen comments: "These identities cannot be so easily disowned because they have emerged from a history that has both received harm and harm others." See "Ecumenical Vocation," 120.

history(ies)? How do we account for it without falling into silencing the past or the "victims" of some of our missiological practices?[27]

Susanna Snyder's analysis of migration, trauma, and spirituality[28] aids reflection on how spirituality can help us revisit this question of "double identity." As she explores spirituality as a path to address collective trauma, Snyder stresses that a key step in this journey is the purging of the self.[29] She recognizes that both privileged and marginalized need at some point to engage with it. For the privileged, this purge involves revealing and letting go of power and of *false images of the inflated self* (for instance, the false notion that Mennonite theologies of nonviolence and peace exonerate us from causing harm). For the marginalized, it involves letting go of *false images of the diminished self* and the powerlessness imposed and internalized as result of being harmed (for instance, Mennonite self-understanding as exclusively "powerless" or victim in the history of marginalization[30]). While the need for one or the other of these two movements may be identified (the

---

27. Again, here my use of "we" is intended to point to challenges that I believe are present within the global Anabaptist/Mennonite communion, rather than implying that all missionary practices have been the same. In the Mennonite family, we do not all share the same responsibilities for practices where mission has allied with the life-harming patterns of colonialism; and the subsequent positionalities of privilege and marginalization are not equal historically and geographically among the different people and communities. My attempt here is to challenge precisely some of the apparent "clear" lines between being marginalized and marginalizing that have become central in the construction of our identities. The aim is to revisit the way we frame our history(ies) of missionary practices and theologies and to look critically at how some life-harming missiological/colonial theologies and practices might have acquired new forms in present discussions and contexts.

28. Snyder, "'La Mano Zurda,'" 227.

29. Here, I am considering a collective "self." While the notion of a collective "self" could carry several limitations, I am focusing on the notion of spirituality as a personal *and* collective experience. Theologian Dorothee Soelle—one of the theologians grounding Snyder's view of the purge of the self as a constitutive dimension of spirituality—describes spirituality as the mystical journey. Soelle argues it involves visiting three different stages or *"vias"*: *via positiva* (opening up to be amazed by God's original blessing); *via negativa* (decentering oneself and letting go of the ego, that is, purging the self); and *via transformativa* (the spiritual journey leads to resisting and seeking to transform the injustices that cause oppression). Snyder's discussion of the "purge of the self" is an analysis of Soelle's proposed *via negativa*. This model of the *three vias* became key in the theological foundation of the WCC's 2013 Pilgrimage of Justice and Peace. See Soelle, *Silent Cry*.

30. This, as with the *false images of the inflated self*, could lead to assuming that one cannot do harm to others—that being marginalized excludes one from the possibility of causing harm.

former for offenders and privileged, and the latter for victims, for example), a "purge of the self" addressing Mennonite history(ies) and identity(ies) would involve a careful exploration of *both*. It means, then, the need to look inside our own global communion—our regional, national, and local churches and communities—to see some of the potential repercussions of these "false images of the self." We need to seek out the wounds and the wounded, and aim at healing and restoration. I would argue that this path is also a key part of nurturing a mission spirituality.

Jeremy Bergen's analysis of the role of apologies as expression of repentance could offer a way forward,[31] especially when it comes to addressing the responsibilities of historical harms.[32] As he describes it, an act of church repentance entails a *confession of sin* (naming a wrong and claiming responsibility for it), *public acknowledgment* (taking a public stance on the past), *commitment to the future* (repentance from the past should indicate the new direction to be walked and the transformations that will take place), and *public witness* (an act of repentance signals both the historical, messy existence and the divine reality beyond the church).[33] Rather than "compromising" the witness of the church, acts of church repentance communicate that "the basis of its hope is not itself [the church], certainly not its good efforts or best intentions, but Jesus Christ."[34] These acts point to the historical particularity of the church as well as its need to humbly proclaim that what it has to offer to the world is not what the church itself contains but what it witnesses to: Christ and the fullness of life he incarnates and brings.

As Bergen shows, an act of repentance is not a simple statement. It is rather a conversion—a transformation that both forms part of a mission spirituality and results from it, following our discussion. This is similar to

---

31. Bergen reminds us that "The early Anabaptists called attention to the biblical themes of repentance and conversion as implying the death of the old self and regeneration by the power of the Holy Spirit, which manifests in holiness of life." See "Ecumenical Vocation," 124.

32. My intention here is not to prescribe repentance as the only way forward, or to decide on what the church has to repent from. More than a final step, for a church to decide to apologize or repent means to engage in a process of discernment and self-critical stance. This is what I think is crucial regarding the intersections between mission and colonialism, as we seek healing and reconciliation—i.e., witnessing to God's life-giving mission. It is crucial to create spaces for such a critical discernment as a global communion.

33. For a more detailed account of theological, ethical and historical aspects in terms of church apologies and repentance, see Bergen, "Whether, and How," 129–44.

34. Bergen, "Whether, and How," 140.

the WCC's emphasis on *metanoia* and the performative exercise in which the church (1) listens carefully to the victims and those who have been marginalized; (2) recognizes and seeks to heal the deep wounds churches have caused; (3) seeks to be changed itself; and (4) seeks to nurture fullness of life in a process that witnesses to the Spirit's transformation.

I return to the argument that led us to this exploration—that certain topics exclusively of concern to Mennonites the Global North are being imposed on Global South Mennonites in a potentially neocolonialistic "move"—with two observations to conclude the present discussion. First, this argument points to the urgent need to revisit past harms perpetrated not just without but also within the Mennonite family, including the marginalization experienced in spaces historically the focus of migration and/or missionary work. Second, it signals the need to help each other reflect critically on how a one-sided view of our identity can lead to harming others. A history of marginalization has led us Mennonites to be less aware of the violence we have done to others. Recognizing that different forms of marginalization are present in all societies (a mission from the margins lens) and seeking to nurture a mission spirituality characterized by self-critical discernment might enable us to overcome simplistic reductions, for instance the ones framed as Global North and Global South tensions—that is, a center-margins relation understood exclusively in geographical terms.

Analysis of the intersections between mission and colonialism is necessary and can lead to recognizing how individual and group identities in global contexts also reflect and are reflected in localized constructions of privilege and marginalization—localized "centers" and "margins." These localized constructions may more directly shape the response to (or the reticence to respond to) the "controversial issues" in the Global South than a neocolonialist imposition. Here a self-critical mission spirituality is crucial for recognizing the continuities and discontinuities of global marginalization dynamics in local spaces, as well as for identifying and addressing these localized forms of privilege and marginalization as we seek to overcome life-harming patterns that compromise our witnessing to God's mission.

We Anabaptist/Mennonites need to affirm the notion of mission from the margins in order to be healed from the colonial paradigm to which we have also ascribed. But those in the center (in the Global South *and* the Global North) need to listen carefully, waiting (more often than not) in silence and in hope that the marginalized have not given up on the ones in the center. We are called to discern together the presence of the Spirit of God and to hold each other accountable for times (both past and present) where we have failed to witness to God's will for fullness of life and a just peace.

May God open us—all—to such transformation by the Spirit as we participate in God's mission in and for the world.

APPENDIX

CONCERN Republication Volumes

The original CONCERN pamphlet series consisted of eighteen volumes that were published between 1954 and 1971. What follows in this index is a complete listing of that content as reorganized in the seven-volume series published by Wipf and Stock.

The Roots of CONCERN: *Writings on Anabaptist Renewal 1952–1957*, ed. Virgil Vogt. Eugene, OR: Wipf & Stock, 2009.

CONCERN *for Education: Essays on Christian Higher Education, 1958–1966*, ed. Virgil Vogt. Eugene, OR: Wipf & Stock, 2010.

CONCERN *for the Church in the World: Essays on Christian Responsibility, 1958–1963*, ed. Laura Schmidt Roberts. Eugene, OR: Wipf & Stock, 2022.

CONCERN *for Church Renewal: Essays on Community and Discipleship, 1958–1966*, ed. Laura Schmidt Roberts. Eugene, OR: Wipf & Stock, 2022.

CONCERN *for Church Mission and Spiritual Gifts: Essays on Faith and Culture, 1958–1968*, ed. Laura Schmidt Roberts. Eugene, OR: Wipf & Stock, 2022.

CONCERN *for Church Polity and Discipline: Essays on Pastoral Ministry and Communal Authority, 1958–1969*, ed. Laura Schmidt Roberts. Eugene, OR: Wipf & Stock, 2022.

APPENDIX: *CONCERN* REPUBLICATION VOLUMES

CONCERN *for Anabaptist Renewal: A Radical Reformation Reader, 1971*, ed. Virgil Vogt and Laura Schmidt Roberts. Eugene, OR: Wipf & Stock, 2022.

The Roots of CONCERN: *Writings on Anabaptist Renewal 1952–1957*, ed. Virgil Vogt. Eugene, OR: Wipf & Stock, 2009.

- Virgil Vogt, "Foreword"
- Paul Peachey, "The Historical Genesis of the CONCERN Project"
- The Original Frontispiece of CONCERN Volumes 1–4

CONCERN 1 (1954)

- Paul Peachey, "Introduction"
- Paul Peachey, "Toward an Understanding of the Decline of the West"
- John Howard Yoder, "The Anabaptist Dissent: The Logic of the Place of the Disciple in Society"

CONCERN 2 (1955)

- Paul Peachey, "Preface"
- John W. Miller, "The Church in the Old Testament"
- Paul Peachey, "Spirit and Form in the Church of Christ"
- David A. Shank and John Howard Yoder, "Biblicism and the Church"
- Appendix: "Close communion—On what lines?"

CONCERN 3 (1956)

- Paul Peachey, "Preface"
- C. Norman Kraus and John W. Miller, "Intimations of Another Way: A Progress Report"
- Hans-Joachim Wiehler, "Preaching in the Church?"
- J. Lester Brubaker and Sol Yoder, "A CONCERN Retreat [CONCERN and Camp Luz]"
- Lewis Benson, "The Call: Journal of Spiritual Reformation"
- Notes on books

APPENDIX: *CONCERN* REPUBLICATION VOLUMES

CONCERN 4 (June 1957)

Paul Peachey, "Preface"

"Epistolary: An Exchange by Letter"

Paul Peachey, "What Is CONCERN?"

John Howard Yoder, "What Are Our Concerns?"

John W. Miller, "Organization and Church"

Herbert Klassen, "Property: A Problem in Christian Ethics"

CONCERN *for Education: Essays on Christian Higher Education, 1958-1966*, ed. Virgil Vogt. Eugene, OR: Wipf & Stock, 2010.

Virgil Vogt, "Editor's Note"

Michael Cartwright, "Foreword"

John Howard Yoder, "Christian Education: Doctrinal Orientation" (1959)

John Howard Yoder, "A Syllabus of Issues Facing the Church College" (1964)

John Howard Yoder and Paul M. Lederach, "Theological Statements for a Philosophy of Mennonite Education" (1971)

CONCERN 13 (1966)

Albert J. Meyer and Walter Klaassen, "Church and Mennonite Colleges"

Joanne Zerger Janzen, "The Bethel Experience in Retrospect"

Walter Klaassen, "Christian Life at Conrad Grebel College"

Henry Rempel, "The Bluffton College Christian Fellowship"

Steve Behrends, "Christian Communal Living on the Tabor Campus"

[Unattributed] "Tabor Christian Fellowship Association"

Glenn M. Lehman, "The Church on Eastern Mennonite College Campus"

Harold E. Bauman, "The Church on Campus, Present and Future: What are the Issues?"

Virgil Vogt, "Afterword"

APPENDIX: *CONCERN* REPUBLICATION VOLUMES

CONCERN *for the Church in the World: Essays on Christian Responsibility, 1958–1963*, ed. Laura Schmidt Roberts. Eugene, OR: Wipf & Stock, 2022.

Laura Schmidt Roberts, "Series Foreword"

Laura Schmidt Roberts, "Introduction"

Gordon D. Kaufman, "Nonresistance and Responsibility" (CONCERN 6, 1958)

Albert J. Meyer, "A Second Look at Responsibility" (CONCERN 6)

David Habegger, "Nonresistance and Responsibility —A Critical Analysis" (CONCERN 7, 1959)

John Howard Yoder, "The Otherness of the Church" (CONCERN 8, 1960)

CONCERN 10 (1961)

Jan M. Lochmann, "Christian Thought in the Age of the Cold War"

Albert Gaillard, "Christians and Marxists"

Katharina van Drimmelen, "Where Are the Firemen?"

John Howard Yoder, "The Christian Answer to Communism"

John Howard Yoder, "Marginalia"

CONCERN 11 (1963)

Karl Barth, "Poverty"

Andrew Murray, "The Poverty of Christ"

R. Mehl, "Money"

Virgil Vogt, "God or Mammon"

John Howard Yoder, "Marginalia"

Melissa Florer-Bixler, "All Economy Is Atheist: Towards a Non-Competitive Hope for the Church in the World"

Appendix: CONCERN republication volumes content list

APPENDIX: *CONCERN* REPUBLICATION VOLUMES

CONCERN *for Church Renewal: Essays on Community and Discipleship, 1958–1966*, ed. Laura Schmidt Roberts. Eugene, OR: Wipf & Stock, 2022.

Laura Schmidt Roberts, "Series Foreword"

Laura Schmidt Roberts, "Introduction"

John Howard Yoder, "Marginalia" excerpt (CONCERN 8, 1960)

John Howard Yoder, "Marginalia" excerpt (CONCERN 5, 1958)

Hans-Ruedi Weber, "The Church in the House" (CONCERN 5)

Quintus Leatherman, "The House Church in the New Testament" (CONCERN 5)

Paul M. Miller, "Can the Sunday School Class Be the 'House' within which the True Church Is Experienced?" (CONCERN 5)

Albert Steiner, "Group Dynamics in Evangelism [by Paul Miller]: A Review Article" (CONCERN 8)

Gerald C. Studer, "Evangelism Through the Dynamics of a Christian Group" (CONCERN 5)

Virgil Vogt, "Small Congregations" (CONCERN 5)

CONCERN 12 (1966)

Leland Harder, "Changing Forms of the Church and Her Witness"

John W. Miller, "The Renewal of the Church"

John Howard Yoder, "Marginalia: A Syllabus of Issues"

Lewis Benson, "The Order that Belongs to the Gospel" (CONCERN 7, 1959)

Susanne Guenther Loewen, "After Yoder: Failure, Authenticity, and the Renewal of the Mennonite Church"

César García, "A Global Communion as a Condition for the Possibility of Church Renewal"

Appendix: CONCERN republication volumes content list

APPENDIX: *CONCERN REPUBLICATION VOLUMES*

CONCERN *for Church Mission and Spiritual Gifts: Essays on Faith and Culture, 1958–1968*, ed. Laura Schmidt Roberts. Eugene, OR: Wipf & Stock, 2022.

Laura Schmidt Roberts, "Series Foreword"

Laura Schmidt Roberts, "Introduction"

Paul Peachey, "Churchless Christianity" (CONCERN 7, 1959)

M. H. Grumm, "The Search for Guaranteed Survival" (CONCERN 8, 1960)

Edmund Perry, "The Christian Mission to the Resurgent Religions" (CONCERN 9, 1961)

John Howard Yoder, "A Light to the Nations" (CONCERN 9)

Paul Peachey, "The End of Christendom" (CONCERN 9)

CONCERN 15 (1967)

John Howard Yoder, "Marginalia"

James Fairfield, "Tongues, a Testimony"

Herb Klassen and Maureen Klassen "You Shall Receive . . . "

S. Djojodihardijo, "An Experience in My Life"

Donald R. Jacobs, "The Charismatic in East Africa"

Myron S. Augsburger, "The Charismatic Aspects of the Work of the Spirit"

Irvin B. Horst, "A Historical Estimate of the Charismatic Movement"

Gerald C. Studer, "The Charismatic Revival: A Survey of the Literature"

Werner Schmauch, "The Prophetic Office in the Church" (CONCERN 5, 1958)

CONCERN 16 (1968)

Henderson Nylrod, "Nasty Noel"

William Roberts Miller, "Pious Jingle Bells and the Coming of Christ"

Marlin Jeschke, "Getting Christ Back Out of Christmas"

John Howard Yoder, "On the Meaning of Christmas"

John Howard Yoder and Virgil Vogt, "Marginalia: The Case Against Christmas"

Hyung Jin Kim Sun, "Global Anabaptist Movement: From Cross-cultural to Multicultural to Intercultural"

Andrés Pacheco Lozano, "Mission and Margin(alization): An Ecumenically-Shaped Anabaptist/Mennonite Approach to Mission"

Appendix: CONCERN republication volumes content list

CONCERN *for Church Polity and Discipline: Essays on Pastoral Ministry and Communal Authority, 1958–1969*, ed. Laura Schmidt Roberts. Eugene, OR: Wipf & Stock, 2022.

Laura Schmidt Roberts, "Series Foreword"

Laura Schmidt Roberts, "Introduction"

Gerald C. Studer, "Second Thoughts on the Pastoral Ministry" (CONCERN 6, 1958)

[Unattributed] "Marginalia" excerpt (CONCERN 6)

A. H. A. Bakker, "Efficiency in the Church" (CONCERN 7, 1959)

Edgar Metzler, "The Need to Which We Minister" (CONCERN 7)

Lewis Benson, "The Church's One Foundation" (CONCERN 8, 1960)

Walter Klaassen, "The Preacher and Preaching" (CONCERN 9, 1961)

William Klassen, "Discipleship and Church Order: A Review and Discussion" (CONCERN 9)

Walter Klaassen, "New Presbyter Is Old Priest Write Large" (CONCERN 17, 1969)

J. Lawrence Burkholder, "Theological Education for the Believers' Church" (CONCERN 17)

Virgil Vogt, "Marginalia" excerpt (CONCERN 17)

Elmer Ediger, "*Studies in Church Discipline*: A Review Article" (CONCERN 5, 1958)

William Klassen, "Some Neglected Aspects in the Biblical View of the Church" (CONCERN 8)

Calvin Redekop, "Postulates Concerning Religious Intentional Ethnic Groups" (CONCERN 9)

Balthasar Hubmaier, "On Fraternal Admonition" (CONCERN 14, 1967)

Don Jacobs, "Walking Together in East Africa" (CONCERN 14)

Samuel Shoemaker, "Dealing with Other People's Sins" (CONCERN 14)

Kimberly Penner, "Toward Ecclesial Practices and Notions of Authority that Embody Radical Hope"

Isaac S. Villegas, "The Ecclesial Flesh of Anabaptist Visions"

Appendix: CONCERN republication volumes content list

CONCERN *for Anabaptist Renewal: A Radical Reformation Reader, 1971*, ed. Virgil Vogt and Laura Schmidt Roberts. Eugene, OR: Wipf & Stock, 2022.

Editor's Note

John Roth, "Foreword"

CONCERN 18 (1971)

Virgil Vogt, "Introduction"

John Howard Yoder, "The Recovery of the Anabaptist Vision"

Harold S. Bender, "The Mennonite Conception of the Church and Its Relation to Community Building"

Harold S. Bender, "The Anabaptist Theology of Discipleship"

William Klassen, "Anabaptist Studies"

Walter Klaassen, "Radical Reformation"

Harold S. Bender, "The Pacifism of the Sixteenth Century Anabaptists"

"Anabaptism: An Introductory Bibliography"

Appendix: CONCERN republication volumes content list

Bibliography

Adams, Ron, and Isaac Villegas. "Post-Christendom or Neo-Christendom?" *The Mennonite*, February 1, 2013. https://anabaptistworld.org/post-christendom-neo-christendom/.

Anabaptist Mennonite Biblical Seminary. "AMBS Response to Victims of John H. Yoder Abuse." https://www.ambs.edu/about/ambs-response-to-victims-of-yoder-abuse .

Appleton, George. "Christian Encounter with Other Religions." *Frontier* 2 (1959) 134–39.

Bergen, Jeremy M. "The Ecumenical Vocation of Anabaptist Theology." In *Recovering from the Anabaptist Vision: New Essays in Anabaptist Identity and Theological Method*, edited by Laura Schmidt Roberts et al., 103–26. London: T. & T. Clark, 2020.

———. "Whether, and How, a Church Ought to Repent for a Historical Wrong." *Theology Today* 73.2 (2016) 129–44.

Bergmann, Sigurd. *God in Context: A Survey of Contextual Theology*. Aldershot: Ashgate, 2003.

Bergsma, Stuart. *Speaking with Tongues: Some Physiological and Psychological Implications of Modern Glossalalia*. Grand Rapids: Baker, 1965.

Cramer, David, et al. "Theology and Misconduct: The Case of John Howard Yoder." *The Christian Century* 131.17, August 20, 2014. https://www.christiancentury.org/article/2014-07/theology-and-misconduct.

Cullman, Oscar. "Πέτρος, Κηφᾶς." In *Theologisches Worterbuch zum Neuen Testament: Pe-R*, edited by Gerhard Kittel, 6:94–112. Germany: Kohlhammer, 1959.

Dostoyevsky, Fyodor. *The Brothers Karamazov*. Great Books of the Western World 52. Translated by Constance Garnett. Chicago: Encyclopedia Britannica, 1952.

Du Plessis, David. *The Spirit Bade Me Go: An Astounding Move of God in the Denominational Churches*. Dallas, TX: N.p., 1961.

Edman, V. Raymond. *They Found the Secret: Twenty Transformed Live that Reveal a Touch of Eternity*. Grand Rapids: Zondervan, 1961.

Enns, Fernando. *The Peace Church and the Ecumenical Community: Ecclesiology and the Ethics of Nonviolence*. Kitchener: Pandora, 2008.

Fox, George. *The Journals of George Fox*. 8th ed. 2 vols. London: London Friends' Tract Association, 1891.

———. *The Works of George Fox*. 8 vols. Philadelphia: Gould, 1831.

"Global Trends: Forced Displacement in 2017." https://www.unhcr.org/5b27be547.pdf.

Goodall, Norman, et al. *A Decisive Hour for the Christian Mission: The East Asia Christian Conference 1959 and the John R. Mott Memorial Lectures*. London: SCM, 1960.

Green, Stanley W., and Rafael Zaracho. *God's People in Mission: An Anabaptist Perspective*. Asunción, Paraguay : Mennonite World Conference, 2018.

Grubb, Norman. *C. T. Studd: Cricketer and Pioneer*. London: Lutterworth, 1939.

———. *Rees Howells: Intercessor*. London: Lutterworth, 1952.

Gruber, Judith. *Intercultural Theology: Exploring World Christianity after the Cultural Turn*. Göttingen: Vandenhoeck & Ruprecht, 2018.

Grumm, M. H. "The Search for Guaranteed Survival." *National Christian Council Review* 79.11 (1959) 406–13.

Haroutunian, Joseph. "The Realization of the Church." *Theology Today* 17.2 (1960) 137–43.

Harper, Michael. *As at the Beginning: The Twentieth Century Pentecostal Revival*. London: Fountain Trust, 1965.

———. *Power for the Body of Christ*. London: Fountain Trust, 1966.

Hershberger, Nathan. "Power, Tradition, and Renewal: The *Concern* Movement and the Fragmented Institutionalization of Mennonite Life." *Mennonite Quarterly Review* 87.2 (2013) 155–86.

Hitt, Russell T. "The New Pentecostalism: An Appraisal." *Eternity* 14.7 (1963) 10–16.

Hock, Klaus. "Grenzziehung und Grenzüberschreitung: The Making of 'Mission' als Thema der Missionswissenschaft." In *". . . ihr werdet meine Zeugen sein . . .": Rückfragen aus einer störrischen Disziplin*, edited by Arnd Bünker and Ludger Weckel, 249–59. Freiburg im Breisgau, Basel, Vienna: Herder, 2005.

Hooft, W. A. Visser 't. "The Asian Churches in the Ecumenical Movement." In *A Decisive Hour for the Christian Mission: The East Asia Christian Conference 1959 and the John R. Mott Memorial Lectures*, edited by Norman Goodall et al., 46–58. London: SCM, 1960.

———. "Asian Issues in the Ecumenical Movement." In *A Decisive Hour for the Christian Mission: The East Asia Christian Conference 1959 and the John R. Mott Memorial Lectures*, edited by Norman Goodall et al., 59–71. London: SCM, 1960.

———. "The Significance of the Asian Churches in the Ecumenical Movement." *The Ecumenical Review* 11.4 (1959) 365–76.

———, ed. *The First Assembly of the World Council of Churches: The Official Report*. New York: Harper, 1949.

Howes, John F., and Otis Cary. *Japan's Modern Prophet: Uchimura Kanzo*. Kyoto: Doshisha University Press, 1958.

Jennings, Raymond P. *Jesus, Japan, and Kanzo Uchimura*. Tokyo: Kyo Bun Kwan, 1958.

Jennings, Willie James. *The Christian Imagination: Theology and Origins of Race*. New Haven: Yale University Press, 2011.

Jeremias, Joachim. *Jesus' Promise to the Nations*. Translated by S. H. Hooke. Studies in Biblical Theology 24. London: SCM, 1958.

Kanagy, Conrad, et al. *Global Anabaptist Profile: Belief and Practice in 24 Mennonite World Conference Churches*. Goshen: Institute for the Study of Global Anabaptism, 2017.

Kaufman, Edmund G. *The Development of the Missionary and Philanthropic Interest among the Mennonites of North America*. Berne: Mennonite Book Concern, 1931.

Kelsey, Morton T. *Tongue Speaking: An Experiment in Spiritual Experience*. Garden City: Doubleday, 1964.

Kim Sun, Hyung Jin. "Forging an Intercultural Mennonite Identity: Personal Reflections on Ethnoreligion in a Global Context." *Mennonite Quarterly Review* 99.2 (2020) 201–5.

Kurosaki, Kokichi. *One Body in Christ*, Kobe: Eternal Life Press, 1954.

Martin-Achard, Robert. *Israël et les Nations: La Perspective Missionnaire de l'Ancien Testament*. Neuchâtel-Paris: Delachaux et Niestlé, 1959.

Miller, John W. "The Renewal of the Church." *Concern* 12 (1966) 32–50.

Miller, R. Edward. *Thy God Reigneth: The Story of Revival in Argentina*. Prescott: World Missionary Assistance Plan, 1964.

Murray, Andrew. *The Full Blessing of Pentecost: The One Thing Needful*. Sheffield: Christian Literature Crusade, 1954.

———. *The Spirit of Christ: Thoughts on the Indwelling of the Holy Spirit in the Believer and the Church*. Edinburgh: Oliphants, 1963.

Nee, Watchman. *The Normal Christian Church Life*. Washington, DC: International Students Press, 1962.

———. *Sit, Walk, Stand: The Process of Christian Maturity*. Fort Washington: CLC, 1957.

Newbigin, J. E. Lesslie. *The Household of God: Lectures on the Nature of the Church*. London: SCM, 1953.

Nichol, John Thomas. *Pentecostalism*. New York: Harper & Row, 1966.

Norman, W. Howard. *An Interim Report on Nonchurch Christianity in Japan*. Nishinomiya: Kwansei Gakuin University Annual Studies, 1958.

Pannabecker, Samuel F., et al. "Mission (Missiology)." https://gameo.org/index.php?title=Mission_(Missiology)&oldid=167790.

Panikkar, Kavalam M. *Asia and Western Dominance: A Survey of the Vasco da Gama Epoch of Asian History, 1498–1945*. London: Allen & Unwin, 1953.

Phillips, McCandlish. "And There Appeared to Them Tongues of Fire." *The Saturday Evening Post* 237.19 (1964) 30–43.

Radhakrishnan, Sarvepalli. "The Spirit in Man." In *Contemporary Indian Philosophy*, edited by Sarvepalli Radhakrishnan and J. H. Muirhead, 475–504. London: Allen & Unwin, 1952.

Redekop, Calvin. *Mennonite Society*. Baltimore: Johns Hopkins University, 1989.

Regehr, Theodore D. *Mennonites in Canada, 1939–1970: A People Transformed*. Mennonites in Canada 3. Toronto: University of Toronto, 1996.

Rengstorf, Karl H. "μανθάνω, καταμανθάνω, μαθητής, συμμαθητής, μαθήτρια, μαθητεύω." In *Theologisches Worterbuch zum Neuen Testament: L–N*, edited by Gerhard Kittel, 4:390–415. Germany: Kohlhammer, 1959.

Sanford, Agnes. *The Healing Gifts of the Spirit*. Philadelphia: Lippincott, 1966.

Sargant, William. "Some Cultural Group Abreactive Techniques and their Relation to Modern Treatments." *Proceedings of the Royal Society of Medicine* 42 (1949) 367–374.

Sawatsky, Rodney. "Editorial." *The Conrad Grebel Review* 8.2 (1990) iii–iv.

Schmauch, Werner. "Das prophetische Amt in der Gemeinde." *Junge Kirche* 19 (1958) 126–31.

Shenk, Wilbert R. "The 'Great Century' Reconsidered." In *Anabaptism and Mission*, edited by Wilbert R. Shenk, 158–77. Scottdale: Herald, 1984.

Sherrill, John L. *They Speak with Other Tongues*. New York: McGraw Hill, 1964.

Smith, William Cantwell. "Comparative Religion: Whither—and Why?" In *The History of Religions: Essays in Methodology*, edited by Mircea Eliade and Joseph M. Kitagawa, 31–58. Chicago: University of Chicago Press, 1959.

Snyder, Susanna. "'La Mano Zurda with a Heart in Its Palm': Mystical Activism as a Response to the Trauma of Immigration Detention." In *Post-Traumatic Public Theology*, edited by Stephanie Arel and Shelly Rambo, 217–40. Cham: Palgrave Macmillan, 2016.

Soelle, Dorothee. *The Silent Cry: Mysticism and Resistance*. Minneapolis: Fortress, 2001.

Soto Albrecht, Elizabeth, and Darryl W. Stephens, eds. *Liberating the Politics of Jesus: Renewing Peace Theology through the Wisdom of Women*. London: T. & T. Clark, 2020.

Spellers, Stephanie. *Radical Welcome: Embracing God, the Other, and the Spirit of Transformation*. New York: Church, 2006.

Sundermeier, Theo. "Begegnung mit dem Fremden: Plädoyer für eine verstehende Missionswissenschaft." *Evangelische Theologie* 50 (1990) 390–400.

Toews, Paul. *Mennonites in American Society, 1930–1970: Modernity and the Persistence of Religious Community*. Scottdale: Herald, 1996.

Torrey, Rueben A. *The Baptism with the Holy Spirit*. 2nd ed. London: Nisbet, 1905.

———. *How to Bring Men to Christ*. Grand Rapids: Fleming Revell, 1911.

Tozer, A. W. *How to Be Filled with the Holy Spirit*. Harrisburg: Christian Publications, 1960.

Uchimura, Kanzo. *How I Became a Christian: Out of My Diary*. Tokyo: Keiseisha, 1895.

———. *Japan and the Japanese*. Tokyo: Minyusha, 1894.

United Nations High Commissioner for Refugees (UNHCR). *Global Trends: Forced Displacement in 2017*. Geneva, Switzerland: UNHCR, June 2018.

Vogt, Virgil, ed. *CONCERN for Education: Essays on Christian Higher Education, 1958–1966*. Eugene, OR: Wipf & Stock, 2010.

———, ed. *The Roots of CONCERN: Writings on Anabaptist Renewal, 1952–1957*. Eugene, OR: Wipf & Stock, 2009.

Vogt, Virgil, and Laura Schmidt Roberts, eds. *Concern for Anabaptist Renewal: A Radical Reformation Reader, 1971*. Eugene, OR: Wipf & Stock, 2022.

Waltner Goossen, Rachel. "'Defanging the Beast': Mennonite Responses to John Howard Yoder's Sexual Abuse." *Mennonite Quarterly Review* 89.1 (2015) 7–80.

Wesley, John. "A Letter to the Reverend Dr. Conyers Middleton." In *The Works of John Wesley*, 10:1–79. 14 vols. Grand Rapids: Zondervan, 1959.

Wilkerson, David. *The Cross and the Switchblade*. New York: B. Geis Associates, 1963.

World Council of Churches (WCC). *Just Peace Companion*, 2nd ed. Geneva: World Council of Churches, 2012.

———. *Together Towards Life: Mission and Evangelism in Changing Landscapes*. https://www.oikoumene.org/en/resources/documents/commissions/mission-and-evangelism/together-towards-life-mission-and-evangelism-in-changing-landscapes.

Yoder, John Howard. "The Otherness of the Church." *Concern* 8 (1960) 19–29.

www.ingramcontent.com/pod-product-compliance
Lightning Source LLC
Chambersburg PA
CBHW060607230426
43670CB00011B/2006